Wrestling with Rest

Wrestling with Rest

*Inviting Youth to Discover
the Gift of Sabbath*

Nathan T. Stucky

WILLIAM B. EERDMANS PUBLISHING COMPANY
GRAND RAPIDS, MICHIGAN

Wm. B. Eerdmans Publishing Co.
4035 Park East Court SE, Grand Rapids, Michigan 49546
www.eerdmans.com

25 24 23 22 21 20 19   1 2 3 4 5 6 7

ISBN 978-0-8028-7626-3

Library of Congress Cataloging-in-Publication Data

A catalog record for this book is available from the Library of Congress.

Unless otherwise noted, Scripture quotations are from the New Revised Standard Version of
the Bible, copyright © 1989 by the Division of Christian Education of the National Council of
the Churches of Christ in the U.S.A. and used by permission.

For Janel
my companion in every season

and for Merv
who has taught me more about grace than he'll ever know

Unless the LORD builds the house,

those who build it labor in vain.

Unless the LORD guards the city,

the guard keeps watch in vain.

It is in vain that you rise up early and go late to rest,

eating the bread of anxious toil;

for the LORD provides for his beloved during sleep.

Psalm 127:1–2

Contents

Foreword

To keep the Sabbath is a radical act of resistance to a culture
that has lost track of the meaning of life.

—Rebecca Parker

You are about to read an unexpectedly bewitching book. It sings of young
people you know, whose lives are familiar. Its prose is winsome, clear, and
truthful. The stories in this volume could come from my ministry with
young people, or from yours. And then, just as you put down your coffee,
maybe around page 10, you realize you've been spellbound.

This book is not about youth. This book is about *us*.

For all his Mennonite niceness—which is as genuine and sweet as a summer tomato on the vine—Nate Stucky is a committed contrarian. He giddily
traffics in the anathemas of our culture. He delights in dirt and worms and
lost causes, seeing in them possibilities for redemption. As the director of
Princeton Theological Seminary's Farminary Project, Stucky teaches his
students to turn the anathema of waste into an elixir of life, compost that
transforms depleted dirt into life-giving soil. He celebrates the anathema of
limits—nightfall, seasons, human frailty—as opportunities to trust God. In
Wrestling with Rest, he dives headlong into the anathema of rest, daring us
to stop—just *stop*—to let God be God. He is maddeningly non-anxious, and
rivetingly on-point.

Wrestling with Rest will restore your hope in youth ministry by wresting
it from the tyranny of "youth activities." This is no simple diatribe against
overscheduled youth (in fact, Stucky refuses to rubber-stamp the "oversched-

uled youth" hypothesis, countering with a refreshingly nuanced, well-researched understanding of the role extracurricular activities play in young people's growing sense of self).

But while this is very much a book about caring for young people, it is also a book about caring for the adults who love them: you, me, anyone who wants to reflect the love and care God has for the teenagers in our midst, but who find ourselves exhausted by our "always on" society. Here be dragons: Heaven knows, at our particular moment in history—a moment when young people feel rising levels of anxiety, racism, violence, abuse, opioids, and countless other crushing problems closing in—they desperately need people to witness to God's love and care for them. Surely this is why we've been called "for such a time as this" (Esther 4:14). There is so much need and so few hours; so many young people struggling to grow up, and so few of us to help them do it.

Surely this warrants our busyness, doesn't it? Busyness keeps kids out of trouble. It reminds us that we're important.

But . . . it's killing us.

Of course, young people know how to rest—they have to learn not to do it. They have to learn to ignore the limits of their bodies, to learn to prolong day into night in defiance of darkness, to constantly feed the twin mongrels of consumption and production nipping ceaselessly at their heels. They must learn, as Stucky puts it, to be "busy being busy."

It turns out that we adults have been their impeccable teachers. In contrast to Europe, the United States has no federal law guaranteeing paid time off, sick leave, or breaks for national holidays.[1] The average American employee leaves almost a week of paid vacation days on the table each year.[2] But it's not just physical time off that matters. Social and intellectual "mental congestion"—the sensory overload made possible by the screens and cellphones that feed our addiction to information and connection—uses up precious brain bandwidth and energy as well. Churches offer little sanctuary here; most youth ministry resources are brimming with recipes for anxiety, ideas for more things we could do with, for, and to youth than we will ever have time to implement, no matter how many lock-ins, service projects, or mystery rambles we plan. Even darkness, "the only power that has ever put the human agenda on hold,"[3] has been banished by the LEDs of our omnipresent technological gadgetry. As Clark Strand, author of *Waking Up to the Dark: Ancient Wisdom for a Sleepless Age*, points out: "No wonder we have trouble sleeping. The lights are always on."

At this point I owe you a confession: I read the section of this book on adolescent sleep deprivation at three o'clock in the morning. (I know.) It occurred to me then, and many times since then, that maybe God sent Nate Stucky into the world to convict us (just me?) of our soul-killing addiction to productivity. People who know Nate in person concur that he is one of those people whose very goodness makes the rest of us want to be good as well. But eventually that requires some Real Talk, because goodness comes at a cost. As Aslan reminds us, only God is good. So becoming like God means relinquishing the flotsam—the accomplishments, the finished projects, the "conspicuous busyness"[4]—that we thought would carry us to shore. And relinquishing even these flimsy security blankets feels like anathema.

Throughout this book, Stucky urges us—with significant backing from biblical narratives, Karl Barth, and other theological heavyweights—to do one radical thing: stop. Just stop. If stepping off the merry-go-round of consumption and production feels like death to us, it's because it is: Sabbath is a practice of dying, of *not* doing the very thing that our survival depends upon, in order to depend upon God instead. In so doing, we loosen our identities from their tether to work, just as the practice of Sabbath liberated the Hebrew people from being defined by their slave-identities. Instead, we become people defined by our trust and dependence on God.

Treating Sabbath as a day of leisure is quite different from the more challenging position on rest that Stucky urges us to consider. Sabbath is neither an earned vacation nor a chance to lounge around sipping lemonade while we catch our second wind before heading into the Monday morning frenzy. Sabbath is more fundamental: it challenges that frenzy's power to begin with. Rest declares to the frenzy that *it* is anathema. Rest reveals our frenzied busyness for what it is: fear. What if we don't use every waking moment to work and produce? How will we survive? Who will take notice? Who will we be?

In the Bible, the word "anathema" is typically translated from the Hebrew word *herem*, which, unhelpfully, can mean *either* "to consecrate or devote to God"—or "to exterminate." The Greek version meant "to offer up" and referred to any sacrifice or offering to a divinity. But since *anathema* often referred to idols, consecrated objects that were so wholly devoted to the gods that you couldn't sell them (if you wanted to be rid of them, you had to destroy them), the word became associated with destruction. By the time the early church used the term, it meant excommunication from the community of believers.[5] Today we use it to mean something unthinkable, something so detestable that we shun it.

Rest is such a concept. Stucky calls it "disorienting grace" with cause: this holy rest is pure gift, but most of us shun it, preferring instead our familiar forms of captivity. We have become attached to our lesser identities, as Stucky calls them, selves we know through our work, based on the illusion of limitless lives. Surrendering those selves—trusting God's work instead of our own—is an incalculable risk. Time and time again, God delivers God's people from captivity to work, in Egypt, in Babylon, in Gethsemane. Time and time again, God shuns the idol of productivity. And time and time again, we welcome it back, binding ourselves to our production value, choosing yield over grace, work over rest, anxious busyness over joyful deliverance. It's interesting that the thirty-nine categories of activities that Talmudic law forbids on Shabbat all have to do with material production: farming, weaving, slaughtering, writing, kneading, building, and so on. As Abraham Joshua Heschel wrote, "Six days a week we live under the tyranny of things of space; on the Sabbath we try to become attuned to the holiness of time."[6]

The twist, made explicit in the Christian Scriptures, is that while death may be our ultimate limit, it is not God's. For Barth, the seventh day of creation points *beyond* time—to a way of being with God that upends our view of rest, limitation, and death by making them conditions for life. As Stucky points out, in Genesis, the seventh day, a day of rest, is humankind's first full day of life. In Jesus's ministry, anything that stifled life—legalism, narrow-mindedness, faithlessness—was put to death on the Sabbath, while

Jesus's teachings and renegade healings on the Sabbath were gifts of liberation and wholeness. Centuries later, Karaite Jews declared the seventh day the most joyous day of the week, a day of blessing and celebration. Despite pockets of legalism, over the centuries the practice of Sabbath consistently released people from their various captivities, so they could experience the liberation of trusting God instead of themselves, even if just for a day.

Nate's first teaching on the research presented in this book was as a teaching assistant in my youth ministry classes. He would come into class with a flotilla of rubber ducks in tow, which he passed out to students when they arrived. It was a nod to a famous *Sesame Street* vignette in which Ernie asks Mr. Hoots, a jazz-loving owl, to teach him to play the saxophone. Noticing that Ernie was still clutching his beloved rubber duckie, Mr. Hoots tells Ernie that if he wants to play the saxophone, "ya gotta put down the duckie." In class, Nate would exegete Scripture, quote Karl Barth, and round up the usual theological suspects to make his case on the importance of Sabbath in youth ministry. But his trump card was Mr. Hoots. If they were serious about wanting to practice Sabbath, Nate told students, first they had to die to their ideals of productivity. First they had to put down their duckies.

I remain Nate Stucky's biggest fan and most noncompliant student. That's how it works, isn't it? Those whom God sends you to teach, teach you. I still struggle with Sabbath-keeping. But somehow putting down the duckie is a doable first step. So before you turn the page . . .

Stop. Just stop.

Now put down the duckie.

Now begin.

KENDA CREASY DEAN
Princeton, NJ

Acknowledgments

They say it takes a village to raise a child. So also a book. I am deeply indebted to so many who have journeyed with me through various seasons of this project. Thanks to the students at Princeton Theological Seminary who sat years ago in a class I taught about young people and Sabbath. So many ideas were refined in that space. Thanks also to the many students who have heard and wrestled with these ideas since.

Thank you to Kenda Creasy Dean, Rick Osmer, and Gordon Mikoski for being the chief architects in my formation as a practical theologian. I pray this work honors your work. I cannot thank you enough for believing in me, challenging me, and welcoming me as your colleague.

To the students, teachers, and administrators who made my research in Chapter 3 possible, know how deeply grateful I am for your endless work on my behalf. Every honest window into the life of a young person is a gift. You gave me that gift again and again and again. This book would have no backbone without your honesty. I only hope I did justice to your stories.

From my research with students, Jake and Ashley Higgins and Sarah DeVries gladly and meticulously transcribed hours of focus groups and interviews. I am exceedingly grateful, even if Jake ribs me about the "Hello, hellooo? Is this thing on?" that began every recording. Thank you also to Zion Mennonite Church, Souderton, Pennsylvania, for the research grant that made my work with the high school students and the transcriptions possible.

My editor, David Bratt, from Eerdmans has been a faithful guide for my first journey of book-writing. Your enthusiasm for the project and your conviction that the church needs this work have been a steady source of encouragement. I also thank you for insisting that I write to an audience that included more than pointy-headed intellectuals.

Dwight Rohrer and Rachel Mast read the entire manuscript when it was in a less friendly and less readable form. Your honest feedback, including all the time involved, was such a gift. I cannot thank you enough.

Jeff Chu and Wes Ellis just kept encouraging me to do this project, particularly in times when progress lagged. God bless you both.

This book is dedicated to two of the dearest friends I have ever had: Merv Stoltzfus and my wife, Janel. Merv, you have been my mentor, friend, and guide for almost twenty years. You have seen this project in a hundred different iterations and offered feedback on the full manuscript. I simply couldn't survive in ministry without you, Merv. You exude abundant life and faithfulness. I'm only trying to do the same.

And Janel . . . how do I adequately thank the one who has most consistently embodied God's faithfulness to me? You have been a constant and faithful companion. You and the kids have seen me die and rise again a thousand times along the journey of this book. How could I repay that kind of faithfulness? I don't think I can. The gift of journeying through life together might just be the sweetest grace of all.

Introduction

The stories we hear when we're young stay with us. They define us, tell us who we are. For good, and sometimes for ill, they inform the ways we live our lives. Sometimes we realize it. Sometimes we don't.

In order to understand this book and the stories it contains, you need to know a bit about my story.

When I was sixteen years old, my youth group from First Mennonite Church, Pretty Prairie, Kansas, went on a service trip to Appalachia. (If the term "Mennonite" makes you think horses, buggies, and straw hats, just stop. Those are either Amish or a more conservative group of Mennonites than the ones I grew up with.)

We were a bunch of farm kids who knew our way around a hammer and a circular saw, and when we got to Harlan County, we did what we knew how to do best. We worked. We also knew how to eat.

At one point during the week, the people who ran the ministry in Kentucky had to make a choice. Our appetites were throwing off their budget. We were eating more than any other youth group they had seen. Should they try to make us eat less?

Ultimately, they decided not to attempt to curb our appetites. Why? As the story was told to me, the director of the whole ministry said something like, "I don't care how much they eat. They're getting more work done than any other group I've ever seen."

We didn't hear that story until after the fact, but when we did, we couldn't have been prouder. You may have heard of the Protestant work ethic. I suppose it's a thing, but I need to tell you a secret about Mennonites. Though most would never admit it, in their heart of hearts, many a Mennonite thinks the Mennonite work ethic puts the run-of-the-mill Protestant work ethic to shame.

This is a story I've been told.

This is a story I've told.

This is a story I've tried to live.

This story shapes my deepest understanding of who I am. In other words, it shapes my identity. Who am I? I am a hard-working, Mennonite farm-kid from Kansas who knows how to get stuff done.

Most of the time, this sense of identity seems like a great gift.

But not always.

Look again at the story of our trip to Appalachia. It follows the contours of countless stories that play out in the lives of countless young people in countless places for countless reasons. Youth work hard; they do something special; and then they receive encouragement and affirmation. They feel the love.

Work hard. Receive reward. Repeat.

What could be wrong with this story?

We love this story. It empowers us. It defines us.

But there's a problem with this story. It begins with us; it depends on our effort; and it leaves virtually no room for failure. In other words, it is a story devoid of grace. It is also a story devoid of rest. Rest actually cuts against the cycle of work, reward, repeat.

If I think about all of this in relation to my children, it shakes me to the core. It disorients me completely. Sure, I want my children to grow up and know how to work hard. I also want them to know beyond the shadow of a doubt that grace is real.

I want my children to know that who they are cannot be reduced to any work they can or cannot do. I want them to know that they were loved before they existed. I want them to know they will always be loved, and I want them to know that love and grace are just part of who they are. I want them to know that love and grace are just part of who God is.

I need a different story, a story that plays out differently than work, reward, repeat. I need a story that makes room for work, but insists that love and grace belong to me and my children no matter what work we can or cannot do.

In my work as a teacher, youth pastor, and parent, I've come to believe that I am not alone in my need for another story. Our world is short on grace. We're also short on rest.

In the last decade or so, I've come to believe that the Sabbath provides us with just such a story. Through the Sabbath, God tells us another story. It's a story that doesn't do away with our work. It's a story that puts our work in perspective. It's a story of rest and grace, but it's not always an easy story to hear.

Think about this. If you've been living your life by the work-reward-repeat cycle, and if that has gone relatively well for you, then rest and grace may upset the cart. Remember the story of the laborers that Jesus told. The ones who started working at the end of the day received the same wages as the laborers who worked the entire day. Why? Because of grace.

That's not fair. And that's the point.

Grace messes with us, especially if we're hard-working types from anywhere who know how to get stuff done. Grace disorients us. But grace also provides us with an extraordinary promise.

Before we existed, before we could do anything to earn it, we were loved. Sabbath tells this story.

Let's see if we can learn it . . . and live it.

Our young people desperately need to hear it.

Wrestling with Rest: Whoever Said This Was Easy?

A Day in the Life of Danny: Blessed Busyness

Danny doesn't have much time for rest, but he doesn't seem to mind.

I met Danny a few years ago, when he was a senior in high school and I was leading a retreat for his youth group. Danny lives in a town close enough to Washington, DC, to allow his parents to commute, yet far enough away for farms, orchards, and livestock to dot the countryside nearby. Danny is tall and slender, understated and confident. He is well-liked by his peers and a clear leader in his youth group. He loves his friends and is an accomplished musician.

Like many young people his age, school, sports, rehearsals, college prep, and friends keep Danny's schedule full. He's learned to manage his time carefully, prioritize wisely, and limit leisure as he pursues a host of lofty goals.

In a single day, Danny juggles AP Environmental Science, AP Psychology, AP Calculus, Intro to Engineering, an online business development course, his application to MIT, rehearsal for a performance at the Kennedy Center, a lacrosse fundraiser, and over three hours of practicing music. In the midst of this busy day, Danny still finds time to pack for an upcoming youth retreat, touch base with friends, and go to the dentist.

Danny is a devoted member of his hometown United Methodist Church, which offers an excellent youth music program that has allowed Danny to participate in youth choirs and orchestras throughout his childhood. The youth choir sings each Sunday during worship and travels on a much-anticipated choir tour each spring.[1]

Danny pursues excellence in all he does, and his church's music program provides yet another outlet for expressing this passion and discipline. Danny's many commitments demand a lot, but he doesn't seem to mind. On the contrary, he wears his busy schedule like a badge of honor. Yet what remains unclear in Danny's life is whether any distinction can be made between the rhythm of life that functions at his church, and the rhythm of life that emerges from the opportunities and demands of Danny's life in school, on the playing field, and on the stage.

Danny's life overflows with good things and good opportunities, which all contribute to an extraordinarily full schedule that the church and society generally applaud. Is this as it should be? Are we right to assume that a full schedule equals a life well-lived? Should the rhythm of the life of the church be distinct from the rhythms—or arrhythmias—of a hyper-connected, consumption-driven society? If so, on what basis?

The degree to which Danny's church contributes to and promotes a rhythm of life which knows no ceasing leads to distinctively theological questions. What does all this time on the go say about Danny's and Danny's church's understanding of who God is? What image of God does such a rhythm suggest? Danny's church takes great pride in its musical program for youth. The leaders among the youth are the ones who are most involved. His church appears to equate greater involvement and increased activity with superior faithfulness. In other words, the norms at Danny's church suggest that the more faithful you are, the busier you'll be.

Does Danny ever question how constant activity influences his understanding of who God is? Is this what faithfulness to God is supposed to look like? Does he ever question the influence of constant activity on his own identity? Does Danny's church ever help him ask such questions, or are Danny and his fellow youth left to assume that the life of faith is a life of continuous motion?

The roots of the word "Sabbath" literally mean "to desist" or "to stop,"[2] yet Danny loves to be on the go. He loves his full schedule, and his church loves to fill it. So, how can Danny know a relationship with God which regularly includes Sabbath rest when his church seems to only echo the broader society in its encouragement to go, go, go?

Texting with Cliff[3]

Cliff is a sophomore at Silver Academy. Like the vast majority of American teens, Cliff texts to stay connected with others.[4] Texting lets Cliff communicate with his friends virtually all the time, yet Cliff realizes that this isn't always a good thing. He recognizes that, in sociologist Sherry Turkle's words, texting "generates its own demand."[5] Though texting lets Cliff get a message instantaneously to his friends, a received text demands a response with similar promptness. Cliff sums up things succinctly—"Texting is pressure"—and he struggles to imagine a scenario where it would be okay to fail to respond to a text. "Ten minutes, maximum," is how Cliff responds to a question about how much time he has for sending a reply.

At first glance, Danny and Cliff appear to lead very different lives. We don't read about Cliff's hyper-scheduled life, and he never mentions any lofty vocational or educational goals. Danny seems to exercise great restraint when it comes to technology. Yet through the differences, a common theme emerges which stands in stark contrast to the Sabbath. In a very real sense, neither Danny nor Cliff ever stops. Cliff never escapes the pressure to text; Danny never steps out of his hectic schedule. In Danny's case we questioned the implications of his endless activity on his understanding of and relationship to God. In Cliff's case, we notice the irony of a technology that promises to keep people connected, but is being used in a way that ultimately fosters discontent and dissatisfaction.

Cliff feels no freedom to exercise his own ability to make decisions when it comes to texting. When asked about possible situations in which it would be acceptable to fail to respond to a text, he can think of only two: "Your class has a test. Or you lost your signal."[6] In both cases, the choice to not respond is imposed on Cliff. He doesn't choose it for himself, and he seems incapable of imagining a scenario in which he would impose a limit on his ability to respond to a text.

Why does this matter? It matters because vibrant relationships depend on limits. In marriage, a person devotes herself to another, thus limiting every other relationship. In faith, God commands that we have no other gods before the one true God. When the limits are removed or ignored, relationships falter.

We catch a glimpse of this in both Danny and Cliff. While Danny's schedule prevents him from knowing and experiencing God's Sabbath rest, Cliff's way of texting ironically prevents him from knowing satisfied relationships with his friends. What choice do Danny and Cliff have but to know some form of ceaselessness as inherent to their identities? What would it take for them to imagine rest as a God-given gift and integral rather than contradictory to who they are?

Sabbath: Disorienting Grace

This book is for anyone who has worked tirelessly in the hope that young people may know themselves as God's beloved children. (It is also for anyone who has worked tirelessly to know her- or himself as a beloved child of God.) It raises a simple but identity-shaking question about our efforts and rest. We've been willing to work tirelessly on behalf of young people. But are we willing to rest on their behalf as well? If that question seems illogical or lazy, I hope you'll keep reading. I've had that reaction, and I still struggle with it; but a real invitation—a divine and holy invitation—continues. It is the invitation to a Sabbath journey, a journey of work and rest, but one that happens to begin, in utterly disorienting fashion, with rest. We have said that we would do anything for the young people we love. But are we willing to recognize that there is work we were never meant to do?

I would caution the reader at the outset that this is not an easy journey. Though books on the Sabbath overwhelmingly use words like "rest," "delight," "pleasure," "recreation," and "rejuvenation," such a Sabbath vocabulary fails to account for either young people's anxious experience of rest or the anxiety and turmoil that frequently accompany the accounts of the Sabbath in Scripture. The Israelites in the wilderness struggle; the Pharisees struggle; Jesus seems to struggle; and Cliff and Danny struggle, too. The Sabbath journey challenges and disorients for very logical reasons. You see, if we've been staking our identity on the fact that we would do anything for our young people, yet through the Sabbath, God invites us to rest and recognize that our endless work can save neither ourselves nor our young, then the foundations of our identity are shaken. We struggle to know who we are.

I'm convinced this is precisely the point.

God's invitation to us for Sabbath rest is an invitation to come and die. It's an invitation that exposes the degrees to which we have trusted our work and ability more than we have trusted God, but then surprises us with the news that our truest identity never depended on what we could do or accomplish. If we're willing to receive God's gift of Sabbath rest—to die to identities founded on mere human efforts—we may rise anew to the realization that we are God's beloved children. We may then find that our labor on behalf of the young people we love finds its bearings and roots not in our productivity or efficiency, but in God's all-powerful grace.[7]

To begin grasping this, let's explore three more Sabbath stories.

Story #1: Sue's Sabbath

Sue Miller has known life—or rather, the lack of life—that results from an existence that knows no Sabbath rest. Sue grew up in southern California, with both her single mother and her grandmother raising her. Sue's mom was a devoted Methodist who worked the night shift to make ends meet; Sue's grandmother was a strong, spunky Mennonite from Minnesota who held vigorously to her faith. Every summer, Sue would fly to Minnesota to spend a month with her grandma, and every winter, Sue's grandma would escape the cold Minnesota winters by spending two months with Sue and her mother in California.

Sue's earliest impressions of the Sabbath all go back to her relationship with her grandmother. While Sue has no memory of her mother even using the word "Sabbath," her grandmother never used the word "Sunday." She only spoke of the Sabbath. "She was very legalistic—very, very legalistic." The fact that her grandmother wouldn't allow her to latch-hook on Sundays left a particularly strong impression.[8] "This is the Sabbath. We don't do this on the Sabbath." As Sue entered adolescence, she found herself more and more dissatisfied with her grandmother's legalism.

After giving birth at seventeen to her son, Alex, Sue followed the path of her own mother by juggling parenthood, education, and career. Sue earned her undergraduate degree in social work, and then spent the next dozen years raising Alex and working at a home for new and expecting teen moms. Half of those years included working an additional part-time job at a bank. In the midst of the demands of single parenthood and career, Sue managed to maintain the weekly rhythm of her own childhood and take Alex to church each Sunday. Looking back, she sees those Sundays neither as a continuation of her grandmother's legalism nor as days of intentional Sabbath practice. It was just something she did.

During those years of raising Alex and pursuing a career in social work, Sue also discerned a call to ministry. The year after Alex graduated from high school, Sue headed for seminary. Her experience with young people in social work, her gifts for ministry, and her strong mind led her to attend a well-respected, East Coast seminary that had a reputation for combining academic rigor and passion for the church. Her first semesters proved to be more of a challenge than she had anticipated.

In spite of the fact that Sue quickly made friends with a few other seminary students, she consistently found herself suffering from impostor syndrome.[9] She felt like a fraud. In the context of other strong students and in the midst of trying to learn unfamiliar theological terms and ideas, Sue constantly felt insufficient and out of place. She would walk into the seminary dining hall, scan the crowd, and think, "Everybody in this room knows more theological language than I do; they know more about the Bible than I do; they know more about—I don't know, fill in the blank, than I do, and in order for me to fit in or to belong here, I need to read every single thing so I know even a little bit compared to these other people."

Impostor syndrome virtually paralyzed Sue in both mind and body. She describes the experience vividly: "[I felt] constant anxiety. My chest was heavy; it was harder to breathe. It manifested itself in a way where my brain was constantly spinning, and I wasn't even able to slow down and focus because I was so anxious . . . trying to appear like I belonged here." Term papers made the symptoms all the more severe. In time, she found herself curled into the fetal position on her bed, contemplating how she would explain to her denomination why she had withdrawn from seminary. Had it not been for the intervention of her seminary friends, Sue suspects she wouldn't have survived those first semesters. She says it felt like pursuing an identity she could never attain.

During Sue's second year of seminary, she learned about an understanding of the Sabbath that starkly contrasted with her grandmother's narrow legalism. This broader view of the Sabbath invited Sue to consider Sabbath not as a heavy-handed burden, but as an opportunity to receive and embrace gifts of rest, grace, and life from God. On this view, Sabbath provides an opportunity for God's people to remember that their lives and their identities ultimately find their rooting and basis in God's grace and provision, not in endless work.

In other words, Sue was reminded that her truest and deepest identity didn't depend on how many books she had read or how well she knew different theologians or theologies. According to Sue, this broader view of the Sabbath "convicted and inspired" her as it opened her eyes to the insufficiency of her grandmother's legalism—a view which in many ways reduced Sabbath to another example of endless human effort.

After a number of weeks of discernment and ongoing conversation, Sue realized what she needed to let go as her way of practicing the Sabbath. Sue decided she would radically trust God's grace and practice Sabbath by letting go of the impostor syndrome. In some sense, her life had come to depend on the syndrome: it drove her identity as a student; it told her she could never be enough. Though it insisted that she always read, know, and do more,

Sue never could have reached a point where she had read, known, or done enough. In this way, impostor syndrome cursed Sue by insisting that she constantly pursue an identity she could never attain. In other words, it held her captive. So, to practice Sabbath by letting go of the impostor syndrome meant "do[ing] something that I thought was going to be impossible."

Sue committed to observing a twenty-four-hour, weekly Sabbath, and during her Sabbath she chose not to do homework and focused instead on building relationships. This practice wasn't easy; it occasionally meant staying up until midnight on Saturday night and waking up early on Monday morning to finish homework. Sabbath practice in and of itself created some of its own anxiety, but it also opened up a vast space—a whole weekly, twenty-four-hour window—through which new life emerged. Suddenly, Sue had time to catch up with family back home; she savored dinner with friends; she attended church more prepared to worship; she took naps. She took naps!

Ultimately, the Sabbath opened a space for Sue to hear God's affirmation of her identity in Christ—an identity that couldn't be earned by endless work, an identity that upended the impostor syndrome, and an identity that had actually been hers all along. When I asked Sue what God had been doing in and through her Sabbath practice, she paused thoughtfully and then said, "Through the Sabbath I heard God tell me, 'You are my beloved child.'"[10]

Sue's Story Is a Church Story

If those of us in the church fail to listen carefully to Sue's story, we may simply smile and feel good about the fact that she ultimately figured it out. But that would be a profound misunderstanding of both Sue's story and the church's place in it. Sue's story should challenge the church to its core. In reality, her story has very little to do with her "figuring it out," and everything to do with her realizing the limits of her own efforts—of what she could "figure out." Sue allowed herself to be embraced by a God large enough to make space for both her work *and* her rest.

To suggest that Sue merely figured things out suggests that the story involves only human effort and action. In reality, Sue's story depends on recognizing the limits of human effort and action. It culminates not in what she accomplished or figured out, but in the relationship between the life of the church and the life of God. As Sue encountered another view of the Sabbath, discerned with others God's call and invitation through the Sabbath, and courageously stopped her ceaseless striving, she discerned God's voice saying, "You are my beloved child."

If we hear Sue's story clearly, we will notice that it depends utterly on God's grace and action, and that it invites a particular kind of human response. Along with Sue, we will recognize Sabbath as a gift that flows from God's grace. We will also recognize that not all human responses to God's grace are equal. To employ explicitly theological language, human response to God's grace may be what Paul calls "the obedience of faith," or it may be sin.[11] Sue's story includes both. On the one hand, her succumbing to impostor syndrome fell short of the fullness of life that God intends for God's people. On the other hand, her Sabbath practice opened her up to life more abundant. On the one hand, legalism prevented Sue from discerning God within the Sabbath. On the other, the renewed Sabbath nurtured not only Sue's faith in God and her sense of vocation, but also her relationships with friends and family.

The church must wrestle with its own sin as well. Sue's story intersects with the church at every point: Sue was born into the church, grew up in the church, raised a child in the church, went to church each Sunday, and was ultimately groomed for formal leadership in the church, yet she never glimpsed God's extravagant grace in the Sabbath. The church must wrestle with the fact that it functionally provided Sue with two misinterpretations of the Sabbath: first, Sabbath equals adherence to a strict set of rules and regulations, presumably because that's what God wants; and second, the life of faith—particularly if you feel called to be a leader in the church—requires constant effort. In this case, responding to God's call eliminates Sabbath as an option because you simply have too much to do.

Both interpretations reduce Sabbath to a matter of human effort; both interpretations crowd out God's grace and action in and through the Sabbath; and both look to human effort and action as the primary basis for human identity. Fear typically provides the foundation for both misinterpretations. On the one hand, the church has feared practicing Sabbath in the wrong way. On the other hand, the church has ruled out regular Sabbath rest, fearing it always had to read more, know more, do more, and be more.

In too many cases, the church not only has refused an identity marked by God's Sabbath grace, but has gone so far as to embrace and showcase an identity characterized by endless labor, refusal to rest, and obsession with productivity and efficiency. The church has too often proclaimed "We will not rest until the job is done!" without recognizing that human effort has never been enough to bring about the Kingdom of God. In profound and challenging ways, the Sabbath forced Sue to face the reality of her false identity while making space for her to be embraced by the identity that was hers in Christ all along.

To say that the Sabbath reframed her identity is to say that it changed her response to the question "Who are you?" Impostor syndrome distorted her identity. Under its influence, Sue would respond to the question "Who are you?" with "Impostor" or "Fraud." Sabbath changed her answer. In its light she could perceive her truest identity. Who is Sue? She is a beloved child of God. Hear this again: The Sabbath forced Sue to face the reality of her false identity (impostor, fraud) while making space for her to be embraced by the identity that was hers in Christ all along (child of God). God extends the same invitation to the church and its youth.

Sue lived through childhood, adolescence, college, career, raising a child, discerning a call to ministry, and almost two years of formal theological education before she had a robust and life-giving encounter with the Sabbath. She had to wait nearly four decades before she experienced the healing, grace, and rest that God gives through the Sabbath for affirmation of her truest identity. Will our youth have to wait that long as well?

Story #2: Sabbath Implosion

While the stories of Danny, Cliff, and Sue lack any sense of intentional Sabbath practice, my story reads somewhat differently. I arrived at seminary having heard horror stories from the spouses of seminary students. Such spouses lamented the entire seminary experience because the demands of seminary effectively removed their student spouses from marriage and family life. As one who came to seminary with a spouse and two children, I made a simple vow at the beginning: I intended to leave seminary with a family and a degree, but if I was forced to choose, I would leave seminary with my family.

Concretely, this meant (among other things) reserving an entire day as a Sabbath day. Having come from the context of six years of youth ministry in a multi-church, multi-denominational setting, I actually found the freedom of seminary Sundays to be a refreshing luxury. Aside from one summer of field education in a church, my "job" didn't require me to work on Sunday, and I could now have that day as a day of rest with my church and family.

This practice sustained me throughout my pursuit of my master's degree, and paved the way for my doctoral studies. When the pressures of school and work threatened, I would cling all the more tightly to my Sunday Sabbaths. I started the first semester of my doctoral studies confident in my ability to maintain a healthy rhythm of work and rest, even in the midst of the pressures of a new degree, higher expectations, and greater unknowns.

Then the end of the first semester of the doctoral program rolled around, and the wheels flew off.

I panicked.

Anxiety overwhelmed me, and I had no rest—I literally couldn't sleep. How could this be?

At this point in my education, I had already named Sabbath as a primary research interest. Now I—the burgeoning Sabbath "expert"—couldn't rest and couldn't navigate any sense of rhythm between work and rest. I thought I knew myself well enough to know how to navigate this new pressure, yet I sat terrified at the end of this semester, facing work that seemed impossible and the real fear that I was having a mental breakdown. I felt like I was literally losing myself, losing my mind. Somehow, even though I continued to practice the Sabbath diligently, I had no rest.

Story #3: Sabbath and Supper

As it turns out, Sue, Danny, Cliff, and I aren't the first ones to struggle with Sabbath. In Exodus 16, we read of another people who knew nothing of regular rhythms of rest. The Israelites have just crossed the Red Sea. God has delivered them from the hands of the Egyptians, and the people find themselves on the Promised Land side of the Red Sea with Egyptian loot in hand. Then the food runs out, and they panic. They soon express a strange desire—for captivity back in Egypt. "If only we had died by the hand of the LORD in the land of Egypt, when we sat by the fleshpots and ate our fill of bread; for you have brought us out into this wilderness to kill this whole assembly with hunger" (Exod. 16:3). God responds by providing food and Sabbath all-in-one.

> Then the LORD said to Moses, "I am going to rain bread from heaven for you, and each day the people shall go out and gather enough for that day. In that way I will test them, whether they will follow my instruction or not. On the sixth day, when they prepare what they bring in, it will be twice as much as they gather on other days.". . .
>
> On the sixth day they gathered twice as much food, two omers apiece. When all the leaders of the congregation came and told Moses, he said to them, "This is what the LORD has commanded: 'Tomorrow is a day of solemn rest, a holy sabbath to the LORD; bake what you want to bake and boil what you want to boil, and all that is left over put aside to be kept until morning.'"
>
> So they put it aside until morning, as Moses commanded them; and it did not become foul, and there were no worms in it. Moses said, "Eat it today, for today is a sabbath to the LORD; today you will

not find it in the field. Six days you shall gather it; but on the seventh day, which is a sabbath, there will be none." (Exod. 16:4-5, 22-26)

The Israelites struggle to follow instructions. In spite of the command that on the first five days they gather only enough for one day and then eat it all, some hold back manna for the next day, only to wake the next morning and find that it is "full of maggots" and has begun to smell (Exod. 16:20, NIV). The seventh day follows a similar script. The Israelites are to rest, yet some go out and look in the field for the manna that should have already been with them in their tents.

Most anyone raised in the church has heard the story of the manna a hundred times. It rings familiar in our ears, and the manna itself figures prominently enough in the story of God's deliverance of the Israelites from Egypt that they retain a jar of it for future generations and place it in the Ark of the Covenant along with the stone tablets that bear the Ten Commandments (Exod. 16:33).[12] But the familiarity of the story shouldn't prevent us from asking a simple question: Why include Sabbath as part of the manna provision? Why not simply provide manna every day? Wouldn't that have been a simpler solution for a hungry people?

As it turns out, God provides more than bread for the life of God's people. In the familiar words of Deuteronomy 8:3, "One does not live by bread alone, but by every word which comes from the mouth of the LORD." A look at the broader story provides some clues about the fullness of God's provision.

According to Exodus 12:40-41, the Israelites had been in Egypt for 430 years by the time God calls Moses to deliver them.[13] While the initial generations of Israelites in Egypt benefited from the rulers' memories of Joseph, the loss of Joseph's memory meant the loss of the Israelites' freedom. Their identity in Egypt then shifts from a people who initially arrive as welcome guests to a people feared and enslaved by those in power. The generation of Israelites who arrive in the desert after God's dramatic rescue would have known themselves and the many generations who preceded them only as a captive people whose worth was measured almost exclusively in terms of productivity and efficiency.

If we think here in terms of human identity, the Israelites' identity seems to shift over the centuries in Egypt. Their deepest understanding of themselves changes. They arrive as grateful guests in the midst of a famine; centuries later, they remain in Egypt as oppressed captives. The identity shift is dramatic—from guest to slave. When Moses first approaches Pharaoh with the request for Israelite freedom, Pharaoh only reinforces his will for the Israelite identity:

> That same day Pharaoh commanded the taskmasters of the people, as well as their supervisors, "You shall no longer give the people straw to make bricks, as before; let them go and gather straw for themselves. But you shall require of them the same quantity of bricks as they have made previously; do not diminish it, for they are lazy; that is why they cry, 'Let us go and offer sacrifice to our God.' Let heavier work be laid on them; then they will labor at it and pay no attention to deceptive words." (Exod. 5:6-9)

Of course, God ultimately comes and dramatically delivers the Israelites from bondage to the Egyptians, yet with the loss of both the Egyptian taskmasters and the false security of endless labor, the Israelites lose the source of their dominant identity. The wilderness again challenges their identity: it challenges them to move from the false security of slavery and ceaseless labor to the true security of radical trust in God.

The problem is that when endless labor is all you know, stopping for Sabbath feels like anything but true security. It feels like anything but freedom.

In the context of this lost or severely confused identity, it seems plausible that God provides the manna-Sabbath combination as a way of slowly reforming the identity of the Israelite people. As we have seen, Exodus 16:4 indicates that God provides manna in this Sabbath way as a means of testing the Israelites' willingness to follow God's instruction. But how much of a test is really being given? What is God really asking of the Israelites?

If nothing else, it seems that God's instruction for gathering manna requires the Israelites to trust radically in God's provision. To gather only enough for one day and then eat all of it requires them to trust that God will provide more the next morning. To gather a double portion on the sixth day requires trusting that the extra portion will not turn foul, and that there will be manna anew on the first day of the next week. To follow God's command for work and rest is to radically trust in God's day-to-day provision. To do this is to presuppose that God is alive and at work in the world. Such trust assumes that humankind's truest identity cannot be found in endless labor, but is found instead in a God who provides not only food to sustain the body, but also rest and space for the flourishing of identities founded on something greater and deeper than mere human effort and productivity.

In other words, and in concert with Deuteronomy 8:3, the entire seven-day rhythm and each of its parts reminds the Israelites that they do not live by bread alone, but by every word that comes from God. Regarding radical trust, the Israelites are challenged to trust the Giver and not the gifts. This leads back to my end-of-semester panic attack.

Trusting the Giver, not the Gift

At first glance, my story seems quite different from the Israelites' story. My panic attack hit right in the midst of my regular Sabbath practice. The Israelites were just learning Sabbath. Yet a closer look reveals a striking similarity. I remember with great clarity the day my panic attack began. It was my first full day back at school after a delightful Christmas break with family and friends. While I had done some schoolwork on break, I remember feeling pleased that I hadn't allowed it to ruin our family Christmas celebration.

I arrived back at school determined to work hard and finish the semester well. I woke up at 5:30 the morning after our long drive back to seminary. I set to work with what I thought were clear and modest goals for what I wanted to accomplish that day, yet as I sat in front of the computer to work on term papers, I froze. The thought that paralyzed Sue Miller now paralyzed me: "I don't belong here. I'm a fraud."

I had one of those days when I hit the delete key on the computer just as frequently as I hit every other key. The day ended, and as far as I could tell, I had accomplished nothing; I had produced nothing. Suddenly, the work that loomed before me seemed utterly impossible. Lying in bed that night, I felt my mind cave in on itself. The same impostor syndrome that plagued Sue Miller now paralyzed me with anxiety, and I seriously questioned not only my identity as a PhD student, but also my own mental stability.

The Israelites arrived in the desert with an identity that depended almost exclusively on their own action and productivity. Yes, God had miraculously rescued them, but with the fireworks of God's deliverance behind them, they found themselves faced with the disorientation of a new normal—a new rhythm. When stripped of the day-to-day security of a productivity-rooted identity—perverse and disfigured as it was—they panicked. The same thing had happened to me. Somehow, in the midst of my study and practice of Sabbath, I allowed my identity to be reduced to my own action and productivity. Work became about what I could accomplish; Sabbath rest became merely another thing that I did. I found myself trusting more in my own productivity and my own ability to practice Sabbath than I was trusting in the Giver of all good work and rest. In the darkest moments of those weeks, I felt utterly isolated from God, others, and myself.

Is Rest Really That Complicated?

Our exploration to this point may seem relatively simple. We're asking about rest—but not just any kind of rest. We're asking about Sabbath rest—but not just any kind of Sabbath rest. We're asking about Sabbath rest and young people. In telling my own story, I already tip my hand about one core conviction: We can't actually talk about the rhythms of Sabbath labor and rest in the lives of the young people we love unless we're also willing to talk about those rhythms in our own lives. The rhythms necessarily interconnect, and the rhythms of the young echo the rhythms of the old with stunning frequency.

It turns out that there's a lot going on here. For one, to say "Sabbath rest" and not just any kind of rest brings God decisively into the conversation. According to Scripture, Sabbath is God's idea; God observes the first Sabbath; God gives the Sabbath commands; and if we're talking about God, we're onto a subject that is by definition beyond our full comprehension. This means that we're talking about the work of theology, the careful study and exploration of God's being and identity.

We're also talking about youth—another subject that is by definition beyond our full comprehension. Each of the young people in our lives comes from a specific setting, a specific family system, a specific set of norms, and a unique experience (or lack) of rest—just to name a few of the particulars. This means that to understand rest and young people, we could draw on the fields of sociology, economics, cultural studies, and human development, among others. The point of unveiling all this complexity is to acknowledge our need for guidance in the exploration.

My experience and training are in the field of practical theology, and the discipline of practical theology provides tools and a framework for our exploration of youth and Sabbath. If you are a faithful, thoughtful pastor, youth pastor, parent, or practitioner, you're already a practical theologian. Practical theology considers the nitty-gritty of everyday life, dares to believe that God is alive and active throughout all the world, and seeks ways of living and loving both within the nitty-gritty and in response to the loving and gracious God who gives life in the first place. From the very beginning, practical theology has been implicitly present in our work.

We got to know Danny. This meant paying attention to his context—to some of the details of his day-to-day life. We learned a bit about his congregation, and we reflected theologically. What do Danny's rhythms and his church's rhythms say about their understandings of who God is? What should those rhythms say? We also got to know Sue. We explored her story and reflected specifically on her lifelong relationship with the church and how it took almost all of those years before she encountered a truly theological Sabbath, one that grew intentionally out of her convictions about who God is and provided Sue with a real sense of experiencing God through the Sabbath.

This is practical theological work.

As we'll see, practical theology provides discipline and structure for our exploration of young people and Sabbath.[14] Or, as my professor and mentor Richard Osmer observes, practical theology provides discipline and structure for exploring *any* dimension of life worthy of consideration.[15] If you want to think more about what it means to be a practical theologian—and, as you'll see, working with young people is fundamentally work of practical theology—read more about it in the Appendix. For now, we can just say that, at its simplest, practical theology can be seen as a way of living faithfully in relationship with God in the world. It does four things:

1. It grows out of everyday, lived reality.
2. It draws on multiple disciplines or fields of study.
3. It takes God seriously.
4. It aims to live faithfully in the world in response to God.

Looking Ahead

The rest of the chapters in this book follow these movements of practical theology. Chapters 2 and 3 draw on the resources of other disciplines and fields of study in order to pay close attention to the everyday, lived reality of young people.

Chapter 2 looks broadly at the question of youth and rest, and it uncovers something of a cruel irony. Though young people depend on rest for health and vitality, social and cultural norms go so far as to mock rest as a sign of weakness. The truth is that young people simply require rest—a lot of rest—for life and for healthy minds, bodies, and relationships. Rest nurtures healthy, integrated young people. Both social and "hard" sciences reveal this need, yet cultural ideals and expectations press young people into a very different relationship with rest. Broadly speaking, the culture idealizes busyness, marginalizes sleep, and employs mobile technology to both of these ends. Chapter 2 explores both the science of healthy adolescence and the cultural realities that too frequently oppose it.

Chapter 3 moves from the broad consideration of adolescence in Chapter 2 to a focused exploration of thirty-nine seniors in high school. Time diaries, focus groups, and interviews gave young people the opportunity to share their experiences and understandings of rest. As these young people reflect on rest, another cruel irony emerges. In order for rest to be rest, it needs to reduce anxiety and stress. But they ultimately acknowledge that rest creates its own anxiety, worry, and pressure. We explore this in Chapter 3.

Chapter 4 puts the longings and anxieties expressed by the young people in Chapter 3 in conversation with an account of the Sabbath that is rooted in Scripture and the theology of Karl Barth. Here, Scripture and Barth help us take God seriously. What emerges is an understanding of the Sabbath as a practice of receiving life through death. Because Sabbath comes as a gift of sheer grace, it challenges all limitless human striving, and it insists on the insufficiency of identities rooted in accomplishment and human effort.

This grace utterly disorients, but this doesn't diminish human accomplishment and effort. Rather, it enlivens the work of humanity by putting it in proper perspective relative to God. Through the Sabbath, God insists that the only adequate foundation for human identity is God's all-powerful love and grace. All lesser identities must pass away. The grace-rooted identity that emerges affirms the message that Sue Miller heard on her Sabbath journey. We are God's beloved children.

In Chapter 5, the final chapter of explicitly theological reflection, we address a potentially thorny question: What about Jesus and the Sabbath? Barth's entire theological project insists on the centrality of Christ,[16] and my own Mennonite tradition has consistently sought to interpret all of Scripture through the lens of Christ.[17] So, how do we make sense of the multiple New Testament passages in which Jesus seems to blatantly disregard the Sabbath? Is Sabbath something that remains for God's people since Christ, or does Christ usher in an era in which Sabbath practice becomes optional? What we will see in Christ is a most radical demonstration of God's grace in and through the Sabbath. It is a grace that surrounds Christ himself as he lay dead on Holy Saturday—a Sabbath day—and into resurrection life on Easter Sunday.

The sixth and closing chapter moves the discussion to the final dimension of practical theology. It will simply ask, "Now what?" How do we live well in the world in a way that responds faithfully to God's grace in the Sabbath? What does faithful Sabbath living look like for youth? What does it look like for us? How do we respond to the insights that emerge in the first five chapters?

In Chapter 6, we'll ask the same question Sue Miller asked: "What do we need to put down so we can receive God's Sabbath rest?" What needs to pass away so that a grace-rooted identity can flourish? Where might Christ's resurrection life be leading us?

A Final Word of Grace

We have considered the urgency and complexity of the question of youth and Sabbath, and we're preparing to look at this question in even greater detail. But before we do, we do well to pause and recall once more our conviction that we do not work or rest alone. God has gone before us; God travels with us; and God follows us on the journey. Guilt, shame, and dread will simply not suffice as a starting point for this exploration. Our starting point must be the grace of a God who has chosen to rest with all creation (Gen. 2:1–3) since the beginning, and who invites us to abundant living and to loving relationships with each other and with the God who created us in the first place.

At the same time, we should be aware that God's grace inevitably leads us down difficult paths, and we do well to anticipate the anxiety we will face as we continue into our exploration of the Sabbath. Anxiety paralyzed Sue on her journey toward Sabbath practice, and it paralyzed me in the midst of Sabbath practice. The degree to which our identities have been co-opted by lesser gods is in all likelihood directly proportional to the anxiety we may expect on our journey into God's identity-transforming grace.

Why? Because through the Sabbath God challenges us to own up to and discard every lesser identity. Lesser identities must die so that new and renewed life may emerge. The stories told in this initial chapter raise a critical point that should be made clear at the outset: Sabbath practice, in and of itself, holds no power for grounding our identity in God. The Sabbath practice of Sue's grandma could not save Sue from impostor syndrome. My diligent Sabbath practice could not save me from the closest thing I have ever known to a mental breakdown. Our hope as it relates to Sabbath, then, is not in Sabbath practice, but rather that through the Sabbath we may encounter a living and gracious God who offers us rest in the first place.

The obstacles to grace are real. The inertia of ceaseless activity tempts us to give up the whole exploration; it makes Sabbath ceasing, even once, a tremendous challenge. As it turns out, receiving God's gracious gift of Sabbath rest might be hard work, but it might also open a vast and fruitful space where we, too, might rest, delight, and hear God affirm, "You are my beloved child."

To say Sabbath is to say grace. May God give us grace to perceive and receive grace along the way.

2 Rest Is for the Weak . . . and You'll Die without It

I was merely doing what youth pastors do: driving the church van with a pile of high school students from one place to another. I don't recall where we had been, but I'm relatively confident we were headed back to the church after some outing or retreat. Then my sense of youth-pastor serenity was abruptly interrupted.

"Stop the van! Pull over!!"

"Oh great," I thought. "Somebody's sick."

Before the van had pulled to a complete stop, Michael, one of the youth, bolted out the side door, vintage 35mm camera in hand. Before I could come up with an appropriate response, Michael had inconspicuously snapped a few photographs of a luxury sports car that was stopped in the lefthand turning lane nearby.

In the moments leading up to what I thought would be a sure loss of someone's lunch, the aforementioned pile of youth had been admiring the sports car as it drove next to our van on the four-lane road. When Michael, our budding youth photographer and car enthusiast, saw the sports car slowing down to make a turn, he couldn't control himself. Our van just had to stop, too. When he landed back in his seat after snapping the pictures, the youth around him erupted in laughter and applause.

In my state of confused amusement, caught a bit between my own impulse to either laugh hilariously or issue some kind of admonition, all I could do was take my foot off the brake and put it back on the accelerator. It all happened so fast that I don't think I ever put the van in park.

It's a random story; it all happened in a matter of seconds; and it reminds me of everything I loved and a bit of what made me crazy about being a youth pastor. Random acts of roadside photography usually don't happen when chauffeuring the women's quilting circle from place to place. With youth, you never know, and I love young people for the ways they open life to the unexpected. Yet, as we drove away, I also recognized that the scenario likely included risk that would have troubled Michael's mother. As Michael stood on the shoulder of a busy four-lane road snapping pictures, he certainly wasn't paying attention to traffic.

The story could have ended quite differently. Thankfully, as I recall the laughter of the youth, the pictures of the sports car after Michael developed them, and my befuddlement at the whole scenario, I can wryly smile, shake my head, and wonder again at this beautiful and bewildering stage of life known as adolescence. How is it that any of us survive it to reach adulthood?

In this chapter we'll focus our attention broadly on adolescence, culture, and rest, and to do this we'll draw on disciplines and fields of study outside theology.[1] We'll consider adolescence in America by asking three broad questions. First, how can we understand adolescence as a critical period of human development? Second, what characteristics of American culture generally mark adolescence? Finally, how do the first two questions relate to rest? This exploration will unveil a challenging irony. While adolescents require rest for healthy functioning, relationships, and development, the broader culture dismissively shrugs its shoulders, assuming that sleep deprivation, busyness, and 24/7 connectivity are simply part of what it means to be a contemporary American young person.

Adolescence: The Beauty and the Challenge

Michael's church-van-hopping photography raises a number of questions about adolescence. What, exactly, was Michael thinking? Was he thinking? To what extent did his friends influence his behavior? What about his romantic interest in the girl sitting next to him in the van? Was this just a case of raging hormones? Could he help himself, or was this a case of the developmental powers of adolescence overtaking Michael? In order to answer these questions and to explore adolescence broadly, we turn to a field of study with enough syllables to impress (or induce Sabbath slumber) at any dinner party: interpersonal neurobiology.

Dr. Daniel J. Siegel works as a leader in this emerging field, and he utilizes its resources to explore adolescence as a unique stage of human development.[2] While interpersonal neurobiology draws on a wide array of sciences, it draws with special prominence—as the name of the field suggests—on neuroscience. However, the science of the brain, which many would consider a traditional "hard" science, ironically and irrevocably points to the "softer" human sciences.[3] The development and structure of the human brain, according to neuroscience, depend on the contexts, experiences, and relationships of the person—thus *interpersonal* neurobiology.

Adolescence, it turns out, cannot be reduced to either biology or behavior, and adolescent development happens in a way that depends on a complex constellation of factors which include genetics, biology, family history, experiences with caregivers, relationships with peers, and the influence of the whole cultural context on the adolescent's life.[4] Within the complexity of these many factors, Siegel makes it clear that healthy adolescence depends on rest.[5]

Both the complexity of adolescence and our questions about Michael's roadside photography point to the mysteries and myths that often surround this season of life. That's why we can begin to have an accurate understanding of young people by recognizing that not all of the rumors about youth are true. Siegel identifies and challenges three such myths. First, he clarifies that raging hormones do not overtake young people. While hormone levels do increase during adolescence, the changes during this period have more to do with brain development than hormones. Second, adolescence isn't merely an obstacle to overcome. In fact, the strengths and gifts of adolescence are strengths and gifts that humanity needs across the lifespan. Finally, Siegel argues that total independence isn't the goal of adolescence. The brain can't function apart from the body, and people can't function without vital relationships with others and their contexts. So the goal is interdependence, not independence. Relationships with adults, and parents in particular, do evolve during adolescence, but young people don't stop needing the positive influence of adults, peers, and others in their lives.

To make his point that the strengths of this season of life are strengths that are needed across the lifespan, Siegel identifies four central features of adolescence:

- emotional spark
- social engagement
- novelty-seeking
- creative exploration

Depending on the young people in your life, these characteristics may elicit joy or despair. They can be a blessing and a curse.

While emotional spark can bring vitality and excitement to life, it can also lead to emotional volatility, unpredictability, or flat-out melodrama. Social engagement leads young people to form new relationships and to relate to others in new ways, but it can also lead them to prefer the company of peers to the company of important adults. Novelty-seeking opens adolescents up to new experiences and sensations, but it can also go hand-in-hand with impulsiveness and the risks that go with it. Finally, while creative exploration can lead youth to identity crises and angst over the meaning of life, it also makes them problem solvers who think outside the box.[6]

In all of this, we highlight some specifics of a truth that youth workers have known all along. Yes, adolescence brings with it real challenges, but the challenges themselves are gifts that brim with potential. Siegel recognizes this:

With the problems our world faces today—the energy crisis, changes in the environment, overpopulation, war, poverty, and threats to the availability of healthy food, water, and air—never before have we so desperately needed a way to think beyond our usual strategies to create innovative ways of sustainable living on our precious planet. My suggestion to you is that the power of the adolescent mind has just that spark of emotion and social drive, just that push to explore new solutions to old ways of doing things, that may save life on our planet.[7]

In the few short years since Siegel wrote these words, the challenges to our common life have continued to grow. Ongoing systemic racism, gun violence, the radical polarization of the political system, gross disparities in wealth distribution, and hosts of other injustices could be added to Siegel's list. These are wildly complex problems that demand new and creative responses—not only rational engagement but emotional investment, not merely Lone Ranger problem-solvers but deep collaboration. Young people bring these gifts—and the world needs them.

The point here is not that young people alone can save the planet. The point is to recognize that our planet and our common humanity desperately need the very characteristics which make youth a challenge and a gift. Understanding the functioning and development of the adolescent brain helps us minimize the risks of adolescence and optimize healthy growth. It also helps adults maintain these strengths in their own lives.[8] But, before exploring the adolescent brain, it's important to note a general relationship between these four characteristics and rest. Aside from the possibility that rest itself may be a novel experience for some young people, each of these characteristics—emotional sensitivity, increased social engagement, novelty-seeking, and creative exploration—could be seen as an obstacle to rest. In order to grasp the importance of rest in the midst of these challenges, we need to dig a little deeper in our exploration of adolescence.[9]

The Adolescent Brain

One of the changes in the brain that leads to the four characteristics of adolescence involves the neurotransmitter dopamine—a chemical that helps the cells of the brain communicate with each other. "Starting in early adolescence and peaking midway through . . . enhanced dopamine release causes adolescents to gravitate toward thrilling experiences and exhilarating sensations."[10] This change in dopamine release manifests itself in three ways: increased impulsiveness, increased susceptibility to addiction, and hyper-rationality.[11]

Michael's roadside photography provides a clear example of the impulsiveness of an adolescent under the influence of evolving dopamine mechanisms. As soon as the thought entered Michael's mind, it was out of his mouth. "Stop the van! Pull over!" The entire scenario ended before any of us had a chance to think about it. As for susceptibility to addiction, all addictive substances—drugs, alcohol, foods with a high glycemic index, and so on—cause dopamine release. During adolescence, however, changes involving dopamine make the highs higher and the lows lower when teens try these substances. This leads to increased susceptibility to addiction. Though impulsiveness and susceptibility to addiction are relatively familiar concepts, hyper-rationality deserves a bit more explanation.

A friend recently told me of his experience as an undergraduate student when he and some others rented a house together in their college town in north Florida. A few weeks before Christmas, as the end of the semester encroached upon them, their lights went out. It was no hurricane or blackout—they had forgotten to pay the electric bill. Yet instead of simply sending payment to restore electricity, they decided they could save money by leaving the power off until after they all returned from Christmas vacation. Of course, they failed to calculate the increased cost of food when the stove and refrigerator are without power. As it turned out, making frequent trips to Burger King and eventually restocking a mold-encrusted fridge cost more than the electric bill. These undergrads were engaging in hyper-rational thinking.

Hyper-rational thinking narrows attention to isolated facts without consideration of the big picture. Whereas impulsiveness lacks thought, hyper-rationality includes it, but the hyper-rational brain disproportionately weighs anticipated reward over possible risk. My buddy and his friends made a calculated decision when it came to their electricity, but they did so by either failing to consider or minimizing the possible downsides of their reasoning. No doubt dopamine played a part in my friend's adventure. His friends also played a part, and they did so at the level of my friend's brain. Socializing makes dopamine patterns more intense. An impulsive or hyper-rational action done in the company of friends releases more dopamine than an impulsive or hyper-rational action done alone.

If Michael had been driving himself alone down the highway, he likely wouldn't have stopped for the sports-car photo shoot. If my friend had been living alone during college, he may have simply paid the electric bill. This social dimension of dopamine remains throughout life; it's simply more pronounced during adolescence.[12] Here we see how biology and behavior necessarily connect. My friend's choice (behavior) to live with friends in a house during college impacted his brain (biology), and his brain then impacted how he lived (behavior) with his friends. So, as we look at youth and rest, we need to recognize that rest involves both biology and behavior. It can't be separated from either human choice or the biological changes of adolescence.

As we look at impulsiveness, hyper-rationality, and the hunger for new experiences, we may be tempted to see them primarily as disadvantages. But we should recognize the advantages they bring: the move from childhood to adulthood depends on them. It depends on young people taking real risks, relating to new people, and pursuing new experiences. Going to college, starting new jobs, learning to drive, and beginning a family—all of these movements toward adulthood and maturity depend on the changes that take place during adolescence.[13]

Integration

In order to understand adolescence in Siegel's terms, we need to explore the concept of integration. In any system, integration happens when distinct parts connect harmoniously.[14] Parts maintain their differences, but they also stay connected for the sake of a larger purpose. For example, in a church, the finance committee and the youth ministry don't do exactly the same work—and they shouldn't do exactly the same work. Ideally, though, the youth ministry and the finance committee have a harmonious working relationship. The question regarding integration is whether they can do their distinct jobs in a way that's connected harmoniously for the sake of the health and vitality of the whole congregation and beyond. We might say that the more mature the church, the more integrated the relationships among the church's various parts.

Something parallel happens in the brain of an adolescent. The different parts of the brain with their distinct functions become linked and work together in more sophisticated ways. For example, the "brainstem and cerebellum . . . regulate basic processes like heart rate and states of alertness," and the "amygdala and hippocampus . . . help with functions such as emotional balance and memory processes."[15] Brain integration, then, both preserves the distinct functions of these parts and harmoniously links them for the sake of the vitality of the whole person.

The workhorse of brain integration is the prefrontal cortex.[16] As it develops, it yields new capacities for the adolescent. Self-awareness, metacognition (thinking about thinking), and abstract thought all become possible in new ways. Here again, these new capacities depend on the experiences of the adolescent. Biology and behavior again connect, but if we realize that behavior directly impacts brain development, we're faced with critical questions.[17] What kind of behaviors best help both brain development and the overall development of the adolescent? What kind of behavior fosters integration? Siegel began asking these questions in his own days as a student.

Mindsight: Seeing In, Out, and Between

While in medical school at Harvard, Siegel made a shocking discovery. In spite of having advanced degrees and careers that depended on interactions with colleagues, students, and patients, many of Siegel's professors lacked basic skills in insight or self-awareness, empathy, and integration. Okay, maybe not that shocking, but the realization led Siegel to coin a term to describe what his professors lacked: mindsight. Mindsight, as the term suggests, refers to the ability to perceive or "see" the mind. Someone with mindsight notices both her own mind and the minds of others.

Mindsight includes three basic skills that are needed just as much in adolescents as in Harvard medical-school professors: insight, empathy, and integration.[18] Insight helps us see our own minds; empathy helps us perceive the minds of others; and integration nurtures healthy connections within ourselves and with others. Fortunately, these skills can be cultivated by making use of what we know about human development.

To understand these concepts, consider Kristin. Kristin is sixteen, and she's been playing soccer since she was four years old. Though she enjoyed it as a kid, as the years have progressed, soccer has become less a joy and more of an obligation. She's a good soccer player, but the game has been feeling less and less like a game. Finally, this spring Kristin and her dad stopped to reconsider her soccer experience. As she reflected on her years playing, she realized both the joy of it in childhood and the absence of that joy in recent seasons. Ultimately, Kristin decided it was time to take a break. In stopping to reflect on her soccer experience, Kristin was practicing the skill of insight.

Insight requires attention to the internal dimensions of experience.[19] Experiences at home, school, work, and sport shape adolescents at the neurobiological level, and their brains continuously process these experiences. But if they never stop to consider or reflect on their experiences, development is compromised, and they never learn the skill of tending to the inner experience of everyday life. Their experiences never become their own. They remain disproportionately in the external realm.

In Kristin's story, before she stopped to reflect on her experience of soccer, it was truer that soccer had her than that she had soccer. She just kept
playing and playing because it was what she had always done. To stop and
reflect with her dad on her experience meant that whether she continued
playing soccer or not, she could have a richer and healthier relationship
with soccer. (Though it's jumping ahead to note this, we may see something
Sabbath-like here. The stopping leads to greater vitality.) Siegel insists that
healthy development depends on this willingness to turn focus inward.
Insight nurtures the basic human skill of paying attention and perceiving
life in greater depth and detail.[20] It cultivates the vision of the mind, and it
fosters the integration of the brain.[21]

"Science has clearly shown that how we focus our attention will grow our
brains in specific ways. Amazingly, when we learn to see inside [ourselves]
with more depth, we can use the mind to change the brain toward a more
integrated function and structure."[22] This ability to see inward then becomes
the foundation for a second mindsight skill: empathy.

If insight helps us make mental maps of ourselves, empathy helps us
make mental maps of others. When practicing insight, we pay attention to
our own inner sensations, images, feelings, and thoughts. In empathy, we
imagine another's inner sensations, feelings, images, or thoughts. We expand our focus beyond another's external behavior and consider what might
be happening at a deeper level. This expanded focus clears the way for in-
depth communication. When people connect at this level, they experience
what Siegel calls attunement, the experience of "feeling felt" by another.[23]

Because Kristin ultimately mustered the courage to honestly recognize
her soccer experience and take a break, it's likely that her dad practiced empathy as they reflected together. Her dad may have had his own dreams for
Kristin's soccer career, but instead of paying attention only to his own sense
of things, he practiced empathy. He sought to perceive what Kristin was perceiving, and feel what Kristin was feeling. These interactions directly impact
the development of Kristin's brain. They also point to the third mindsight
skill: integration. As we noted above, integration happens when distinct
parts connect harmoniously.

We see a glimmer of this in Kristin and her dad. Though different people, they connected and worked together to help Kristin discern her soccer future. Kristin's dad brought his own unique perspective, yet as they worked together, they were able to move forward in a way that was beneficial not only for Kristin's relationship with soccer, but also for the relationship between Kristin and her dad. So, integration can happen both within people (for example, in the brain) and between people.

Of course, we know that not every relationship stays in a state of perfect integration. Sometimes (brace yourself) the finance committee and the youth ministry don't connect harmoniously. Sometimes parents and teens struggle to relate. When integration is compromised, things tend to move toward one of two extremes: chaos or rigidity.[24] This could have easily happened with Kristin and her dad. He could have failed to practice empathy, doubled down on his own dreams for Kristin, and rigidly demanded that she continue playing soccer. This could have led to emotional, relational, and psychological chaos.

No one lives in a state of constant integration. Integration is a constant task; it is a journey more than a destination; and within the emotional, social, bodily, and neurological changes of adolescence, many questions arise. How will young people respond to new relationships, new physical sensations, new abilities in thought, mind, and body? How will they connect the new experiences with the experiences of their past? How will youth integrate experiences with peers and parents? What behaviors and practices promote integration and well-being?[25] Siegel offers seven such practices that grow out of everything he knows about the teen brain, relationships, and human development.

Siegel's Simple Seven

1. **Time-In**: Simply stated, "Time-In" cultivates insight. It involves regularly and intentionally shifting one's focus from the external world of activity and distraction to one's inner experience of life. Time-In fosters

the ability to be present to oneself. From a neurological perspective, regular Time-In fosters the growth of integrative brain fibers.[26]

2. **Sleep Time**: The human brain and body simply cannot function properly without adequate sleep. Sleep deprivation impacts virtually every dimension of life, including the brain. We will discuss this more below.

3. **Focus Time**: This involves focusing on a single thing over an extended period of time. It involves minimizing distractions, and it cultivates the skill of paying attention. "The brain is built to focus on one thing at a time, processing it into more elaborated forms, connecting it to similar items, linking it to others, and then consolidating all of the neural firing into long-term structural changes."[27]

4. **Downtime**: Downtime stands at the opposite end of the spectrum from focus time. If focus time fixes attention in an intentionally narrow way, downtime gives the brain a chance to recharge and unwind, and the brain needs regular downtime just as much as it needs focus time. Research shows that the brain benefits from unstructured time, free from the pressures of achievement, competition, and evaluation.

5. **Playtime**: Fun, play, and laughter also help the brain grow. They foster creativity and new ways of being in the world and relating to others. Siegel makes a critical distinction between what he means by playtime and the highly structured world of competitive youth sports. While those times can also have a benefit, the mind also needs more spontaneous play in a noncompetitive, nonjudgmental atmosphere.

6. **Physical Time**: "Moving your body grows your brain."[28] Physical exercise nurtures the brain, improves mood, and fosters mental health and well-being. It has also been linked to creativity.

7. **Connecting Time**: The quality of our connections with others has been shown to directly impact health and happiness, and Siegel points out that these connections extend beyond interpersonal connections to time spent connecting with nature. Intentional time with others and with the natural world provides a context for practicing attunement and empathy. It gives people the opportunity to practice paying attention to the full range of human communication, including facial expression, vocal

inflection, body language, and gestures. Human life and development utterly depend on the interconnectedness of people to each other and to the earth.

Recognizing Rest

Siegel's "Simple Seven" bring to light the critical place of a variety of forms of rest within adolescent development. These seven practices provide a developmental and neurological critique of the limitless striving that we discussed in the first chapter. Healthy development and strong brain functioning require Downtime, Playtime, and Sleep Time, all of which can be interpreted as forms of rest. Even Siegel's Time-In practice pushes back against common tendencies toward limitless achievement or activity. When Siegel describes Time-In, he recommends twenty minutes per day of quiet self-reflection. While such self-reflection may in fact be hard work, it also signals a clear break from external distraction and action.

In addition, Siegel's emphasis on self-awareness, empathy, and integration effectively resists the consumerism-driven caricature of youth that reduces young people to unlimited producers (of grades, résumés, rewards, degrees), insatiable consumers (of products, experiences, substances), or some combination of the two. Self-reflection draws a line between experience and identity; it allows people to have their experiences rather than being their experiences—like it allowed Kristin to have soccer instead of soccer having her. Empathy fosters compassion and helps prevent people from reducing others to objects of experience or consumption. Integration preserves difference while maintaining connection. Integration, empathy, and insight require the capacity to name and be present to emotion, not seek escape from it. Rest nurtures all of this.

So, it should be easy, right? Rest nurtures healthy, integrated people. So we'll all stop and rest more. Probably not. We know it's not that easy. We know it's not as easy as recognizing the need for rest and then lying down for a nap, and, as we have already seen, the core characteristics of adolescence—novelty-seeking, creative expression, social engagement, and emotional spark—lend themselves more to all-nighters than to regular rhythms of rest. It will take more than mere recognition of young people's (and our) need for rest to lead us to celebrate rest as integral to our vitality and identity. It will require a holding environment that helps make it possible.

We turn now to the holding environment—the broader culture and its assumptions about rest. We begin with one specific form of rest: sleep.

Adolescents and Sleep: Do They Really Go Together?

In 1965 seventeen-year-old Randy Gardner set a world record by going without sleep for eleven days. Though others have attempted and claimed to accomplish similar feats since Gardner, Gardner's case stands out because of Gardner's youth and because of the extent to which his condition was monitored throughout his sleeplessness. Among those keeping watch was Stanford sleep scientist William C. Dement, who chronicled the effects of Gardner's self-induced insomnia:

> [Gardner] became irritable, forgetful, nauseous, and, to no one's surprise, unbelievably tired. Five days into his experiment, Randy began to suffer from what could pass for Alzheimer's disease. He was actively hallucinating, severely disoriented, and paranoid. He thought a local radio host was out to get him because of changes in his memory. In the last four days of his experiment, he lost motor function, his fingers trembling and his speech slurred.[29]

Gardner survived and recovered, but the trauma of sleeplessness and the fear of what could happen during future record-setting attempts ultimately led the Guinness Book of World Records to stop tracking duration of sleeplessness as a record. An exceptionally rare genetic disorder suggests that the Guinness Book made a wise choice. Fatal Familial Insomnia affects only about twenty families worldwide. It typically presents itself in adults in their thirties, and the condition makes it impossible for its victims to sleep. Its symptoms include fevers, tremors, profuse sweating, uncontrollable muscular jerks and tics, feelings of crushing anxiety and depression, and psychosis. "Finally, mercifully, the patient slips into a coma and dies."[30]

The facts that a rare genetic disorder causes Fatal Familial Insomnia and that Randy Gardner ultimately recovered from his self-induced insomnia may lead us to the popular conclusion that sleep deprivation is a bit like middle school: inconvenient, but not fatal, and most recover. The science of sleeplessness suggests otherwise. Consider, for example, the influence of fatigue on driving. Every year, sleepiness factors into over a million accidents in which a half-million people are injured. Sixty thousand suffer debilitating injury. Eight thousand die . . . and young people are disproportionately likely to drive drowsy.[31]

This should give us pause.

Sleep is a matter of life and death.

Consider again Randy Gardner. His case proves all the more enlightening for the simple fact that he undertook his self-imposed trauma during adolescence. Without much difficulty, we can see the four characteristics of adolescence in Gardner's chosen experience. He clearly sought a novel, emotionally intense, socially engaging experience which allowed him to creatively explore a realm that, as far as the Guinness Book of World Records was concerned, had never been humanly explored before. The fact that Gardner embarked on the sleep deprivation as part of a school science fair and under the observation of the science community only highlights a necessarily cultural component to the experiment.

Sleep and culture influence each other like biology and behavior, yet sleep science reveals a dilemma. Though healthy adolescence depends on healthy and adequate sleep, the broader culture not only makes attaining sufficient sleep a significant challenge, but it occasionally goes as far as glorifying sleep deprivation and looking down on the need for sleep as a sign of weakness and inferiority.

Not so long ago, sleep scientists believed that as children grew into adolescence, their need for sleep decreased. Inspired by the work of the aforementioned William C. Dement, Mary A. Carskadon carried out a research project on adolescent sleep at Stanford University in the 1970s to prove this very theory. To her surprise, the research challenged common assumptions. She discovered that while the timing of sleep phases changes during adolescence, the amount of sleep needed remains the same.[32] Beyond this, the fact that some teens report being sleepy during the day, even when their nighttime sleep stays the same, has led some sleep scientists to argue that the total need for sleep during adolescence actually increases.[33]

However, in spite of the fact that adolescent need for sleep remains constant or increases, actual sleep among adolescents tends to move in the opposite direction. Adolescent sleep behavior follows three dominant trends: older teens sleep less than younger teens; the timing of sleep is delayed in older versus younger teens; and weekday to weekend sleep discrepancy increases with age.[34] Though the National Sleep Foundation recommends that teens sleep between 8.5 and 9.25 hours each night,[35] the actual sleep that teens get averages between seven and seven-and-a-half hours per night.[36] This means that the "average" young person gets between one and two hours less sleep per night than needed.[37] The next logical question is why.

Sleep Deprived, but Why?

While research shows that peers, extracurricular activities, and employment all impact young people's sleep, no factors exert more influence than parents and school. Imagine fifteen-year-old Henry, a sophomore in high school. Henry's parents have given him more control of his own schedule, including his bedtime routine. When Henry was a sixth-grader, his parents made sure he was in bed by 9:00; now he turns out his light between 11:00 and 11:30.

Given cultural norms and changes in sleep phases, the delay for "lights out" comes as no surprise. At the same time, now that Henry's in high school, he has to get up earlier. In middle school, the school day started at 8:20. High school begins at 7:30. Henry's story illustrates a very common collision between sleep and culture among teens. Henry loses in this scenario for at least three reasons:

- He sets his own bedtime. Yes, Henry may like it, but research shows that teens get more sleep when parents maintain influence over bedtime.[38]
- His natural sleep rhythms shift to a later time. Scientists have discovered that during adolescence, the "sleep window" shifts between ninety and 120 minutes. This means that on average a young person accustomed to falling asleep at 9:30 and waking up at 6:30 as a ten-year-old will undergo biological changes that shift sleep hours to a point where the body naturally tends to stay up until 11:00 and not wake up until 8:00.
- He's in high school now, and it starts earlier.

The first two bullet points compromise Henry's sleep in the evening. And the third one reduces his sleep in the morning. Though school districts across the country are beginning to wake up to this reality,[39] Henry's life still illustrates the perfect storm that is the norm for countless teens in America.[40]

Again, Henry's total sleep need doesn't decrease; it simply shifts to a later timeframe.[41] The reduction in sleep brings with it real consequences.

Sleep Deprived . . . So What?

If we step back and look at the broadest contours of the sleep research, it appears that, in general, adolescents get an hour or two less per night than they should. That may lead us to ask, "How much damage can a single lost hour of sleep really do?" A sleep doctor in Tel Aviv sought to answer this very question.[42] Dr. Avi Sadeh and a team of researchers randomly divided a group of seventy-seven fourth- and sixth-graders into two groups. For two nights, kids slept according to their normal routines while Sadeh and his team measured their sleep by night and their brain function by day. The next three nights, kids in one group were told to go to bed earlier; kids in the second group were told to go to bed later. Again, the team measured total sleep by night and brain function during the day.

In the end, the group that went to bed earlier averaged an hour more sleep per night than the other group. This was no surprise. What did surprise Sadeh and his team was the impact of the single lost hour on brain function. After just three nights of losing a single hour of sleep, those who went to bed later lost the equivalent of two years of brain maturity. In other words, those lost hours caused the sleep-deprived sixth-grader to function cognitively like an average fourth-grader.[43]

So it's no wonder that sleep loss has been linked to lower grades, compromised attention, and increased behavior problems in young people.[44] As Daniel Siegel already informed us, the brain depends on adequate sleep for healthy functioning. In fact, the brain actually processes memories and grows during sleep in ways that don't happen when a person is awake, and the more emotionally intense an experience a person has while awake, the more important sleep becomes for consolidating or making sense of the experience.[45] Again, given the increased emotional sensitivity of adolescence, one can make the case that sleep becomes all the more important.[46]

In this light, compromised brain function and lower grades make perfect sense. Yet as far as the impacts of sleep deprivation are concerned, compromised academic performance is just the tip of the iceberg. Sleep deprivation in adolescence has been associated with obesity across the lifespan, ADHD, mood disorders, substance abuse, violence, reduced immune function, increased stress, poorer school attendance, lower grades, and an inability to regulate affect, not to mention sleepiness.[47]

Before we shame school districts, parents, or adolescents for sleep loss among teens, we need to recognize the complexity of these issues. For example, think about school transportation. Most school districts utilize early high-school start times so that the same buses can haul both high school and elementary students. Buses make an early run to pick up older students, and then make a later run for youngsters. The same routine marks the end of the school day. Using this method requires roughly half the number of buses and bus drivers compared to sending all students to school at the same time. Any decision to change school start time for older students necessarily impacts politics, finances, athletics, and family life, not to mention academics. Sleep practices and culture inextricably intertwine—and too often the natural, biological, and developmental needs of young people collide with cultural norms and expectations.[48]

We also need to consider sleep deprivation in terms of adolescent development. We could read the sleep science and respond fearfully to the threat of emotional instability, compromised academic performance, obesity, and susceptibility to ADHD. But if we focus on these external symptoms of sleep deprivation without also considering internal consequences, we miss a critical integrative point. Compromised functioning as a result of sleep deprivation risks not only external symptoms but integration within the self. The work of identity formation by way of self-reflection is compromised. Sleep-deprived young people not only struggle to relate to the external world; they struggle to relate to themselves.

Sleep Is for the Weak

From one perspective, we might easily and in many cases rightly assume that those involved in setting school start times seek what is best for students. They, too, find themselves caught in the midst of a complex system with its own set of implicit and explicit values, and they work to the best of their abilities to ensure the best possible education for students. On this view, sleep stands as something of a benign and expendable commodity. Yes, it is necessary, but it will be sacrificed if need be for the sake of convenience and inertia. All of this presents challenges enough for contemporary adolescents in pursuit of adequate sleep and healthy development.

Unfortunately, a closer look at cultural ideals reveals a more sinister view of sleep. The declaration on a mug at a trendy coffee shop in Princeton, New Jersey, sums up in five words one dominant cultural perception of sleep: "Sleep Is for the Weak." Granted, the intent may be tongue-in-cheek, yet the message can't be separated from the broader context of a town that includes one of the most prestigious universities in the world. The subtext suggests that the elite and the strong willingly deprive themselves of sleep for the rewards which sleep prevents.

A recent best-selling book on child development offered a similar assessment of American culture's perception of slumber: "Sleep is for wusses."[49] Here, sleep evolves from a benign commodity into a crutch, a sign of weakness and inferiority. Refusal of sleep signals strength, determination, and even the American dream. Again, cultural ideals and developmental needs collide. Our apparent approval of widespread sleep deprivation suggests that as a culture, we've actually mistaken a lesser form of life for life in all its fullness. The foreignness of a well-rested existence has made tiredness the new norm. If we stop to reflect on it, we may recognize the sleepiness in young people's eyes not as a sign of normal adolescence, but as a signal that all is not well.

Too Busy to Rest: It's Obvious, Right?

In 1981—before cell phones, home computers, and iAnything—psychologist and professor David Elkind published a text that has now sold more than a half-million copies and garnered a Twenty-Fifth Anniversary re-release: *The Hurried Child: Growing Up Too Fast Too Soon.* The back cover of the revised edition issues a warning against "the crippling effects of hurrying." It cautions that "a new generation of parents has inadvertently stepped up the assault on childhood," and that in spite of parents' best intentions, they were over-scheduling and hurrying their young into "overwhelming pressures, pressures that can lead to low self-esteem, to teenage pregnancy, and even to teenage suicide."[50]

Fearful parents bought Elkind's book in droves, and "over-scheduling" became a new watchword among well-read caregivers. Books like *The Over-Scheduled Child: Avoiding the Hyper-Parenting Trap* and *Reclaiming Childhood: Letting Children Be Children in Our Achievement-Oriented Society* joined the chorus feeding the popular perception that over-scheduling and hyper-busyness rampantly and negatively impact our culture and particularly our young people.[51]

In the world of youth ministry, we've pulled our hair out trying to schedule retreats, youth Sundays, confirmation events, and fundraisers, only to have two freshmen and one sophomore show up because every other young person was playing league soccer, working a part-time job, training to be an Olympic swimmer, or taking SAT prep classes. The sleep research only makes it all the more obvious. Our young people are chronically sleep deprived because they are so . . . ridiculously . . . busy.

Not necessarily.

In spite of the deep conviction that over-scheduling and hyper-busyness rampantly ruin our lives and the lives of our children, another body of research in the social sciences paints a more complex picture. Sandra Hofferth from the University of Maryland has examined the question with some care. She and her colleagues wanted to test Elkind's thesis. Though we know that young people are busier with programmed activities now than in decades past, we really don't know if over-scheduling or "hurrying" young people actually does any harm[52]—because the research hadn't been done. For this reason, Hofferth studied young people from late childhood to early adolescence (ages nine to twelve) to find out how many kids are hurried, how hurriedness varies by class and family structure, and, most critically, whether the most hurried are also the most stressed.[53]

To answer these questions, Hofferth and her colleagues divided young people into four categories of hurriedness according to how they spent their time across a two-day reporting period: hurried, focused, balanced, and uninvolved. The categories created a spectrum of involvement, with "hurried" kids being busiest (having more than four hours of structured extracurricular activity during the two-day reporting period) and "uninvolved" kids being least busy (having no structured extracurricular activity).[54]

Although Hofferth and her team expected to find the highest levels of stress among the busiest kids, their research actually uncovered more instances of low self-esteem, symptoms of withdrawal, and an inability to get along with others among kids with no activities than in the hurried, focused, and balanced groups.[55] Similarly, the parents of the uninvolved youth also showed higher levels of stress regarding their children.[56]

Hofferth's work challenges many popular perceptions of over-scheduling and busyness. First, it challenges the notion that over-scheduling and busyness are reaching epidemic proportions (around 25 percent in her research).[57] Second, it challenges the notion that the busiest young people are also the most stressed out.

At this point, we might fairly ask, "If we're not as busy as we think we are, and our busyness looks like it might do more good than harm, then why are we talking about it?" Before we address this important question, and before we sweep over-scheduling and busyness under the rug as non-issues, it's important for us to recognize that a significant minority of young people do suffer in part because of over-scheduling.

Multiple studies reveal that over-scheduling does present real and measurable challenges. Hofferth's project also recognizes this. Even though the busiest group showed fewer and less severe symptoms of stress than the group with no activities, it was the focused and balanced youth who showed the fewest symptoms of stress. In other words, there does come a point when busyness seems to increase stress.[58]

Other research confirms Hofferth's basic argument. One study looked at the influence of after-school programs on disadvantaged children and found that after a year, those who participated in after-school programs performed better academically and had higher motivation than those who did not.[59] Another study examined data from a nationally representative sample of five- to eighteen-year-olds and found, like Hofferth, that those involved modestly—less than twenty hours per week—in organized activities functioned better across a number of measurements compared with those who did no extracurricular activity. For those who did participate in activities for more than twenty hours per week (3 to 6 percent), the benefits declined, but rarely to a point that functioning measured lower than for those who were involved in no activities.[60]

In her work with affluent suburban youth, University of Columbia psychologist Suniya S. Luthar tested the hypothesis that rampant over-scheduling leads to high distress and substance abuse among young people. She found little support for this theory and instead discovered much stronger correlations between various family factors and negative outcomes. Specifically, young people's relationships to and perceptions of their parents had a much greater influence on their well-being than did over-scheduling per se.[61] Here, because of its impact on the parent-child relationship, the over-scheduling of parents appears to impact the well-being of the child more than the over-scheduling of the child.

In summary, the research on busyness and adolescence indicates the following:

- A number of popular texts across recent decades express concern for over-scheduling and hyper-busyness among young people and suggest that hurrying young people detrimentally impacts child development and well-being.
- Research in the social sciences challenges the "over-scheduling" theory in a number of ways.
- The number of "hurried" young people doesn't likely occur in epidemic proportions. Research confirms that a significant minority (approximately 25 percent in Hofferth's work) of young people do qualify as hurried. This research suggests that the benefits of extracurricular activities diminish at a certain level of intensity and duration of involvement, particularly when combined with an uncomfortable level of parental pressure or expectation.
- The young people who appear to function most poorly are actually those with no activities.
- Research shows a number of positive outcomes for young people who are involved in extracurricular activities, particularly if that involvement takes place in a balanced or focused way.

The point of all of this ties back to our broader practical theological framework for addressing the question of youth and Sabbath. We're working here at exploration and interpretation. Many of us have a long-standing assumption and fear that over-scheduling negatively impacts our youth. Elkind's work and work like his taps into these fears, yet research simply doesn't rubber-stamp the "over-scheduling hypothesis." Yes, there is a point when over-scheduling negatively impacts well-being, and we must surely remember this, but more is going on here than a simple cause-and-effect between busyness and well-being. The research on over-scheduling challenges us to broaden our exploration.

A Bigger Question: The Cult of Busyness

Ten years after David Elkind published his manifesto against over-scheduling children, Juliet Schor published another work that interpreted the American sense of hyper-busyness. Her book, titled *The Overworked American: The Unexpected Decline of Leisure*, made a simple argument: Americans are busier than ever because they're working more than ever.[62] Yet in a way that parallels the scholarly response to Elkind, research challenges Schor's argument.

The more compelling argument regarding contemporary culture, work, and leisure deals with our evolving conception of busyness itself. In a nutshell, we—like Danny in Chapter 1—wear busyness like a badge of honor. At some deep psychological level, in a place deeply influenced by our broader culture, we like to be busy. It's part of who we are. It's embedded in our identity.

People ask, "How are you?"

We respond with some pride, "Good. Busy."

Busyness has become a good and a value in and of itself, and whether we're busy or not, cultural ideals compel us to esteem busyness and even feign it as a sign of prestige and importance.

This hasn't always been the case. Jonathan Gershuny, a leader in the field of time-use research, takes us through the past century or so to demonstrate the way that busyness has evolved. Gershuny pairs economic changes since the turn of the nineteenth century with time-use data since the 1960s to argue that the real shift in contemporary life isn't simply one that actually makes most people busier. In fact, the shift involves fundamental changes to popular perceptions of busyness. Whereas busyness would have been a hallmark of the working class in 1900, by 2000 busyness made its way up the social strata to point to those at the top. If busyness goes hand-in-hand with the upper class and the privileged, then busyness suddenly becomes a desired commodity.[63] People want to be busy.

But there's more going on here than our simple desire to be busy. It's also true that efficiency has been on the rise over the last century. (Think Henry Ford and the assembly line.) The more efficient we are, the more we produce at work; the more we produce at work, the more we must consume at leisure.[64] Gershuny comments, "The surprising result . . . is that if working hours remain constant, any growth in real output per hour of production must be matched by a compensating growth in the extent of consumption per hour."[65]

Suddenly, it seems, we have a model that helps explain why a modest amount of free time can remain, yet the feeling of busyness can increase. As a society, we busy ourselves in our leisure time by consuming all that we produce in our work time, and thus the "ever less leisurely leisure of both rich and poor" that Gershuny describes.[66] The force of busyness thus encroaches upon contemporary culture in at least two ways. On the one hand, we esteem busyness as a sign of power and privilege; on the other hand, busyness disturbs our leisure time by way of increased consumption of goods and services.

Indeed, labor and leisure statistics suggest just such a shift.[67] In a May 2013 article in *The Atlantic*, Derek Thompson compiles a number of statistics—without reference to Gershuny—that affirm Gershuny's work. In the US in the past sixty years, the average number of working hours per year has *decreased* by two hundred hours per worker. But when you break the statistics out to those who make the most and the least money, the picture becomes more complex. Since 1980, those who make the most money have seen an increase in work time of nearly seven hours per week. Those who make the least, however, have seen a slight decline in hours of work per week.

Thompson notes trends that echo Gershuny. "Half a century ago, 'making it' partly meant that you wouldn't have to work so hard. That's no longer the case. As income inequality has grown, so has an inverse phenomenon called 'leisure inequality,' in which free time is allocated to poorer, less educated Americans."[68] In fact, research on young people and busyness tells a similar story. American teens average 6.5 to 8 hours per day of total free time.[69]

However, young people's participation in commerce—particularly by way of technology—helps them feel busy whether they're involved in structured activity or not. Our exploration suggests less a situation of widespread, harmful over-scheduling and more a situation where busyness has become a badge of honor, inextricably tied to economics and signifying prestige, power, and upward mobility in the eyes of the culture at large.

It is less and less socially acceptable to be anything but busy.

Downton Abbey vs. Cadillac

The PBS drama "Downton Abbey" and a recent commercial by automaker Cadillac illustrate busyness at both ends of the twentieth century. "Downton Abbey," with its depiction of the Grantham and Crawley families, their staff, and their massive estate, offers a picture of different socioeconomic classes at the beginning of the twentieth century. The extended leisure of the Grantham family signals precisely their standing among the society's privileged and elite.

The service staff of the household, on the other hand, embodies work and busyness at the other end of the spectrum—cooking, cleaning, tending to the needs of the Granthams and their guests, and generally typifying the life of the working class. The whole scene portrays Gershuny's description of economics, work, and leisure from a century ago.[70] In that context, busyness was associated with the working class, not with the power and privilege of the leisurely elite.

Depicting economics at the other end of the century, Cadillac released a commercial in 2014 to tout its new luxury electric car, the ELR. The commercial opens with actor Neal McDonough overlooking a large backyard pool. As he speaks, he moves purposefully through his expansive contemporary home, gives his daughter a high-five, hands the paper to his wife, instantly changes from khaki shorts and a polo shirt into a business suit, and ends up in his new Cadillac in the driveway. The script lauds the American work ethic, snubs surplus vacation, and ironically associates a home built for leisure with a determined work regimen that explicitly limits it. McDonough says,

> Why do we work so hard? For what? For this [gesturing to a large swimming pool in the backyard]? For stuff? Other countries—they work . . . they stroll home . . . they stop by the café . . . they take August off. Off!
>
> Why aren't you like that? Why aren't we like that?
>
> Because we're crazy, driven, hard-working believers, that's why. Those other countries think we're nuts. Whatever. . . .
>
> It's pretty simple. You work hard, you create your own luck, and you gotta believe anything is possible. As for all the stuff? That's the upside of only taking two weeks off in August. N'est-ce pas?[71]

Consider the way the commercial depicts the relationship between upper-class life and busyness: endless work and the upper-class life necessarily go together. Both the constantly moving cinematography and the content of the commercial proclaim a clear message: hard work, less leisure, and constant, focused motion signal the life of luxury and privilege. Contrary to the norms for Lord and Lady Grantham, cultural norms in the twenty-first century associate busyness with prestige, not the humble working class.

Before we cast the Cadillac commercial aside as a harmless example of determined American capitalism, we should consider it in light of Siegel's work on adolescent development. Of Siegel's seven practices for healthy development and integration, McDonough embodies exactly one: focus time. The commercial spot suggests that downtime, sleep time, time-in, physical time, and connecting time must never get in the way of ceaseless focus. Playtime gets relegated to two weeks in August. Yet again, the culture resists rest for being opposed to its ideals. Rest gets in the way of who we strive to be; it's most certainly not integrated into the American dream.

For the Love of Busyness

The sum of the research suggests that the real opponent to rest in contemporary culture isn't merely busyness, but our love of busyness. Yes, young people have more structured activities on their schedules than in decades past, but this is only half the story. The other half is our need to stay busy. We stay busy because we want to. Busyness has become a socially constructed good and a value that symbolizes the privileged class.

Our love of busyness helps explain the "Sleep Is for the Weak" mug in the Princeton coffee shop. The strong, privileged, and powerful are too busy and important to sleep, and the rest of the world tries to catch up. This explains why our love of busyness and our loss of sleep are two sides of the same coin.

If we or our young people feel busy, the research suggests that in most cases this sense doesn't come from a jam-packed schedule. Notable exceptions exist, but for the majority, the problem of feeling busy appears to stem less from structured time and more from unstructured time and the cultural lauding of busyness. In other words, the research seems to indicate not so much a lack of time, but a loss of our collective ability to track time. We're too busy trying to be busy. We lose time; it slips away; and we're unsure of where it goes or why we feel so frazzled. Perhaps the smartphone in our pocket, the laptop on our desk, and the tablet in our hand hold a clue.

Growing Up with Technology

Meet Caleb.

Caleb lives in Massachusetts; his grandma lives in Iowa. For three months now, when Caleb talks on the phone with his grandma, she thinks he has a cold. It's no cold. His voice is changing.

Caleb is on the early side of adolescence—body stretching upward, with feet almost as big as his dad's. Sandy blonde hair parted to one side. Glasses. He's almost fifteen.

Caleb dreams of becoming a YouTube star. He's already been working at it. Two years ago he started a channel that features how-to videos. His first posted video, edited down for length, came in at almost twenty minutes.

Caleb experimented with different kinds of content—building Lego sculptures, throwing a perfect fastball—before he landed on his preferred genre. He builds popular movie props and costumes using simple crafting materials and common household items.

Slowly, Caleb attracted a following. He gained a few subscribers. As time passed, Caleb refined his skills—learned new painting and detailing techniques, improved his videography and editing, and developed something like his own brand.

Friends at school learned about his channel. When they came over to his house, they wanted to see his modest workbench/production studio. They occasionally text him with ideas for videos.

Eventually, Caleb monetized—started making pennies a day, then dimes. With his channel synced to his email and his phone, he could track comments and analytics any time and anywhere. He knew how many people were watching his videos, how many subscribers he had, and how much money he was making.

Though this may come as a surprise, the road to YouTube stardom hasn't been perfectly smooth. About a year ago, Caleb slumped into a chair at the dining room table, clearly frustrated. He was ready to quit. Not enough people were subscribing. Viewers weren't spending as much time with his videos. He was back to earning pennies a day.

And then he had to deal with the trolls. Brace yourself for another surprise, but people say ridiculous things online. Hate speech and foul language are just the tip of the iceberg.

Caleb—and Caleb's parents—saw it all. It was a journey they traveled together.

In, through, and beyond his YouTube channel, Caleb is figuring out who he is.

I don't tell Caleb's story because it's exceptional. I tell it because it's common. Caleb, like all young people, is doing the work of adolescence, and there's simply no telling Caleb's story or his experience of adolescence apart from technology. It intersects virtually every dimension of his life.

His YouTube channel is but one dimension. YouTube, friends, phone, parents, laptop, siblings, digital camera, life dreams: each of these connects in some way to all the others. Life and technology. Technology and life.

Technology: What Can We Say?

To venture into the territory of technology is to take a risk. Things written about technology usually have a shorter shelf-life than milk. Such writing tends to be obsolete before it's published.

So, why even address the question of young people and technology? It needs to be addressed because we'll never understand young people, rest, or the relationship between the two if we don't at least glance at technology. Technology's presence is too pervasive to ignore.[72]

Yet because technology changes so quickly, it's wise for us to consider it from a particular vantage point. Here we aim not for the perfect strategy for dealing with the latest smartphone, but for guiding insights into the relationship between young people and technology, particularly as it links to the question of rest and the journey through adolescence.

At this point we have yet to define technology. The Oxford Dictionary says technology is "the application of . . . knowledge for practical purposes."[73] This definition demonstrates the vastness of technology: a horse-drawn plow is technology as much as a smartphone. Both the plow and the smartphone apply certain kinds of knowledge for particular practical purposes. The plow helps the farmer tend the land. The phone helps with communication, research, entertainment, and a host of other things.

For our purposes here, we'll focus primarily on electronic technology, and even more specifically on mobile technology (cell phones, smartphones, smart watches, etc.).

Back to the Characteristics of Adolescence

Earlier in this chapter, we named four prominent characteristics of adolescence: increased emotional intensity, social engagement, creative exploration, and novelty-seeking.

Caleb demonstrates each of these characteristics in a way that connects intimately with technology. His experience with YouTube elicits a broad range of emotions: the excitement of new subscribers or affirming comments, the struggle of coming up with new ideas for content, the satisfaction of completing a new video, the frustration of statistics that aren't as good as he wants, the hurt inflicted by trolls.

These heightened emotions often come from the social dimension of his experience with technology, both positive and negative, and sometimes in successive moments. In one moment, a troll leaves a hateful comment. In the next moment, a friend responds to the hateful comment in a way that defends Caleb. Friends come over and want to see his production space; they encourage him. All of this showcases the social engagement that is native to adolescence.

The emotional intensity and the social engagement, of course, can't be separated from the creativity that lies at the heart of Caleb's project. He builds; he creates; he paints; he details; he films; he edits; he adds sound and visual effects. That creativity then becomes the set on which emotions and social engagement are rehearsed.

And, of course, the whole endeavor is a brand-new experience that emerged just as Caleb began the journey of adolescence. As much as it may make his parents queasy, he's literally growing up on YouTube.

Increased emotional intensity, social engagement, creative exploration, and novelty- seeking: it's all there, with technology touching every moment.

Intimate Technology

When it comes to technology, professionals disagree about the newness of the challenges that technology presents. Some say that technology, with its pervasiveness and sophistication, challenges us in ways that no other humans have experienced in the history of the universe. Others say that the challenges are old, that technology just has a way of presenting the challenges in new ways.

Regardless of the newness of the challenges, it's worth at least noting the level of intimacy between people and technology. Think of a person who knows you better than anyone else in the world. What does that person know about you? Your likes and dislikes? Your schedule? Your circle of friends? Your location? Your face? Your touch? Your eyes?

These are intimate dimensions of our lives. Very few people know us to this degree.

And yet this intimacy is exactly what technology offers. It promises to know us and respond to us as it learns all of these things. It recognizes our touch and our face. It knows our favorite stores and our social circles. It knows where we are. It (auto-)completes our sentences.

It also promises to connect us intimately with others.

In naming this intimacy, my point isn't to pass judgment. This level of familiarity is an aspect of technology that can do tremendous good and tremendous harm.[74] My point concerns young people and the necessary work of integration during adolescence.

What will it look like for young people to have technology rather than for technology to have young people?[75] What will it look like for young people to use technology in a way that fosters healthy and integrated relationships rather than dysfunction and chaos?

Sleeping with Screens

We've already said that healthy adolescent development depends on sleep. Here, too, technology intersects an intimate dimension of our lives.

Imagine another scene at Caleb's house.

It's 9:15 p.m. Technically, Caleb was supposed to be in bed fifteen minutes ago. His parents sit on the couch and watch TV. Caleb slouches in an easy chair, phone in hand. His gaze is fixed; he sits perfectly still except for the regular swiping of his thumb across the screen of his phone. He's watching other people's YouTube channels.

His parents suddenly realize that it's getting late. "Caleb! Do you see what time it is? Go take your shower and get to bed."

Caleb manages to procrastinate a bit more, but by 9:45 he's finally upstairs in bed. His phone charges on the desk in the kitchen. For a few hours, the walls of his house separate Caleb from mobile technology.

An hour after Caleb goes to bed, his dad turns out the lights in the kitchen as he gets ready for bed. On his way out of the kitchen, a flash of light catches his eye. Caleb's phone has just lit up with a text from Katrina to Caleb and their friends. "Anybody up?"

Given our intimacy with technology, it's no wonder that a growing body of research points to the challenges that mobile technology poses to sleep. In one study, 62 percent of teens confessed to using phones after lights out. Those who did so were more likely to feel tired the next day.[76] College students respond to text messages and calls after falling asleep. Some go as far as sleeping with their phones under their pillows.[77]

Researchers at Harvard have even documented cases of "sleep texting"—similar to sleepwalking—in which people send and receive texts during their sleep and then have no memory of the activity the next morning.[78]

One clear difference in the research is between those who bring devices into the bedroom at night and those who don't. Children with devices in the bedroom at night average an hour less of sleep per night. Teens average a half-hour less.[79]

Caleb and Katrina sit at two different places in the research. Caleb sleeps as Katrina taps out a text on her phone. And while no kid should be judged for a single late-night text, questions about the relationship between technology and teens remain. Identities are taking critical, foundational shape in both Caleb and Katrina.

For this one moment on one night, sleep is part of who Caleb is in a way that it doesn't appear to be for Katrina.

Busyness, Technology, and Limitless Consuming

Imagine Caleb again. Fifteen minutes past his bedtime, he's slouching in the chair and scrolling through videos while his parents are lost in the TV. Now imagine the daily dinner scene at restaurants or homes in every corner of America. Couples or families share a meal, but no one looks at anyone. If there was conversation, it's over. Now each person stares at a two-dimensional rectangle of light.

Now think back to the research on busyness. Productivity goes up, but work hours remain constant. The quantity of free time more or less stays the same, but because more has been produced, there's more to consume during free time. Free time gets busier and busier. People consume entertainment, cheeseburgers, organized sports, unorganized sports, ballet, drama, social media, and YouTube. As this happens, identities continue taking shape. Boredom (which can breed new ideas), stillness, and moments not spent consuming become more and more foreign to who we are.

Is it any wonder, then, that with a few spare moments before bed or a pause in the conversation at dinner, we reach for a screen and consume a bit more?

Who are we? We are consumers, youth and adults alike. Why? Because there's plenty to consume. And important people stay busy. There's no end, no limit, to all our consuming. We produce; we consume; we're busy being busy.

This is the opposite of a life marked by Sabbath. Unless, at some point, we're willing to do one radical thing.

Just stop.

The Crux of the Matter

It's no accident that Caleb's phone sits on the desk in the kitchen when he heads off to bed. Caleb's family has set a clear limit. If Sabbath sets a limit to work ("six days you shall work, one day you shall rest"), then perhaps Caleb's family has marked out a daily "technology Sabbath" (fifteen hours max with a screen, at least nine without).

Here again, this limit echoes Daniel Siegel's notion of integration. Following Siegel, we could say that an integrated relationship between Caleb and his phone would mean that the two remain distinct. Caleb still uses his phone, but they don't become one inseparable thing. Caleb is not his phone; the phone is not Caleb. But for this to occur, there have to be clear boundaries between the two. There has to be a Caleb who's separate from the phone.

And this isn't easy.

The phone generates its own momentum. It (and the apps on it, and the developers behind the apps) would love to have Caleb stay connected 24/7. Plenty of young people tend more toward this extreme. (They say that Steve Jobs didn't want the iPhone to have a power button.)

Integration requires work, thoughtfulness, and intention. Healthy relationships with technology, friends, and relatives depend on boundaries. Or, to put it another way, healthy relationships depend on limits, and more often than not, limits have to be set in opposition to the momentum of other broad trends.

The momentum of busyness threatens to overrun all our days.

In some ways, it's easier to sleep less; it's easier to allow ourselves to be constantly consumed and distracted by busyness; it's easier to stay connected to technology 24/7. Yet if we look at ourselves or our young people long enough, we realize the risk. We recognize the chaos and the lack of integration that creep into our lives when we fail to abide by limits.

Our very identity bends toward chaos when we live without limits. It becomes more and more difficult to distinguish between us and our sleep loss. It's just part of who we are. It becomes more and more difficult to distinguish between us and our busyness. It's just part of who we are. It becomes more and more difficult to distinguish between us and our technology. It's just part of who we are.

Remember again the affirmation that Sue Miller was given when she received God's invitation to Sabbath rest. That Sabbath rest drew a line between Sue and her schoolwork. It set a limit. Because of this, Sue became more integrated. She had her schoolwork; her schoolwork no longer had her. Her identity became clearer. Before she was a student, she was a beloved child of God.

That affirmation depended on the limit that was set on her schoolwork. It depended on that rest.

Conclusion: Rhythm, Rest, and the Risk of a Lost Identity

Musicians and music theorists have long considered how notes, rests, and music relate. The music happens, they say, in the rest between the notes. If you change the duration and frequency of the rests, you alter the identity of the song.

Imagine the theme from the movie *Jaws*. It begins with only two notes a half-step apart. Buhhh-Dunt . . . then silence . . . then the same two notes . . . Buhhh-Dunt. As the pace increases and the rests get shorter, our sense of impending danger rises. All the action and the essence of the music takes place in between the notes. If you play the exact same notes without the rests, the song utterly loses its identity.

The forces that exert themselves on contemporary adolescence may not be removing rest altogether, but they're certainly altering the duration, frequency, and quality of the rests. And yes, it is messing with both the identity of young people and the identity of the culture as a whole. In this context, the drone of restlessness prevents the richness, depth, and artistry of integrated living that emerges only in the context of regular and sufficient rest.

We could find young people all over the country who don't quite fit the data. The data itself tells us that 12 percent of young people don't even own a cell phone, 20 percent get recommended amounts of sleep, and some portion of young people surely decry boredom as their problem more than busyness. The point is not to universalize the data. The point is to recognize broad trends and to see those markers that have become, to some extent, an assumed part of adolescence. The importance of these trends lies not in their universality, but in the ways that they signal that rest has too often become contradictory to the culturally assumed identity of adolescence. Cultural trends make it all too easy to look at hyper-connected, sleep-deprived, harried young people and think, "Yup. That's what adolescence is supposed to look like." Such a viewpoint makes rest antithetical rather than integral to adolescent identity. It also prevents young people from engaging the practices (sleep, time-in, downtime) that lead to health and vitality in the first place.

As we turn the page to the next chapter, we turn the page—in my opinion—to an extraordinary and humbling gift. In this chapter we've explored adolescence through a relatively broad lens. In the next, we zoom in on the beauty and the struggle of a very particular cohort of young people. They will share their understandings and experiences of rest, and as they do, we'll have to ask ourselves to what extent we're responsible—both for good and for ill—for their perceptions and experiences. How have our lives and our example led them to where they are?

Do they have any sense that rest might be integral to their identity or to God's?

Do we?

3

Anxious for Rest . . .
Anxious at Rest

During a recent spring semester, thirty-nine seniors at a progressive Christian high school in eastern Pennsylvania generously shared their lives with me.[1] They described to me their experiences and understandings of rest, and during this relatively short time, they shared remarkable and diverse stories. In academic terms, I did empirical research. In pastoral terms, I tried to listen well and ask good questions. (For the record, I don't think you can actually pull apart the academic and the pastoral.)

This chapter tells the story of my relationship with these thirty-nine young people. More accurately, it tells the stories of these young people and their experiences and understandings of rest and the Sabbath. As a glimpse of the whole, I begin by offering a snapshot of three.

Matthew: Matthew's life looks like a mash-up of the lives of Danny and Cliff from Chapter 1. Like Danny, Matthew faithfully attends church and youth group, and his faith community clearly influences his rhythm of life. He recently enjoyed volunteering as a counselor for junior-high students at an outdoor educational camp put on by a local Christian school. Like Cliff, Matthew has a relationship to texting that makes it unclear whether he controls his phone or his phone controls him. By any standard, Matthew's sleep habits leave him attempting to function on a substantial sleep deficit. During my research, Matthew offers me a particularly close look at one week of his life, and during those seven days, Matthew averages less than six hours of sleep per night; he texts well over two hundred times per day; he spends the typical seven hours per weekday in school; and he works twenty-six hours at a part-time job.

When the weekend rolls around, Matthew should be ready to crash. Instead, he pulls an all-nighter at his church youth group's lock-in. Matthew never stops moving. Even when I speak with him, though he sits in a chair, his leg bounces continually up and down.

Jennifer: Like Matthew, Jennifer holds a part-time job. After that, the similarities break down. While Matthew's perpetual motion tends to attract attention, Jennifer avoids the spotlight. She tends toward the back of the room. She's reserved, but also courageous. Thanks to a work-study program at school, Jennifer puts in her hours at her job during the school day. She sees the local daycare where she works as a place where she can truly be herself and where she feels connected to both God and others. She finds her relationships with the children deeply meaningful. Jennifer doesn't attend church regularly, yet Sunday lunch stands as a highlight in her week.

Each Sunday, her "Pop-pop" (grandfather) makes spaghetti, and her extended family gathers for a meal and an afternoon together. She comments, "Everybody comes over to my house and . . . we just basically spend half the day with each other, and I feel like that's a pretty good gift."[2] Jennifer has a cell phone, and she occasionally texts, but she can also go entire days without texting. She sleeps almost nine hours each night.

But Jennifer also knows stress and anxiety. Her parents are divorced, and her relationship with her father is strained. She worries about finances; her part-time work helps support her single mom and her siblings. As she considers rest, she writes, "I feel like my tiredness is more emotional and mental than physical."[3]

Jessica: Jessica excels at everything, or so it seems. She's confident, yet humble—a varsity athlete and a member of the school concert choir. Teachers laud Jessica's discipline and talent. They brag about her. She fits the scholarly definition of a "highly devoted" youth—someone whose faith influences virtually every sphere of her life.[4] For as long as Jessica can remember, she has felt called by God to move to Africa, adopt African children, and do women's advocacy work. Her passion for Africa led her to visit the continent as an eighth-grader, and her sense of call appears clear and compelling.

I interview her on the eve of senior speeches—a much-anticipated capstone to the careers of Jessica and her classmates. She feels guilty about spending money on a dress for her senior speech because she knows that money could have gone to Africa. Her family maintains a very clearly defined Sabbath rhythm, but Jessica is trying to figure out how to appropriate her family's tradition and practice into her own faith. Ironically, she articulates a pragmatic understanding of rest. Rest is useful; it helps her get stuff done; it provides a chance to work through the pressure and stress that go along with being a high achiever. Regarding Sabbath, Jessica appreciates her family's tradition, but she thinks they hold a view that's a bit stricter than she would choose.

Matthew, Jennifer, and Jessica hold many things in common. They're all members of the same graduating class; they all attend the same high school; they all live within a few miles of each other; and they all think of themselves as Christians. But amid all the commonalities, their relationships with rest and the Sabbath diverge widely. Matthew knows very little rest, and he likes it that way. In his words, "I'm one of those people that, like, always needs to be doing something."[5] Jennifer rarely goes to church, yet she senses something like Sabbath rest in her weekly family mealtimes with Pop-pop. Jessica's family maintains a very distinct Sunday, yet her skill for juggling multiple talents and the opportunities those talents afford have led Jessica to see rest time as an opportunity for productivity in another register.

As I try to communicate the story of these young people's relationships to rest and the Sabbath, it becomes immediately clear that one story will not suffice. The narratives that they tell of their lives and the place of rest within those narratives are too diverse. Yet amid the complexity, uniqueness, beauty, and hardship, one motif appears and reappears too often to ignore. We see hints of it in Jennifer and Jessica, and we may even see it in Matthew's leg bouncing ceaselessly up and down.

When these young people reflect on their lives and describe their understandings and experiences of rest generally, and of Sabbath rest more specifically, they usually do so in reference to stress, anxiety, pressure, and worry. They define rest in these terms: in order for rest to be rest, it needs to reduce anxiety and stress. They long for this kind of rest, yet as they wrestle with their experiences of it, they ultimately confess a cruel irony. Though they long for a rest that relieves the pressures and worries of life, rest creates its own anxiety. As another participant, Michael, put it, "Most of my day is stressful, like school generally is stressful, work is stressful; even sometimes relaxing is stressful."[6]

What, then, can they do? How have they come to a place where the rest they crave doubles back on them to create its own anxiety? Is it any wonder that they welcome opportunities to escape their worries?

Getting Started

As I began my work with these thirty-nine young people, I faced a daunting and exciting challenge. How could I best give them the opportunity to share their experiences and understandings of rest?[7] I didn't want them to give me the answers they thought I wanted to hear. I hoped for a genuine glimpse into their lives, but I realized this was asking a lot. Thankfully, I was able to connect with a remarkable teacher at the school who incorporated my research into a class he was already teaching. This meant that participation in at least some pieces of my project would be required as part of the class.

My first request of the students was substantial. I asked all thirty-nine to complete a seven-day time diary.[8] When I asked them to do this, they weren't yet aware of my interest in rest or the Sabbath. They simply knew I was interested in how they spent their time. With only that interest in mind, they filled in a time diary with everything they did, including sending and receiving text messages, for a full seven days. These diaries revealed much, but I still needed the young people to do more work in order to get at their understandings and experiences of rest.

I gave the completed time diaries back to the students along with yellow highlighters. Then I asked them to go through their diaries line-by-line and highlight every instance of rest, using their own definition of rest. If they thought running was rest, they should highlight it. If they thought napping wasn't rest, they shouldn't highlight it. After this, the next thing I asked them to do with their time diaries was to again go through them line-by-line and indicate any times when they felt they were particularly connected to God or others, and any times when they felt they were particularly themselves. In asking this last question, my goal was to see if or how students might distinguish different kinds of rest. Would they mark some instances of rest as times they also felt connected to God or others? Would rest help them feel like themselves?

After the completing and coding of the time diaries, our substantive conversations could begin. The time diaries provided a starting point for many hours of focus groups and interviews, and throughout each conversation, I sought the answer to one primary question: How did they understand and experience rest? Along the way, we also talked about the Sabbath as a particular kind of rest that connects people deeply to God.

In the end, I experienced the blurring between the academic and the pastoral, which I referred to in the first paragraph of this chapter. I learned much from these high-school seniors. They helped me do serious research, and along the way they opened up their very lives to me. They took an interest in this question of rest in a way that demonstrated the relevance of the subject matter to them—it went far beyond the requirements of a class assignment.

My goal in this chapter is to share as honestly and compellingly as I can what these young people shared with me.

Rest as Escape

Screen Time

As I initially read time diaries of all thirty-nine youth, a pattern quickly emerged concerning screen time and rest. A vast majority—nearly 85 percent—highlighted some form of entertainment media or screen time as rest. This included watching television, movies, video games, Facebook, YouTube, and Netflix; and of these genres, youth highlighted watching TV or movies most frequently.[9] When asked why these qualify as rest, a select few looked to entertainment media as an outlet for connecting with friends or family. For them, a movie or a television show provided something of a shared experience.

But the most dominant responses described these media as rest because they provided distraction or escape from other dimensions of life. In other words, screen time provided a time to check out. Amanda, for example, said she highlighted watching TV "because you can kind of just turn your mind off and zone out . . . so I counted that as rest."[10] Jessica and Vince reiterate Amanda's sentiments.

Jessica: It's relaxing.

Vince: You kind of get to escape the stress of everyday life. . . . When I watch TV or something, I kind of just focus on that and not anything else.

Jessica: You can zone out from life.

Vince: Exactly, zone out.[11]

Throughout their diaries, these youth vary immensely in the number and variety of things that they highlight as rest. Gabe, for example, highlights only two things: showering and watching TV. He doesn't mark either of these activities as times when he felt connected to God or others, or as times when he felt like he was particularly himself. Danielle, on the other hand, highlights profusely, marking almost forty different activities as rest—everything from snacking to talking with friends to choir to study hall to playing guitar. With very few exceptions, when Danielle experiences rest, she also feels connected to God or others, or feels especially like herself. But watching television stands in stark contrast to these other experiences of rest. While watching, Danielle doesn't feel particularly like herself; she doesn't feel connected with others; and she doesn't feel connected with God. Rather, it's a time merely to escape and zone out.

Comments that link rest and something like escape quickly accumulate. These youth employ a variety of phrases to express this sentiment: zoning out, taking a break from reality, turning your mind off, taking myself out of the world, completely shutting off from the world, getting to escape life for a while, getting away from everything, and escaping reality. While youth employ phrases like these beyond screen time (e.g., playing an instrument as rest and escape), they apply them with particular frequency to movies, TV, and the like.

As these youth expand on their understanding of the relationship between entertainment media and rest, the relationship between rest and anxiety comes into clearer focus.

> **Michael**: I can easily just plop in front of the TV and relax and stuff, but if I want to take quiet time, I have trouble doing that because I feel like I'm doing nothing and like "Oh, I could be getting work done" or something, and it's really hard for me to do that. . . . It is a challenge sometimes to actually make the effort to just be quiet for once and do nothing.

Taylor agrees.

> **Taylor**: Rest is very anxious for me because even though I try to, I still stress out about the things I have to do or I want to do and it

constantly keeps me going so I don't rest. . . . My rest is watching TV when there's noise or listening to music when there's noise, so when I'm actually quietly trying to rest, it's not good for me.[12]

Note the matrix here involving stress, anxiety, work, and rest. Watching TV or listening to music qualifies as rest—they highlight it in their time diaries as such—because it keeps stress and anxiety at bay. It helps them relax. Rest that includes quietness or doesn't include doing something of some kind brings on its own anxiety, because in those cases Michael and Taylor can't help but think about the work that isn't getting done.

The prospect of "just being quiet" or "quietly trying to rest" is "challenging" and "not good."[13] The point here is not to reduce rest to stillness and quiet, but to recognize the understandings and experiences of rest that these young people describe. Rest of a certain kind (in this case, watching TV or listening to music) provides an escape from stress. Rest of another kind—the quiet of doing nothing—turns out not to be very restful because it creates its own anxiety.

Listening to Music

Echoing Taylor, Kaitlin looks to the relaxation of TV or listening to music as rest and stress relief: "School is definitely stressed. . . . Just when I am at home normally is what I would consider rest—when I am just relaxing and watching TV or listening to music, when nothing really stressful is going on."[14] Brian makes a similar move when I ask him what he highlights as rest and why. "Besides sleeping at night and napping, I [highlighted] friends—kind of like hanging out, that's always restful—[I] don't have to worry about anything."

As Brian reviews his time diary, he notices a pattern: he regularly highlights listening to music before doing homework. This makes him laugh because he sees this music-listening as sheer procrastination. Even with homework looming, he describes this time listening to music as "one of the most restful times." When I press him for more explanation, he says the music offers him a time for "zoning out."[15] By listening to music, Brian can temporarily escape the demands of homework.

As Jessica, Vince, Michael, Taylor, Kaitlin, and Brian reflect on their experiences with TV, movies, and listening to music, they express a common understanding of rest. Rest is rest if it lets them "escape the stress of everyday life," if it reduces stress and anxiety, or if it provides a space where they "don't have to worry about anything." A movie, TV, or music provides enough noise to ward off both the anxiety of work and the anxiety of quiet and stillness.

But, as Taylor expands on her experience of listening to music as a form of rest, she discloses a significant distinction between, say, watching a movie and listening to music. Listening to music involves Taylor in a way that Netflix doesn't. In one conversation, I ask what a total stranger would miss about her if the stranger only had access to her time diary. Taylor remarks,

> Probably my relationship with God. Because when I listen to music, that is kind of my time with God, and [the stranger] wouldn't see that. . . . They wouldn't know what kind of music I am listening to unless I write it down, or how much time I spend, because usually it is only like ten minutes, but that ten minutes is still special to me.[16]

Not surprisingly, Taylor marks listening to music in her time diary both as a time of rest and as a time when she feels connected to God. In so doing, she makes a distinction between at least some listening to music and watching TV or a movie, which she never marks as a time of feeling connected to God. While both provide something of an escape, music functions both as an escape and as a time to connect with God. Music invites more of her into the experience of rest than the mere zoning out of watching TV.

John talks about listening to music in a similar fashion. When I ask one focus group if they feel that technology, broadly speaking, makes Sabbath rest more or less possible, a handful initially reply that it makes Sabbath rest less possible. But as they take time to consider, they offer a more complex view. John turns the discussion to the prominence of listening to music in his life—an experience that technology enables.

> I listen to music every chance that I get. I can't fall asleep if I don't have music. I bring my speakers into the bathroom when I shower. Skateboarding, writing papers, I listen to music. . . . That would be my Sabbath rest, you could say.[17]

In a comment that echoes others' distaste for the quiet, John notes that he can't go to sleep without music. As we will see below, John looks to skateboarding and the music that accompanies his skateboarding as rest that provides an escape from the demands of school, family, and stress.

Like Taylor and John, nearly a third of these youth identify listening to music as rest, and again, they do so in a way that distinguishes listening to music from watching TV or movies. Whereas no youth indicate feeling connected to God while watching TV or movies, nearly a third who highlight listening to music as rest also mark it as a time when they feel connected to God. Youth were also more likely to mark listening to music as a time when they felt particularly like themselves, as compared to their time watching TV or movies. The implication here seems to be that listening to music provides an escape from other realms of life even as it provides an outlet for self-expression.[18] We will see the mixture of rest, self-expression, and escape to an even greater degree as we follow John's lead to skateboarding and other forms of creative expression.

Creative Expression

In shifting to creative expression as a form of rest, we shift farther down a spectrum of personal involvement. In terms of bodily participation, creative expression involves youth in a way that a TV show or a movie does not. We also shift to an iteration of escape that stands in contrast to the apparently mindless distraction of screen time. A movie can create emotion for youth;

creative expression invites young people to discover and express their own emotions. Here, perhaps youth escape into reality rather than away from it.

As these youth looked through their time diaries, over and over again they highlighted a wide variety of creative expression as rest: singing in choir, taking photographs, painting, knitting, crocheting, writing, journaling, making ceramics, playing guitar, cello, and piano, playing in the orchestra, and tie-dying shirts.[19] More than 40 percent highlighted some form of creative expression as rest, and two-thirds of these marked these times of rest as also being times to be yourself or to connect with God or others. Danielle feels connected to others, God, and self while she plays guitar; Adam feels like himself and connected to others through ceramics; Megan feels like herself while doing photography; and Andrew speaks with eloquence and theological depth as he describes the connection he feels to God and others while playing music:

> I sometimes play hymns and just sing. I feel like I'm talking to God. . . . I think music is a talent I was given not only for me to just feel restful, but maybe to glorify God, too. To be used as his tool, so I play for church, and I just feel so accomplished. Not that I played well, but that people were moved . . . and maybe connected to God. So, music—I just feel like it's not just me. Maybe just singing hymns and playing, I feel the presence. I don't really feel it, but it must be there. It's not my own talent.[20]

One can feel Andrew trying to express mystery beyond words. Music, in fact, helps him do this. "I can express my feelings in music. If I'm really mad, I can just play the rock music sometimes. It just relieves my stress. Something I've been holding onto is just gone after that. And that is really rest for me."[21] Again, we see one of these youth connect the dots between rest in this vein and anxiety, stress, worry, and pressure.

Similar to Andrew, Taylor identifies music as rest "because music is my stress reliever, and it makes me feel calm and at peace."[22] Danielle says that "anything music-related" provides an escape "where you just forget about homework or anything."[23] Creative expression also provides an outlet for self-expression whereby these youth experience enjoyment, passion, and love. Heather comments, "I highlighted ceramics [as rest] . . . because I just enjoy doing that. It's a time where I can just kind of get everything out."[24]

When I ask a focus group about creative expression and why so many highlighted it as rest, students have a conversation that repeats many of these same ideas:

Me: What is it about these things [forms of creative expression] that leads people to label them as rest? Vince?

Vince: You can just express every emotion that you have in your body, whether it be anger or happiness or whatever, as freely and any way you want. For example, some people, when they're painting, they just go all out. They don't even care what they're painting. They just throw their emotions down onto paper.

That's what art is—emotions translated to paper. As far as guitar or skateboarding—same thing. You can just release any kind of emotion or stress or anxiety that you have built up inside of you, and that's peace.

John: It's just something to be different and express myself, like he said. I can be skateboarding and be so pissed off . . . [that] at the end of the day, I could end up smashing my skateboard . . . I can just put my foot down on the board and snap it in half, and I get my energy out that way.

Or I can be scared . . . so scared to do this trick, but I'm gonna do it anyway and then be like, "Why was I so scared?" It's just so easy . . . or if you're in a relaxed mood, your whole skateboard flow is, like, relaxed, and you're not, like, hyped about everything and tense, it's just flow, like pop onto this, pop onto that.

You can express yourself—any feeling—through this. People looking [on] wouldn't notice it, but you in your head, you can just . . .

you can paint your stuff down on the skateboard and do it however you're feeling.

Jessica: You can work through whatever you're stressing about.

Me: What else, Jessica?

Jessica: I think it's just a way to express yourself and work through whatever you're going through and just work things out. I feel like people enjoy those things, so it's just a time to relax and get away from work or stress and just do what you love. A lot of those are things that people are passionate about here. . . .

Me: It seems like there's a pattern here where stress can go down and joy can go up. Does that sound right?

Many: Mmh, yeah.

John: You can just be yourself. You don't have to worry about what others think. It's just something that brings you self-joy. . . . It's where you can express yourself and be yourself. You don't have to put the mask on for anybody. You can take it off and be yourself.[25]

From these comments, one gets the sense that Jessica, John, Vince, and the others long for more outlets and opportunities for simply being themselves and for expressing their emotions, or, as John poetically states, to "paint your stuff down."

The idea of escape comes through as well. Creative expression allows these youth to "get away from work or stress." It provides freedom from those for whom they feel they have to put on a mask. Here their skateboarding or painting bears on their relationships with others. Though some of these youth—as already noted—do sense a connection to others through creative expression, that sentiment doesn't come through in the conversation with

74

Vince, John, and Jessica. Their creative expression has much more to do with relating to themselves than to others. John even says, "People looking [on] wouldn't notice."

Altogether, these youth offer a picture of creative expression as an escape from the pressures and stress of life and as a safe space for expressing the full gamut of life's emotions. These youth release anxiety and stress while doing something they love. In contrast to the predominantly mindless escape of consuming a movie or a show on Netflix, creative expression appears to consume many of these youth by offering total engagement of mind and body. At the same time, their experience and description of creative expression as rest raises challenging questions.

Do Vince, Jessica, and John have any sense that God might be near as they paint, skateboard, or play music? Why do they frame creative expression—a space where they can just be present to their emotions and be themselves—as escape in the first place? Shouldn't rest that restores be central to one's sense of reality rather than seen as an escape from it? As they express their longing for more such opportunities, one hears an echo of Siegel's "Time-In" practice—time and space for being present to experience and emotion. They hunger for more, but it eludes them. Perhaps they're too busy being busy.

Everyone's Busy

Early in my conversations with these students, I ask what their time diaries reveal about them. A one-word answer follows: "Busy." I ask Megan why, and she responds, "'Cause I have something in every time slot, and I never have free time to just rest."[26] When I get to Heather, she echoes Megan. "I would say 'busy' like Megan, going from one thing to the next. . . . I was kind of sick this past week, so I would just go home and sit on the couch because I was so tired. But that's not really what I would do on an average week. I'm always going and going and going."[27] Heather's sentiments could have come straight from the research on busyness in the last chapter.

She resists the sedentary life that she thinks her time diary suggests. The real Heather is on the move. Her last line suggests an intimate link between identity and busyness. Who is Heather? Heather is always going and going and going, or at least that's how she wants to portray herself. Though she may not intend it as such, the connection that Heather implies in her phrasing captures a dominant theme among these students as they consider rest. Who are these youth? They're busy; busyness partially constitutes their identities and their understandings of rest; and they look to anxiety and stress as gauges for the relationship between busyness and rest.[28] We saw this implicitly in their watching TV and movies, listening to music, playing music, and skateboarding. Here, the prominence of busyness as either reality or ideal becomes explicit.

Busy Culture

As my first focus group with the students concludes, I ask if there were questions I didn't ask but should have. Heather comments, "Why is it that we don't have enough time to rest? . . . What is making our lives so busy?"[29] I'm struck by the fact that this seems like a new question to her, and I ask her if she has an answer to her own question. "Not necessarily." This leads me to ask the whole group for a show of hands as to how many of them think they're busier than they think they should be. About half of them raise their hands. Jennifer's hand stays in the air.

Me: Okay. Jennifer?

Jennifer: Well, I feel like I'm busier than I should be, but I still don't think that I need to change it. I guess—I feel like it's this way for a reason. . . .

Me: What do you think the reason is?

Jennifer: I don't know. I just—I just feel like it's God's plan, like, I don't know. Like there's a reason for everything, and you might not know it, but there's still some, like, he's doing it for something.

Me: So, just—I'm not sure. Say it one more time so I make sure I understand.

Jennifer: Well, like, I don't know. Like I feel I am busier than I should be, but I don't think it's really a problem that I need to fix because I believe that God is putting me in this situation for a reason, so I shouldn't be trying to change it 'cause I know there's, like—he's doing it for, like, a better outcome, I guess, I don't know. Does that make sense?

Me: Okay . . . I think that makes sense.

Stephanie: I would agree, and I also think—

Me [interrupting]: You would agree?

Stephanie: Yeah, I agree with what Jennifer said, and I also think something, like, someone or something is planning, like, better plans for me in the future. Like putting, not a burden on me now, but having me be able to juggle what I'm dealing with now, but I also feel like it is, like we're on the East Coast kind of thing, so kind of like a—

Me: Cultural thing?

Stephanie: A cultural thing. 'Cause when I go out west to Utah in the summer, they're so much more laid back about everything. And they don't—like the group that I worked for out there, they just wake up when they wake up, have breakfast, and then we just plan our day.

They just—everything's so much slower and . . . they really enjoy the time they have.[30]

Jennifer and Stephanie offer a complex view into their attempts at making sense of the busyness of life. They reflect both theologically and culturally. Thanks to Stephanie's experience in Utah, she recognizes that busyness as she experiences it in the northeast United States isn't a fundamental dimension of reality. Other people in other parts of the world live their lives in ways that don't succumb to busyness in the same way.

Both Stephanie and Jennifer clearly desire a larger purpose and sense of meaning in and through the busyness they experience. They hope that busyness isn't the greatest power, and they cautiously acknowledge their dissatisfaction. Jennifer is "busier than she should be," and Stephanie implicitly suggests that the pace and intensity of life in her context falls short of what she experiences in Utah. Yet neither wants to attribute ultimate meaning, power, or purpose to busyness. Jennifer willingly looks to God for this sense of purpose and meaning; Stephanie more cautiously names "someone or something."

Jennifer and Stephanie aren't the only ones who engage in this kind of reflection on the question of busyness. Brian also engages the topic, yet his theological assumptions differ significantly:

I think [God] wants us to rest, but I also think he wants us to do a lot of things that we don't do, and I think the culture that we live in doesn't allow the rest that we need—that he wants us to have. So whether that's just sitting down and thinking—just, like, reflecting on your life or just doing whatever. . . . Our work schedule and school and everything else that we do doesn't really allow what God intends us to have.[31]

Like Stephanie, Brian recognizes that busyness has a cultural dimension. In a way similar to both Stephanie and Jennifer, he considers busyness theologically. Yet Brian approaches the question of busyness not with the assumption that God intends or plans busyness, but rather that God intends rest. However, thanks to cultural influences—work, school, and "everything else"—humans fail to rest, even as they fail to do "a lot of things."

Regardless of these students' assumptions about the relationship between God and culture, none of their approaches to the question of busyness provide an alternative. Jennifer, Stephanie, and Brian all assume that at least in their context, busyness is the norm. Maybe Brian's view assumes that people should just try harder, but the reality is that they don't. All three also talk about busyness as a force greater than themselves. Maybe God works through it; maybe God opposes it; but the fact and force of busyness remain.

Ashley expresses this sentiment as concisely as any of the students. "It is kind of sad that people can't take a day, but it's kind of just how the world is."[32] More than one student comments matter-of-factly, "Everyone's busy." The comments quickly accumulate.

> **Adam**: I feel like it's hard for people to find time nowadays to rest on the Sabbath because everyone's busy and everyone's . . . moving all the time. Everyone has stuff to do, more to do.

> **Melissa**: I agree with the fact that, like you pointed out, it's a challenge 'cause rarely do people find a chance to sit down and rest nowadays. Everyone's busy.

> **Brian**: Um, yeah, I'd say—I mean, school isn't too bad right now, but volleyball ran me in[to] the ground pretty hard. And then it's kind of like we have to have a schedule, 'cause there's only so much time to fit the season in . . . we had sixty games in the span of ten days.[33]

These comments show the students linking busyness and identity both within culture more broadly and within their self-understanding. These students see busyness as a cultural reality; they see it as a force larger than themselves; and they see it as inherent to the identity of the culture that surrounds them—the culture of which they are a part.

From their commentary on busyness, one gets the sense that these teens have virtually no free time. Busyness snatches every moment of their days. Yet we already know this isn't exactly the case. Watching movies and TV, playing video games, listening to music, skateboarding, and creative expression all find their way into their time diaries. This indicates that busyness doesn't equal a total absence of unstructured time. It means, instead, that unstructured time must be filled. If busyness is the badge of honor that Jonathan Gershuny claims it is (see Chapter 2), then it only makes sense that free time isn't free. To some extent, busyness has simply become a part of who they are.

Busy at Rest

Given the link between busyness and identity, it comes as no surprise that many youth have come to define rest as inclusive of constant motion. Anxiety, stress, and worry forcefully re-enter the picture at this point. Nicole goes so far as to defend work as rest:

> A lot of people say work is not rest-like, a job. . . . But for me, I started in a job recently and at first it was not restful at all, 'cause I'm still learning the systems. But it's at a daycare, and yesterday was probably one of the most relaxing days I've had in a while. . . .
>
> Now that I know the people and the kids, it's really easy, because I can just play with the kids all day. That's definitely restful, even though you're still constantly trying to do something and keep them under control. . . . In my old job, I worked as a janitor, so I was obviously doing stuff, but I had way more time on my hands. . . . I could take as much time as I wanted.
>
> So for me that was not restful at all, because my brain could just wander, and for me that's not good because I just—it goes everywhere, and I end up psyching myself out on certain issues, or I get so worried about homework, so when my brain is occupied, it's better.[34]

For Nicole, rest clearly involves a sophisticated equation. Rest equals being busy, but not too busy, and not being mindlessly busy. It means engaging her mind enough to keep it occupied, but not so much as to create anxiety, and not too little so as to create unwanted space for "psyching herself out." Being inactive or having a surplus of time "was not restful at all."

This is not a picture of stillness. It may be holy work, but it doesn't appear to be "holy stopping." Others understand rest similarly.

Jessica suggests an understanding of rest that parallels Nicole's in its preference for a certain level of activity. During an interview, I try to get a clear idea of her perception of rest by asking her if she thinks that Sabbath rest would be more mental or physical:

> **Jessica**: I don't really think either one is necessarily more important. I feel like I could go for a run and that could be stress-relieving, even if I'm like thinking about a lot of things, mentally not resting, but I'm working through it. I think that is beneficial, even if—

> **Me**: So that could be a resting of your mind?

> **Jessica**: Yeah, like my mind's not resting, but it's still, like, the effects of resting, 'cause I'm still working through it and getting all of that processed so I'm not stressed about it anymore. . . . I think relieving stress is resting. It has the same effect of resting, 'cause if I would just rest and not think about it, even when I stopped resting, I would still have all of those problems there, so I think working through it would be better.[35]

Jessica defines rest according to its effectiveness in solving problems and relieving stress. The rest she describes here actually includes the constant motion of both mind and body. Again, the view of rest portrayed here is one that knows little stillness or ceasing, and it must, by definition, reduce stress.

In the same conversation in which they discuss creative expression, Vince, John, and Stephanie agree that rest might in fact be physically exhausting. I ask them about their understanding of the relationship between rest and busyness.

> **Vince**: As far as being busy, like, if you're engulfed in something you really enjoy, I feel like that can be mental rest for you because you can be so involved with that that you forget about everything else.

> **Me**: Like John engaged on his skateboard?

> **Vince**: Yeah, like John engaged on his skateboard. He's really focused, and he's exerting a lot of energy into doing kick-flips, at the same time; that's peace for him, so you can't go wrong there—[it's] stress relieving.

> **John**: It's my getaway.

> **Stephanie**: I agree with Vince. If you love what you're doing, then if you're exhausted at the end of the day from what you're doing, I think that's rest.[36]

On the one hand, they seem incapable of imagining a rest that wouldn't involve extreme exertion. On the other hand, they have a logical reason for avoiding stillness in rest. Nicole has already provided some clues about this, and Stephanie helps clarify. In an interview, she expands on her active understanding of rest. She explains that if she's alone with her thoughts with nothing to do, anxiety rushes in.[37]

During another focus group, James reiterates the dangers of rest that fails to include enough doing:

> For me it depends on what kind of rest I'm doing. If I'm resting where I'm not doing anything, a lot of times my brain will—I'll just be thinking so much that I'll get stressed out or I'll think, "I should be doing this right now," and then I feel guilty.

A lot of times [when] I get home from volleyball, I'll have about an hour and a half of light where I can do things, and I'm like, "Alright, I got all this stuff I want to get done," but I'm tired, and I'll decide just to rest. And then I feel real guilty about it, not toward anybody else, it's just, "Aw, I should've got all this stuff done." So it's just—it's more like I feel like I'm almost wasting time when I'm not doing something.[38]

Like Stephanie, James says that the problem with "not doing anything" is that it creates its own stress and anxiety. The solution: Adopt a method of rest that includes continuous motion, even extreme exertion. Keep your mind occupied. Stay busy at rest.

We should recognize that these youth employ more than just the language of anxiety, stress, and worry as they define rest. With the possible exception of James, each of the young people quoted in this section includes a noteworthy element in their matrix for attaining rest within busyness: love, self-expression, enjoyment, and passion come up frequently. Nicole finds work restful because she knows what she's doing and she enjoys it; Jessica, though she doesn't say it explicitly, clearly takes pleasure in running; Vince speaks of being "engulfed in something you really enjoy"; John speaks passionately about skateboarding as a form of self-expression; and Stephanie extols loving what you do, even as it leads to bodily exhaustion. But questions remain. Is this rest? Is this Sabbath ceasing? What kind of identity does never-ending activity, even in rest, shape and reflect? To what extent has a mind-set of endless productivity overtaken their identities?

As we consider the sum of the conversation around the theme of busyness and rest, we can note the following:

- Youth are busy or at least feel busy and feel pressure to appear busy. They struggle to imagine life or reality otherwise.
- If busyness is too intense, youth become stressed, worried, and anxious.
- If they're not busy enough, this also leads to anxiety.
- Rest within this matrix of busyness amounts to any activity that relieves

stress, anxiety, and worry, distracts from stress, anxiety, and worry, accomplishes something, or otherwise prevents the disorientation of prolonged stillness.

Since setting aside the busyness of life either leaves stress unaltered or even creates its own anxiety, rest ends up being another manifestation of busyness, and the fact that stopping for rest makes these young people anxious only confirms the place of busyness and activity in their overall identity.

One wonders if rest, busyness, and identity defined in these terms prevent these youth from asking critical questions. What if the anxiety that rest causes points to a misplaced identity? What if the anxiety and stress of stillness lay bare the degree to which they've embraced the values and norms of society? Given that the majority of these young people regularly attend church, this combination of rest, busyness, and identity raises critical questions about the church as well. Is this the rest that the church desires for its young people? Is this the rest that makes space for young people to hear God affirm their identity as God's children? Is this the rest that adequately reflects the grace of God? Or is this a rest that merely reflects the value system and preferred identity of a limitless consumer society?

At this point, our exploration tempts us to lay the blame for young people's restless existence squarely at the feet of the culture "out there," but the truth is that we can't draw neat lines between the culture "out there" and the rhythms, values, and expectations in our homes and churches. We know this, and so do these young people. When they talk about their experiences and understandings of rest, no factor influences these things more than their families.

It All Starts at Home

During a session with all thirty-nine students, I ask everyone to write down the name of someone who makes Sabbath rest either more or less possible. I also ask them to write down how they know this person, and what they would tell the person if he or she was sitting with them in the room. Contrary to the schools of thought that look to social groups or friends as the primary influence in the lives of young people,[39] only two of these students identified a peer as one who makes Sabbath rest either more or less possible. The majority—three out of four—named a family member, and of those who did, the vast majority named parents. (In addition, one young person wrote down the name of a boyfriend, but she did so because the boyfriend made Sabbath rest more possible by providing an escape from her parents, who made Sabbath rest less possible.)

These students, who are complex and unique in their responses, affirm overwhelmingly the tremendous influence of their families on their experiences and understandings of rest. Even though the nature of this influence varies greatly, parents and families provide the primary frame of reference for these young people as they describe rest and the Sabbath. They may resist, affirm, or both resist and affirm the influence of their families, but they unquestionably look to families, and to parents in particular, as a starting point for telling their stories as they relate to rest. In fact, for many, the intersection of rest and family serves as a starting point for the anxiety, stress, worry, and pressure that they have discussed.

Setting Sunday Apart

At the beginning of this chapter, Jennifer and Jessica gave us a glimpse into the varied yet powerful influence of families. Jessica's family maintains perhaps the strictest Sabbath practice of any of the youth in her class, and her family does this in a way that can't be separated from the influence and teaching of the church. On Sunday morning, Jessica's family goes to church, and they set aside the entire day in a way that tries to do Sabbath justice to others. They avoid shopping or eating out, and they spend time together as a family—Jessica's parents even prefer that she not go out and spend time with friends in deference to family time. The pace of life for Jessica's family clearly changes on Sunday. "We usually get home [from church], eat lunch, and then take a nap or something and just be lazy all day."[40]

The rhythm of Jennifer's family life also changes on Sunday, but it plays out differently. The explicit influence of the church figures much less prominently. They don't typically go to church, and their Sunday tradition begins with the previously mentioned spaghetti lunch made by Pop-pop. I first learn about this when Jennifer writes her answers to my questions about who makes Sabbath rest either more or less possible and what she would tell that person. In response, Jennifer writes affectionately about her Pop-pop:

> He is a man who is always on the go, working his hardest 24/7. But on Sundays during lunch, spending time with him is the most relaxing thing. B/c of his cancer, my family has grown so much closer, and we spend a lot more genuine time with each other. [If he was sitting here,] I'd tell him he is the reason why I take Sabbath rest more seriously. I feel closer to God when I'm with him.[41]

Already we see a curious theological contrast between Jessica and Jennifer. On the one hand, Jessica's family observes a strict Sabbath, and they do so because of the explicit influence of the church. Historically, the Mennonite church of which Jessica is a part would emphasize each dimension of Jessica's family's Sabbath practice—attending church, emphasizing family time, and not participating in commerce. Yet Jessica doesn't articulate any sense of connection to God that specifically coincides with her family's Sabbath practice, and she doesn't seem to sense that God is doing much in or through her family's Sabbath. On the Sunday that Jessica records in her time diary, she goes to church, but she neither highlights it as rest nor indicates feeling connected to God while at church. She does highlight taking a nap, sharing a meal, and playing a game with her family as rest on this Sunday, but she doesn't indicate feeling connected to God during those times, either.

This has nothing to do with any overall lack of attentiveness on Jessica's part to God's action or presence. Remember that she's the one who has felt called by God since her earliest childhood to move to Africa, adopt children, and do women's advocacy work. She also indicates in her time diary that she feels connected to God on a daily basis during her times of personal devotion each night before bed. Jessica clearly assumes the action of God in the world and in her life, yet as she describes her family's Sabbath practice, any explicit sense of God's activity slips off the page.

Jennifer, on the other hand, observes the Sabbath in a way that many churchgoers might struggle to affirm or recognize. Nonetheless, she sees her family's Sunday time together, and particularly the presence and influence of her Pop-pop, as a means by which she experiences a sense of closeness with God.[42] Although this theological distinction is apparent, both Jessica and Jennifer come from families that approach Sunday as a distinct day.

James also comes from a family that sets Sunday apart. He responds to my question about who makes Sabbath rest more or less possible by listing his dad as someone who makes it less possible. When I ask him about this during an interview, he articulates the extent of the influence:

> I don't think of Sabbath rest as necessarily Sunday. And so for me it's like he [James's dad] is always going. He's a workaholic. He's a mason. It's kinda just in his blood. It's the way he's always been. I always feel like even if he's not there, I always feel like I should be doing something just because it's what he would want me to do. . . .
>
> I feel like I can't go home and just sit down and rest after school. I always have to be doing something. I always have to be going . . . so I feel bad if I'm just sitting inside. So for me, that's what makes it [rest] hard to get.[43]

The question about Sabbath rest leads James away from talking about Sunday. James perceptively recognizes the influence of his father on his own ability to rest even when he's not with his dad.

James feels his father's influence all the time—an influence that inhibits his rest and leaves James feeling pressured and anxious. James also recognizes the connection between labor and identity, and he suggests that his father's identity as a "workaholic" mason prevents rest from happening. To some extent, James actively projects his perception of his father's identity onto himself.[44] His father is "always going," and James feels guilty if he doesn't follow suit. For James, his family's tradition of setting Sunday apart stands as something of an irony. They go to church; they generally abstain from work on Sunday; and they clearly do so in an attempt to observe the Sabbath. Yet, as James comments, "I don't think of Sabbath rest as necessarily Sunday." He remains unconvinced that his Sundays equal Sabbath.

Through James, Jessica, and Jennifer, we see families that intentionally set Sunday apart as a distinct day. Each of these families does this in ways that suggest a Sabbath rhythm of life, and Jessica, Jennifer, and James are all working to make sense of the Sabbath in reference to these family traditions and practices. But the mere fact of Sunday as a distinct day hasn't resulted in comparable experiences of Sunday either as a day of rest or as a time for feeling connected to God.

For better or for worse, for these three, regular participation in the life of a church correlates with the *absence* of a rich Sabbath experience. James and Jessica attend church regularly with their families, yet Jessica describes Sunday in mundane terms, and James simply doesn't experience Sunday as Sabbath rest. Jennifer, on the other hand, doesn't regularly attend church but offers an account of both experiencing rest and feeling connected to God by way of her family's practice of setting Sunday apart.

Perceived Parental Pressure

Other students lament the fact that the influence of family—and parents, in particular—leads not to a slower Sunday pace, but to a level of intensity, work, and pressure that exceeds that of other days. James has already expressed the pressure he feels by way of his father's influence, and other students echo this sentiment. Stephanie's mom and stepdad employ a common logic: During the rest of the week, jobs require the majority of waking hours. The weekend provides the coveted space for getting work done around the house that can't get done otherwise. Stephanie says, "From the minute my mom and stepdad wake up, they are doing something constantly throughout the day . . . especially on the weekends."[45] This creates a scenario for Stephanie in which she feels pressure to follow her parents' lead. Stephanie's experience and description of work, rest, and pressure, like James's, find their basis in the patterns and practices of parents. And James and Stephanie are not alone.

When discussing the challenges of Sabbath rest during one focus group, Nicole shares about the pressures and stress she feels from her family:

> I think my family probably makes it [rest] the hardest 'cause I'm the oldest, and they've never really done the whole college thing yet . . . so especially the college decision and all that stuff . . . was really stressful, and now end-of-the-year stuff is really busy.
>
> But when I finally have a break, and I'll be sitting and just not doing anything, my mom will just yell at me to go clean something or go do homework that's not due for a week. . . . I understand they're just trying to help, but it makes it really stressful, and I can't rest even when I have time to rest 'cause I'm stressed out about what I have to do.[46]

While Stephanie has expressed the pressure she feels to follow in her parents' footsteps, Nicole feels pressure from her parents because she's embarking on a journey that isn't familiar to them. After listening to Nicole, Melissa concurs: "I get a lot of stress from school and pressure from parents. . . . When I do finally have time to rest, they pressure me to do something else."[47]

Here again, we see the difficult irony faced by these young people as they consider rest. Though they define rest in terms of anxiety, stress, worry, and pressure, and they long for rest that will reduce these things, rest again creates its own anxiety. Complex factors lead to this double bind, yet in the cases of James, Stephanie, Nicole, and Melissa, the double bind can't be separated from their families of origin and their parents in particular. At the moment when rest appears within reach, parental pressure—real or perceived—induces the stress and pressure that insist they must keep going.

Others feel a sense of pressure by virtue of the life circumstances which surround their parents. Because of such circumstances, Betsy views the question of rest as a matter of fairness:

[M]y mom's a single mom, she constantly has to work, [and she] . . . does not have rest. So I feel like I have to do the same thing, because I'm kind of the second in line in our family. . . . She doesn't have time to rest, so why should I?[48]

Yet again, the patterns and practices of the family provide the starting point and the frame of reference as Betsy articulates her own experience and understanding of rest. Her relationship to rest clearly mimics the pattern she sees in her mother. But imitation and similarity aren't the only ways to define rest when considering familial influence. Others seek a relationship to rest that contrasts with the example they see in their parents.

Suspicion of Rest

Some families go so far as to look suspiciously at these students when they rest. John explains this at an unexpected time during a focus group. I ask how friends, family, school, and church make Sabbath rest more possible. After a few quiet moments, John breaks the silence.

John: They don't.

Me: You said they don't?

John: Yeah—my family doesn't. It's like if you take a nap during the day. It's looked down on because you could be doing something. It's like, "Why are you falling asleep? What's wrong with you? Are you sick, or were you doing something that you shouldn't be doing and now you're falling asleep? . . . Why aren't you going out and mowing the lawn or doing something with your time?"[49]

Note the specifics of my inquiry. While my questioning route includes asking students about how friends, family, school, and church make Sabbath rest *less* possible, I intentionally begin the questioning in the positive. I ask, "How do your friends, family, school, and church make Sabbath rest *more* possible? How do they help make that possible for you?"

The fact that the question meets with silence and eventually a negative response says something about the interrelatedness of young people, their families, and Sabbath rest. We see another example of students being given the opportunity to comment on peer influence, yet responding instead in relation to the impact their families have. This doesn't mean that these students remain uninfluenced by their peers. Instead, it indicates the ongoing significance of families and parents in their lives as they navigate the question of rest. In John's case, he perceives suspicion on the part of his family when he tries to rest.

In all likelihood, this also indicates a broader cultural and societal ideal that sees rest as secondary if not contrary to the good life. As the trendy coffee mug mentioned in the last chapter proclaimed, "Sleep Is for the Weak." Busyness and activity are held in esteem; rest is viewed with suspicion. And John isn't the only one who comes from a family that views rest with suspicion. This sense of preference for activity and productivity comes through overtly and contentiously as some consider families and rest. As I move toward wrapping up one of the focus groups, I ask a key question:

Me: Any other questions that I should have asked but I didn't?

[Pause]

Joseph: Why do parents make it [rest] more difficult?

Me: Yeah—why do they?

Joseph struggles to articulate his frustration.

Joseph: I don't know . . . while I'm trying to rest, it makes it more stressful, and it's just really irritating. Like you're just trying to—your parents—they don't realize what they're doing, but when—and if you try to tell them, it's just like it doesn't really work.

Justin: I think it just depends on the jobs that they do. My dad's a lawyer, so he's constantly working. My mom works for a hospital, so she's constantly on the phone too.

Joseph: Then they want to know, like, how come you aren't doing more with your time—it's like—talk about rest.

Justin: I think it just depends on the environment you're in.

Me: Yeah—and some of you said adults make it easier.

Justin: My dad calls me lazy all the time. He tells me, "Do something with your life."

Joseph: He [Joseph's dad] told me to get a real job.[50]

Joseph and Justin attribute sentiments to their parents that fall in line with the industrious, hard-working culture that surrounds them. Such sentiments associate rest with laziness and inefficiency when you could be "doing more with your time." The words that Justin attributes to his father about "doing something with his life" reinforce the notion of the counterproductivity of rest. And again, we see the longing for rest and the struggle that rest creates.

To be even-handed, many students named a variety of ways that their families make rest possible. In addition to what Jessica and Jennifer have already mentioned, Heather insists, "I can't imagine Sabbath rest without family. I—you know—when I'm relaxing and just, like, sitting in the living room talking with my family, that's Sabbath rest."[51] Elizabeth explains that her mother encourages her to get all her homework done on Saturday so that she has time to relax on Sunday.

Some parents do chores or other work to give these students more time to rest. Others appreciate the understanding that their parents display about their need to sleep. "[My parents] do let me sleep in a lot, and they do realize that I—and my sister—that we need to sleep. . . . They don't look down on us sleeping until twelve o'clock on Saturday as a problem there. They're okay with that because they realize we need it."[52]

In listening to these young people, we recognize that their understandings and experiences of rest don't fit into any tidy package. We've heard stories that include intentional Sabbath practice and stories that don't. We've heard from young people whose families epitomize their idea of Sabbath rest as well as from young people whose families make rest nearly impossible or who even appear to ridicule them for wanting to rest.

Still, accounting for the influence of families on rest stands as a daunting challenge. "Family" means thirty-nine different things to these thirty-nine different students. Yet in each case, family provides the primary frame of reference for the identity-forming that the students are clearly undergoing, and it provides the primary frame of reference for their articulating experiences and understandings of rest. As we have seen, often that identity formation as it relates to rest results in stress, pressure, and even outright suspicion of anything that hints at Sabbath or rest.

Conclusion: Listening to a Hidden Longing[53]

As we bring this chapter to a close, we listen once more to these remarkable young people. If we listen closely, we can detect a latent longing that weaves its way through their voices and stories. It's a longing for a particular kind of rest—a rest vast enough to encompass body and mind and lead the way to fullness of life.

During an interview with Stephanie, I ask her what she would do, where she would go, and who she would be with if she had twenty-four totally free hours to do anything. She talks about going out West with her mom and sister. In the course of our conversation, she talks to me about her ongoing journey with depression and anxiety, and so I ask her how that journey has related to her experience and understanding of rest.

> **Stephanie**: In my 24 hours . . . if I was there and I had nothing to worry about, I could just lay in the grass and think about nothing. But if I'm like at home, I could be resting, but my mind is going a mile a minute. . . . I'm relaxed, but my mind is never relaxed . . . unless I have no worries at all.
>
> Like this summer, I'm going out to Utah for an internship again. When I'm out there, I'll worry for the first two weeks about what's going on at home, but then when I get in the groove of working with the organization I will have no worries at all . . . until I'm alone in my little house thinking by myself.
>
> If I'm not physically busy, then I'm mentally busy.

> **Me**: It sounds like you can have bodily rest or mental rest, but it's really hard for you to have both at the same time.

> **Stephanie**: Yeah. Yeah.

> **Me**: Would the ideal rest be both?

> **Stephanie**: That'd be so nice. [Pause.] That'd be so nice. During track season I feel that a lot, just because after track practice I'm physically exhausted so that's already there, and after I have all my homework done, and all my responsibilities done, and I can just lay in bed, and I'm so physically exhausted that I can't even think—that is rest. That is the ultimate rest, and I love it, and I can just go right to bed.
>
> Ideally, if I could have the best way of rest, it would be physically and mentally resting with no worries at all.

> **Me**: Would you like more of that kind of rest than you get?

94

Stephanie: I would love that, but then at the same time, I feel like just 'cause I'm used to it, it would be weird to have both. It's kind of a blessing and a curse at the same time.

Me: If you got more of it, you might be anxious 'cause you're getting more of it?

Stephanie: Exactly. Should I have more stuff to do? Do I have more stuff to do? Why am I relaxing when I could be doing such and such?
So I think I cause more work for myself than is really out there.

Me: Why?

Stephanie: Just because my family is fast-paced, and, like, my mom, if she's not at work, she's at home doing something. So she's always doing something. So is Steve [Stephanie's stepdad]. So is everyone.
So I feel like if I'm not using my time wisely, then I'm basically wasting a chunk of time [when] I could be doing something valuable.[54]

Like so many others, she defines rest in terms of worry and productivity. If nothing else, Stephanie longs for an all-encompassing rest, a rest large enough for her body and mind, a rest large enough to overcome worry. She does not know such a rest; she's not sure she wants to know such a rest; but she seems *to want* to want such a rest. She also hints at the radical implications that such a vast rest would bring. It would be "weird." In some very concrete ways, such a rest would challenge her core assumptions about life and identity. She has been raised to associate work and value. She says, "If I'm not using my time wisely, then I'm basically wasting a chunk of time that I could be doing something valuable." She senses that an all-encompassing rest challenges this value structure to the core. She longs for an all-encompassing rest, even as she senses its impossibility within her current sense of reality and worth.

In theological terms, she has absolutely no conception of rest as grace. Note her best description of the all-encompassing rest she desires. It comes only after she utterly expends herself both physically through track practice, and mentally through homework and taking care of "all her responsibilities." Stephanie epitomizes the tension at play in so many of these young people as they consider rest. On one hand, they long for rest; they contemplate an all-encompassing rest and reply, "That'd be so nice. That'd be so nice." Yet even as they are tempted to love such an offer, they recognize they would not know what to do with it. "It would be weird." It would create its own anxiety.

Stephanie is not alone in her struggle with disorienting grace.

In an interview with James, he also hints at a latent longing for Sabbath rest, even as he recognizes the great challenge it poses. I ask James if he thinks that Sabbath rest is an important thing to talk about.

James: I think it's something we miss the point about. We think of it as just Sunday, but I don't think that's exactly what it was created for. I think Sunday is a day of rest, but I think we also need something totally different than just a rest, like an actual, you know, Sabbath rest. I think those are two different concepts.

Me: What's the difference?

James: I think you have like a Sunday which is like *rest* rest, and that day you get off of work, and so maybe you think you shouldn't do anything that day, so you get the rest. So that's a good thing in and of itself. You need time off, so there's your day off, but you might not really be resting in God's presence, and I think that has its own resting, healing power in itself, but that's even more hard to reach. . . .

Like, I think rest, rest is hard, but Sabbath rest is even harder to get.

Me: Why do you think that is?

James: I think just because . . . you have to just let everything go, and that's hard to do . . . 'cause even when you're resting, you can still be worrying about stuff . . . but, like, what you're saying about Sabbath rest, I think you need to totally let things go and try to engage.

Me: Have you experienced Sabbath rest?

James: I'd say probably not much, if any.[55]

These are high-functioning, articulate, self-disciplined, delightful young people who regularly say they feel connected to God. Their parents and their school have good reason to be proud. They're known for many good things. In talking with them, I noticed that they very rarely gave the impression that they were anxious. To the contrary: they more often struck me as the type of young people I would hope my own kids grow up to be. At the same time, these same conversations laid bare three layers of concern. First, our conversations reveal a baseline level of anxiety and stress in their lives, particularly as they consider rest. This, in and of itself, troubles me. But what I find more unsettling is the second, deeper concern: that they never question this constant level of stress and anxiety. They assume that it's just a part of life. Third and finally, they've learned to not let it show.

Stephanie epitomizes this when she tells me matter-of-factly, "I'm very relaxed. . . . Even if there's chaos going on around me, I try not to let it influence [me]. I might be harboring a storm inside me, but I will not let it come out. 'Cause I don't want it to reflect on the people I'm involved with or . . . I don't want them to feel like they need to be in chaos if I'm in chaos."[56]

James and Stephanie don't speak for all young people; even they recognize that their context differs from other contexts. Yet in listening to their longing, we may recognize a longing deep in the heart of humankind. Even as James and Stephanie express their hesitant hopes, we get the sense that such rest lies beyond their grasp. And perhaps they're right. Perhaps the rest they long for can't be grasped; perhaps it can only be received as a gift of grace.

Too many of these youth live under the assumption that their lives depend upon their own productivity, utility, composure, giftedness, care, and achievement. With these assumptions, rest as grace becomes utterly contrary to their sense of self and identity. What would it look like for them to know that their lives depend more on a loving and gracious God than on their own efforts, or that their own efforts find their proper basis and foundation in God's love, grace, and rest? It might look like Sabbath, and that might look—at least at first—like anxiety in an entirely new register.

If we can affirm along with the Judeo-Christian tradition that the Sabbath provides within time a foretaste of the end of time, we can simultaneously affirm that anxiety and despair absolutely will not have the last word. Yes, the journey with God into the Sabbath may yield anxiety along the way. But it might also pave the way for a grace-rooted identity like nothing our young people have ever known.

The picture that these young people have painted raises questions about whether they ever encounter a time and space for hearing, receiving, and living this truth. As we saw in James and Jessica, the mere fact of having Sunday traditions that set this day apart fails to guarantee this time and space. Busyness can't provide this space. Entertainment media can't provide this space. We're reminded again of Sue's experience of her grandmother's Sabbath legalism, in which a form of Sabbath practice was merely a thin veneer over another example of endless human effort. As we turn to Sabbath, Scripture, and Karl Barth in the next chapter, we will come face to face with a Sabbath that begins not with endless human effort, but unequivocally with the action and interaction of a loving and gracious God.

4 On the Seventh Day, God Rested

Sabbath: A Practice in Death

In a brief but pointed account of the Sabbath, pastor, professor, and author Barbara Brown Taylor unflinchingly refers to Sabbath as "a practice in death."[1] While she also mentions the pleasure and rest that accompany the Sabbath, she contends by way of the conviction of experience that Sabbath includes "a yin and a yang."

"People flock to [Sabbath] for the rest part—the hammock part—but once they get into it, there's the looking into the night sky part, which is, 'Why am I here?'"

Brown Taylor identifies productivity as the thread that connects Sabbath, death, and identity. Americans associate productivity with fame and money. Productivity provides "a universal means of valuing one another." The challenge of the Sabbath, then, is its "unproductivity." Being unproductive undercuts our primary ways of evaluating ourselves and others. In the light—or shadow, perhaps—of the Sabbath, we struggle to know ourselves or our purpose. We struggle to know why we're here. On the Sabbath, productivity dies, and those who practice Sabbath must ask disorienting questions.

Who are we if we're not producing something, if we're not achieving, if we're not doing?

These questions ring with haunting familiarity on the heels of the stories about young people and rest that we heard in the last chapter.

Brown Taylor's interpretation of the Sabbath provides something critical to any conversation on Sabbath and young people. The few resources on youth and Sabbath that do exist paint a picture more in line with what Brown Taylor refers to as the "hammock" part.[2] These resources lift up Sabbath as rest, recreation, and rejuvenation. It's harder to stomach Sabbath as death.

We know exhaustion; we know we long for rest; we sense that Sabbath offers something we need. Yet when we get there, Sabbath brings us up short. To borrow again Brown Taylor's imagery, we lie restless and anxious in the hammock.

We have seen anxiety repeatedly in the previous chapters. We saw it in the first chapter in Sue's impostor syndrome; we saw it in my end-of-semester breakdown; we saw it in the sleeplessness, pursuit of busyness, and consumption via technology in the second chapter; and we heard it in the stories of thirty-nine young people who longed for rest as an escape from anxiety even as they acknowledged the anxiety that rest creates.

Brown Taylor helps us draw all the previous discussions on the relationship between rest and anxiety to their logical conclusion. She names explicitly what Nicole, Stephanie, and Brian from the last chapter already sense intuitively.

If Sabbath is going to live and thrive in our lives, something else will have to die.

Brown Taylor helps us clarify what Sabbath is and is not. She pushes back against a view of Sabbath that sees it merely as an escape from reality and candidly names the life-and-death struggle that goes hand-in-hand with the Sabbath. This chapter wrestles theologically with this very issue. It looks for God in and through this issue. How does the Sabbath not skirt death but lead us on a journey through death toward resurrection life? How might God graciously lead us in and through the Sabbath to recognize and embrace our true identity as God's beloved children?

In this chapter, we continue developing a theology of the Sabbath. In the terms of practical theology that we outlined in the first chapter, here we take God seriously. We dare to believe that God has done and is doing something in and through the Sabbath, and we ask, What *does* God do in or through the Sabbath? What does the Sabbath reveal about who God is? What does Sabbath reveal about who we are or who we are called to be? To begin answering these questions, we turn to three sources:[3]

- Scripture's very first story in Genesis
- the theology of Karl Barth (rhymes with smart, not Garth)
- the story of God's deliverance of the Israelites from Egypt in Exodus

The Seventh Day

The vast story of the Sabbath contained in Scripture doesn't begin with death.[4] It begins with brand-new life in the creation narrative in Genesis; it begins with God's own rest on the seventh day.[5] When Swiss theologian Karl Barth begins forming his doctrine of the Sabbath, he too begins in Genesis and grounds his understanding of the Sabbath in his interpretation of the seventh day of creation. We follow his lead.

Barth's exploration of the seventh day of creation comes in the context of his broader interpretation of the entire creation narrative found in Genesis 1:1–2:3. In his interpretation, Barth approaches the broader creation narrative as a "pure saga."[6] In so doing, Barth attempts to enter the text on its own terms. Its primary purpose is neither scientific nor historical.[7] Instead, the text stands at the very beginning of the Bible's first book to convey absolutely vital convictions about God, creation, and the relationship between the two.[8] The text reveals God as One who brings order from chaos, who calls creation into being with a word, and who at last on day six creates humankind in the image of God and gives humanity the commission to fill the earth and steward it.

Barth spends well over a hundred pages exploring the first six days.[9] Throughout, he insists that God's goal and purpose for creation is to make possible the covenant relationship between God and humanity in Jesus

Christ.[10] In other words, God creates the heavens and the earth so that God can be in relationship with the whole creation, and with humankind in particular.

The first six days already reveal the initial contours of this relationship. God has set the stage with the great diversity of creation,[11] and on the sixth day God creates humans as inextricably part of the created order, yet placed in unique relationship to both God and the rest of creation. Within this saga, humans are blessed and addressed personally by God (Gen. 1:28-30); they are created in the image of God (Gen. 1:26); and they are charged with filling the earth and caring for it (Gen. 1:28). Even so, day six closes with a proclamation of the goodness of the whole creation. "God saw *everything* that God had made, and indeed, it was very good. And there was evening and there was morning, the sixth day" (Gen. 1:31, italics added).

Not Finished Yet

As Barth turns the page to the seventh day, he begins, "Creation is finished, but the history of creation is not yet concluded."[12] There is more to the story than the first six days. As he interprets the seventh day, he insists—over and against earlier theologians who only included the first six days in their doctrines of creation—that the seventh day necessarily belongs with the broader account of the creation of the heavens and the earth. It is one story, and any omission of the seventh day necessarily leaves one's doctrine of creation incomplete and unfinished.[13] That's why the question for the seventh day remains the same as the question put to the previous six days. What does the seventh day reveal about God, creation, and the relationship between the two?

The NRSV translation of Genesis 2:1-3 lifts up a dimension of the text that Barth emphasizes. Note the confusing use of the word "finished": "Thus the heavens and the earth were *finished*, and all their multitude. And on the seventh day God *finished* the work that God had done, and God rested on the seventh day from all the work that God had done." The first use of "finished" appears to point backward to the work of the first six days. That work is finished. And yet, on the seventh day, God "finished" the work that God had done. How do we make sense of this? How is it possible that on the seventh day God both finished the work and rested from all the work that God had done?

Barth insists that the finishing and the resting cannot be separated. But this doesn't mean that God continues creative activity on the seventh day. Rather, God completes or finishes creation on the seventh day by way of a new divine act—an act that stands distinct from God's work on the first six days.[14] This new divine act "confirms and confronts" creation, "and this confirmation and confrontation consisted in the fact that 'God rested from all [God's] work.'"[15] By resting from work, God initiates within time and within the created order a particular relationship between God and creation. What does this mean? In order to grasp Barth on these points, we must follow his theological interpretation of the seventh day. What does the seventh day tell us about God? Early in his exploration of the seventh day, Barth names two divine characteristics that the seventh day reveals: God's freedom and God's love.

"The first feature of God revealed by [God's] rest on the seventh day is [God's] freedom."[16] Barth argues that in order for an act to be an act, it must be performed within limits. It must, in fact, be our act. Never-ending activity gives agency to the activity. Technology provides a contemporary example. In order for a person to be free in relationship to a smartphone, for example, the person must control the phone and not vice-versa. Otherwise, the person gives agency to the phone, lets the phone call the shots, and the person—in Barth's words—becomes "entangled in a process imposed upon [the person] and subjected to its higher necessity."[17] This isn't a picture of freedom. In fact, Barth insists that "a being is free only when it can determine and limit its activity."

On the seventh day, God reveals God's own freedom by determining and limiting God's own activity. God does not continue creating and creating because in so doing, God would not have been free, but would have been held captive by the creative activity. God sets a limit to God's own activity; God rests, or Sabbaths, and thus reveals divine freedom.

Recognize that this understanding of freedom utterly contradicts most contemporary definitions. Many assume that freedom happens only in the absence of limits—unlimited time, unlimited money, unlimited information, unlimited data. But Barth insists that God reveals a different kind of freedom on the Sabbath. God puts the phone down, so to speak. God isn't held captive by God's work, but is free to be in relationship to it.[18] This leads to the second divine characteristic revealed on the seventh day.

"The second feature of God revealed in the rest of the seventh day is [God's] love."[19] Barth argues that love lands. Rather than darting about from infatuation to infatuation, love chooses a particular subject. "The reason why [God] refrains from further activity on the seventh day is that [God] has found the object of [God's] love and has no need of any further works."[20] Without Sabbath—without ceasing from work—God "would be a being without love, never ceasing, never finding time for any creature, never satisfied with any."[21]

Again, technology illustrates. At the end of the school day, sixteen-year-old Audrey gets into her mother's car only to find her mom engrossed in her phone, trying to finish a work-related email. Audrey can't help but think, "You love your work more than you love me."[22] This isn't the love that God showed through the Sabbath. The love of God is a love that lands. God loves creation, has time for creation, and determined in advance to set limits around creative work for the sake of love and covenant relationship.[23]

Barth's writing on divine freedom and love brings focus to the previous discussion regarding God's confirmation and confrontation of creation on the seventh day. At the close of day six, God, figuratively speaking, has a question of cosmic proportions to contemplate.[24] How will God relate to the very good creation? Barth suggests two options. First, God could simply continue unlimited creative activity. Yet, as already noted, such a God would not then be free, but would rather be bound to that unlimited activity. The activity, in essence, would control God in that scenario. Another option would be for God to simply turn away from creation and return to "the inner glory of [God's] being and existence before creation and without the world and [humankind]." In this scenario, God creates the heavens and earth, and then leaves them alone.[25] Such a god brings to mind a heartless manufacturer who produces something, ships it, and maintains no ongoing relationship with the product.

The seventh day shows us that God is anything but a heartless manufacturer.[26] Look again at Genesis 2:2: "And on the seventh day God finished the work that God had done, and God rested on the seventh day from all the work that God had done." On the seventh day, God finishes, and God rests. The finishing and the resting cannot be separated. It is God's rest that finishes and completes creation. God doesn't depart from creation but draws near to it in and through God's Sabbath rest. In other words, creation remains incomplete and unfinished apart from God's Sabbath rest. It is, again, a seven-day story, not a six-day story.

Thus, the relationship between God and humankind utterly depends on God's Sabbath rest, given to creation—including humanity—with the invitation to ongoing participation. Humankind stands incomplete and unfinished apart from God's Sabbath rest. The relationship of God, humankind, and all creation begins with Sabbath rest.[27]

Sabbath and Covenant

The broader point regarding the Sabbath is that it tells us something critical about the relationship between God and creation broadly, and more specifically about the relationship between God and humankind. In keeping with his broader theological work, Barth sees the seventh day in light of the covenant relationship between God and humankind enacted in Jesus Christ. In Barth's terms, creation provides the "external basis" for the covenant. The Sabbath stands prominently in Barth's theology because he sees it as the commencement of the covenant history.

On the seventh day, the relationship between God and creation begins. God "was satisfied [on the seventh day] to enter into *this* relationship with *this* reality distinct from himself, to be the Creator of *this* creature, to find in *these* works of his Word the external sphere of his power and grace and the place of his revealed glory."[28] On the seventh day, God chooses creation.

God chooses *this* creation, the one we now inhabit. God did not abandon creation; God did not get lost in limitless creating. God chose this creation, including humankind, to be the place where God would reveal God's power, grace, and glory.

The seventh day reveals all of this. Creation stands incomplete apart from this, but with it, the covenant history begins and creation finds completion in the Sabbath rest of God. It finds its completion in its observation and subsequent remembrance of God's resting. Humankind's first full day of existence is the seventh day—the day of God's rest—which means that the first act of God that humanity has the privilege of witnessing is God's rest.[29] Correspondingly, the first obligation laid on humankind is to "keep the Sabbath with God, completely free from work."[30]

Of course, there will be toil, and sin soon enters the picture. Barth wrestles with this reality. Yet prior to addressing sin explicitly, he lifts up the eschatological dimensions of the Sabbath day. Eschatology looks at last things or the end of time. It concerns "the consummation of God's purposes for the whole creation,"[31] and Barth sees an image of this consummation here on the seventh day.[32] It is an image of God and all creation at rest together in perfect communion. The Sabbath, in this way, points to the end of time, the *eschaton*. Here, the author of Genesis gives us a snapshot of the end of all things embedded in the saga of the beginning of all things.

"The last day will be a Sabbath day, and [humanity's] final time will be a time of rest . . . , and indeed of rest in fellowship with the rest of God himself, of participation in the freedom, rest and joy of [God's] true deity."[33] Thus, the covenant relationship between God and humanity begins and ends with Sabbath rest. If we let the Sabbath truly confront us, we will recognize the limits of human achievement and accomplishment.

We didn't bring ourselves into existence. God did.

We didn't bring about our completion through Sabbath rest. God did.

And our effort and toil cannot bring about the last Sabbath at the end of time. Only God can and will.

This means that as the Sabbath confronts us with our limits, it simultaneously confronts us with the grace of God. This radically reorients human labor and achievement. It may even stir in us the anxiety that has already been named. We and our young people busy ourselves with endless work or distraction. Stopping brings its own anxiety. It threatens.

We will address this below. Before we do, we face the full scope of the disorienting grace that the Sabbath is.

Sabbath as Sheer Grace

The exceptional goodness of creation rests not in the striving, accomplishment, or labor of creation.[34] The goodness of creation rests solely in the goodness and pronouncement of the Creator. It rests in God. Creation is very good because it has been made by a good, gracious, and holy Creator and pronounced to be very good by the Creator. God pronounces humans to be good prior to any labor or striving on their part, and Barth argues that the narrative of the seventh day brings with it the inference that "creation, and supremely [humans], rested with God on the seventh day . . . even though [the first humans] had not as yet any work behind [them] from which to cease." That's why human participation in Sabbath rest on the seventh day of creation couldn't be based in human accomplishment. It could be grounded only in God's work and invitation.[35]

At this point in the saga, humans simply can't see Sabbath rest as something earned or merited. The only work that humans have to reflect on at this point is God's. Humankind hasn't done anything yet. From the beginning, then, God gives Sabbath rest as a gift of sheer grace.

Along these lines, neither the Sabbath rest of God nor the corresponding Sabbath rest of humans should be seen as a "question of recuperation after a toilsome and well-done job." If this were the case, Sabbath rest could be seen as a reward. Instead, Sabbath rest provides the gracious foundation for all of life. "It is this [Sabbath rest] which gives perspective and depth, meaning and luster, to all [our] weeks, and therefore to [our] whole time, as well as to the work which [we] perform in [our] time."[36]

The First Sabbath, Sin, and Christ

The seventh day offers us a remarkable and beautiful picture: God and all creation at rest in the light of God's extraordinary grace. It's tempting to just quit reading at this point, but we know better. The chapters that follow raise challenging questions. What about sin? How is it, exactly, that a good and all-knowing God can rest at this point in the saga? It seems that the broader story reveals a number of good reasons that God should keep working.

Humans, as we learn in a few short verses, struggle mightily with following God's instructions. Forces that oppose God's good and gracious intentions for creation soon enter the scene. In simplest theological terms, sin enters the picture, and humankind rejects freedom by failing to live within the limits God established for the sake of their flourishing.[37] By the end of Genesis 4, murder is on the scene; midway through Genesis 6, God's heart is grieved at the wickedness of humankind.

What kind of God ceases work and rests when it appears there is so much more work to do? Barth wrestles with this question by drawing on the riches of the Christian tradition. He seeks a specifically Christian answer—one that looks again and again at reality in the light of Christ. The earliest believers did just this. Not long after Jesus's earthly ministry, his followers began affirming Christ's intimate involvement in creation. The prologue to John's Gospel expresses this profoundly and beautifully:

> In the beginning was the Word, and the Word was with God, and the Word was God. He was in the beginning with God. All things came into being through him, and without him not one thing came into being. . . . And the Word became flesh and lived among us, and we have seen his glory, the glory as of a father's only son, full of grace and truth. (John 1:1–3a, 14)

Barth draws on this understanding of Christ and creation to answer the question about sin and Sabbath. "As God created heaven and earth through Christ or in Christ, so [God] has created all things with a view to Christ. On the seventh day God was well pleased with [God's] Son. [God] saw creation perfect through Christ; [God] saw it restored again through Christ; and [God] therefore declared it to be finished, and rested."[38] Here again, we look at God's rest on the seventh day eschatologically, with a view to the end of time. Though sin would enter the story, God could rest on the seventh day because God already knew that sin would not have the last word.

God already knew that all creation would ultimately be redeemed in Christ. According to Barth, "God does not only look upon the present of [God's] creation, nor does [God] only look back to that which [God] did in creating it. God knows its future."[39] This may sound abstract, but parents and youth pastors do this all of the time. We don't merely see our youth for what they are today. We don't narrowly perceive the bad choices they make at home, school, or on a youth retreat. We already perceive something more. We sense that the current struggle won't have the last word.

Similarly, from the beginning, God sees creation perfected in Christ. God sees creation in the light of extraordinary grace. Barth says, "In a world created in this way, with the inclusion of the divine rest on the seventh day, the sphere of grace is not a foreign body."[40] The seventh day opens the created order to the "sphere of grace." God's grace belongs to creation.

The God of creation is also the God who takes on flesh in Jesus Christ, and the two dimensions of the one God do not contradict each other. As a seven-day story, the saga of creation includes both the bringing into being of the heavens and the earth, and the completion, confrontation, and confirmation of creation by way of God's rest. It includes creation and God-in-relationship to creation. Because it includes God-in-relationship to creation by way of God's Sabbath, the seventh day already anticipates and provides a basis for the redemption of the world in Jesus Christ.

Thus, when Sabbath enters the narrative of the relationship between God and humanity on the seventh day of creation, it comes before humanity has done any work. It comes with no rules and regulations; it comes before the law. The law will come and will prove necessary, but the first Sabbath of God with creation strongly suggests that rules and regulations simply cannot contain the vast and radical grace that God gives through the Sabbath.[41]

Holy Sabbath!

At this point in our exploration, the extraordinary nature of the Sabbath should be clear. Through the Sabbath, God comes uniquely to creation. Through the Sabbath, we uniquely experience God's remarkable grace. Though the seventh day belongs to the creation saga, it is also set apart. This "set-apartness" points us to yet another dimension of the Sabbath.

Jewish theologian Abraham Joshua Heschel writes, "One of the most distinguished words in the [Hebrew] Bible is the word *qadosh*, holy; a word which more than any other is representative of the mystery and majesty of the divine."[42] In the creation narrative of Genesis 1:1–2:3, the term *qadosh* is applied to only one thing: "And God blessed the seventh day and made it holy [*qadosh*]" (Gen. 2:3). Exodus 31 and Ezekiel 20 draw on the same root, *qdsh*, but in a way that links holiness, Sabbath, and God's people. "The LORD said to Moses: You yourself are to speak to the Israelites: 'You shall keep my sabbaths, for this is a sign between me and you throughout your generations, given in order that you may know that I, the LORD, sanctify [*qdsh*] you'" (Exod. 31:12–13).

At its roots, the term *qdsh* simply and quite appropriately means "set apart." God insists that God alone sets God's people apart. God alone makes God's people holy. The "set-apartness" of God's people cannot be separated from the "set-apartness" of the Sabbath. This connection comes through again in the Ten Commandments. As Heschel points out, within the sum of the commandments, "the term holy is applied to one word only, the Sabbath."[43] This takes place in both Exodus and Deuteronomy:

> Remember the sabbath day, and keep it holy [*qdsh*]. Six days you shall labor and do all your work. But the seventh day is a sabbath to the LORD your God; you shall not do any work—you, your son or your daughter, your male or female slave, your livestock, or the alien resident in your towns. For in six days the LORD made heaven and earth, the sea, and all that is in them, but rested the seventh day; therefore the LORD blessed the sabbath day and consecrated [*qdsh*] it. (Exod. 20:8–11)

Observe the sabbath day and keep it holy [*qdsh*], as the LORD your God commanded you. Six days you shall labor and do all your work. But the seventh day is a sabbath to the LORD your God; you shall not do any work—you, or your son or your daughter, or your male or female slave, or your ox or your donkey, or any of your livestock, or the resident alien in your towns, so that your male and female slave may rest as well as you. Remember that you were a slave in the land of Egypt, and the LORD your God brought you out from there with a mighty hand and an outstretched arm; therefore the LORD your God commanded you to keep the sabbath day. (Deut. 5:12–15)

The two versions of the Sabbath commandment provide two different reasons for the Israelites' observation of the Sabbath. The Exodus version invites the Israelites to imitate God. None of the other Ten Commandments do this, but here God's Sabbath at creation provides the reason for the Sabbath of God's people. God's people are to remember the Sabbath because God did it first.

Deuteronomy 5, on the other hand, looks to God's deliverance of the Israelites from captivity in Egypt. Why Sabbath? Observe the Sabbath because there was a time when you couldn't, but God brought you out from there with a mighty hand and an outstretched arm.

Note the similarity between the two different versions of the command. Both look to God's activity and not human activity as the basis and rationale for Sabbath observance. This fact becomes all the more prominent when we recognize that in both Exodus and Deuteronomy, a statement of God's saving activity provides the prologue to the giving of the commandments. "I am the LORD your God, who brought you out of the land of Egypt, out of the house of slavery" (Deut. 5:6; Exod. 20:2). In every case, God's action and grace provide the basis for human response. God has already acted graciously; God's people now have the invitation to respond in grateful obedience; and Sabbath observance simply reflects the holiness, the set-apartness, that God brings about.

What about Death?

Before going any farther, we pause to return to where we started this chapter. We began with Barbara Brown Taylor and the idea that Sabbath is "a little death." At this point in the chapter, it may appear that death has vanished. But this is not entirely so.

If we understand death as the ultimate limit, then we must recognize the death implicitly present in what has already been discussed regarding freedom, love, and God's Sabbath rest on the seventh day of creation. With every limit, something dies in order that something else may live. When God limits God's work at the end of day six, the continuation of that work "dies," yet this death brings about the life of God's rest. Bondage to work dies; freedom toward work lives. The possibility of a distant God dies; the reality of an immanent God who seeks covenant relationship lives. The life-and-death implications of the Sabbath will become even clearer as we continue.

The Human Side of Sabbath-Keeping

Our exploration of the Sabbath thus far—following Barth's lead—has been focused overwhelmingly on God. This follows the movements of practical theology outlined in the first chapter.[44] Here we do our best to take God seriously. We have asked along with Barth, What has God done and what does God do in and through the Sabbath? What does the Sabbath reveal about who God is?

Our framework for practical theology prevents us from stopping at this point. We must continue forward into a preliminary exploration of faithful human response.[45] In light of God's action in and through the Sabbath, what does Sabbath look like in terms of human action? For this exploration, we again follow Karl Barth.[46] We will see Barth make a move that parallels Barbara Brown Taylor's. Sabbath includes life and rest—the hammock part—but it also requires death. It challenges human identity to the core.

The seven days in Genesis 1:1–2:3 and the Sabbath commandments in Exodus 20 and Deuteronomy 5 already make one thing clear: the human side of Sabbath-keeping must draw its power and purpose from the grace and invitation of a living God. In terms of life and death, our vision of Sabbath apart from God's action and grace must die, and our vision of human thriving apart from Sabbath must also die. Why? Because we've seen that Sabbath comes about only by God's action and grace, and humanity remains incomplete apart from God's Sabbath rest.

As we follow Barth into the realm of human action, he will once again issue a great word of caution regarding human action by shining an insistent light on God's being and action. Barth ultimately does provide guidance for faithful human response, but we should be forewarned that Barth will not supply "three easy steps" for faithful Sabbath practice.

At every turn, Barth resists giving specific instructions about Sabbath dos and don'ts. He offers direction, not prescription, and he does this because of his theological convictions. He insists that the whole point of the Sabbath is to bring us into direct contact with the living God, who is always, by definition, greater than our understanding of God. Sabbath rules are convenient. They may even be necessary, but they tempt us to reduce God to the rules or guidelines.

We just want to know we did Sabbath right, but as soon as that thought runs through our minds, we've already missed the point because we've reduced Sabbath to what we do or don't do and squeezed God out of the picture. We've planted our identity in what we can do rather than let God shake and shape our identities through the Sabbath.[47] Thus, when Barth turns to the Sabbath commandment, the human side of Sabbath-keeping, he cannot help but begin again with God's grace.

God's Omnipotent Grace: The Meaning and Basis of the Sabbath

Barth writes about the Sabbath commandment at the very beginning of a longer section on special ethics.[48] In some way, this makes sense. Ethics has to do with right human action, and Barth is preparing to write about the human side of Sabbath-keeping. But his choice to start ethics with the Sabbath also conveys a deep irony. He's starting a longer section on human action by writing about the absence of human action: rest.

In doing this, Barth merely repeats the heart of his interpretation of the seventh day. God meets human existence not with the immediate expectation of work, but rather with the invitation to grace by way of Sabbath rest. Human work also comes at God's command, but it can be understood only in the light of God's grace. Grace comes first. This leads Barth to assert, "The Sabbath commandment explains all the other commandments. . . . It is thus to be placed at their head."[49]

While this may surprise us, Barth makes this move because he believes that God's omnipotent grace serves as the only proper meaning and basis of the Sabbath. This means, first and foremost, that the Sabbath points neither to itself nor to those who observe it, but rather to the all-powerful grace of God. It does this insofar as it points to God's mighty and gracious acts throughout salvation history. "The meaning of the special holy day [the Sabbath] and the basis of its special observance lies in the fact that it is the indication of [i.e., it points to] the special history of the covenant and salvation."[50] Sabbath points all the way from the beginning of time at the dawn of creation to the great consummation when time will be no more.

If we scan the history of salvation in Scripture, we find that Sabbath shows up with great frequency. As Barth has already pointed out in his exegesis of the seventh day, and as we saw in the Exodus 20 version of the Sabbath commandment, the Sabbath points us directly to God's Sabbath rest on the seventh day. As the Deuteronomy version of the Sabbath commandment and the story of God's provision of manna in Exodus 16 indicate, the Sabbath also points to God's deliverance of God's people from captivity in Egypt.

Sabbath also points to the life, ministry, death, and resurrection of Christ. Jesus's ministry on the Sabbath uniquely highlights his gracious mission,[51] and his death and resurrection take place on the days that surround the Sabbath. The Passover within Holy Week points back to God's deliverance of the Israelites through the Exodus and the provision of manna and

Sabbath in the desert. When Jesus speaks of the forgiveness of sins within the words of institution, he brings to mind the forgiveness promised in the year of Jubilee—a year utterly grounded in the Sabbath.[52] After the crucifixion, Jesus's body lies lifeless in the tomb on the Sabbath day,[53] and his closest followers maintain their Sabbath observance (Luke 23:56). Finally, on the first day of the week—the day following the Jewish Sabbath—Christ rises from the dead. Early in the course of church history, the first day becomes the Lord's Day, the day to gather, break bread, and celebrate Christ's life, death, and resurrection.[54]

The Sabbath from a Christian perspective, then, points us to this vast history, from creation to resurrection to consummation. When we say "Sabbath," we say all these things.

Thus, the force of the Sabbath's uniqueness comes by way of God's omnipotent grace. God gives Sabbath to humankind not as a reward for a week of work, but as a gift. The first full day for humankind—the seventh day of creation—is a day of Sabbath rest, apart from any human effort or achievement. Similarly, the salvation history comes about by God's omnipotent grace; creation exists by God's omnipotent grace; deliverance from captivity comes by God's omnipotent grace; daily bread in desert places comes by God's omnipotent grace; Christ comes in omnipotent grace; and the last day, the *eschaton*, will come about by God's omnipotent grace.

To observe the Sabbath in this light is to receive the omnipotent grace of God. It is to allow ourselves to be confronted by the force of this grace. We cannot earn this rest. We are free to accept it, but we are not free to refuse it, because in refusing grace we also refuse freedom. We may choose to refuse this grace, but in refusing we render ourselves not-free, captive to lesser gods. In refusing this grace, we refuse the limits that mark our freedom. We refuse our truest identity.

In Barth's terms, then, the scope of the Sabbath is enormous, pointing to both salvation history and the end of time, "and if we remember that in both instances we are concerned with its relationship to the particularity of God's omnipotent grace, we shall understand at once, and not without a certain awe, the radical importance, the almost monstrous range of the

Sabbath commandment."[55] If we are willing to celebrate the Sabbath according to its meaning, we will find ourselves in direct confrontation with the omnipotent grace of God stretching from creation to consummation. This is the "monstrous range" of the Sabbath command. It points us directly and repeatedly to God's all powerful, all-gracious action on our behalf, and this omnipotent grace provides the only proper meaning and basis of the Sabbath commandment. In its light, we cannot help but celebrate.[56]

Barth has now set the stage for a second question: On what basis do we observe the Sabbath? In other words, why do we observe the Sabbath in the first place?

Renouncing Faith: The Death of Our Lesser Identities

When Barth shifts from considering the meaning and basis of the Sabbath commandment to considering the proper basis for human Sabbath observance, the shift is slight, and the answer to the first question irrevocably informs and enlightens the second. The question he poses of Sabbath observance could just as easily have been spoken by Vince or Stephanie from the previous chapter. "Why do we do this whole Sabbath thing in the first place?"

Barth will insist that we "do this whole Sabbath thing" as an act of faith that utterly surrenders our life and being into God's hands.[57] This is the response that Sabbath grace invites. It invites faith, a particular kind of faith, that willingly abandons every understanding of ourselves other than one rooted in God's grace. Barth calls this "renouncing faith," and he argues that it provides the only adequate reason for keeping the Sabbath.

Painted starkly in the terms of life and death, faithful Sabbath observance—i.e., observance that is full of faith—requires the death of every understanding of ourselves not rooted in the life, grace, and action of God. This is renouncing faith. It is faith that renounces every identity other than the grace-rooted one we find in God. This renouncing faith bears concretely on everything we do even as it calls into question all other possible reasons for keeping the Sabbath. To hear Barth properly, we must recognize already that he isn't calling for death for death's sake. Death does not get the last word.

What we saw implicitly in our exegesis of the seventh day we now see explicitly: If God sets a limit, the limit is for the sake of freedom, grace, and life. Yes, the limit likely means the death of some thing, identity, or expectation, but the aim and goal of the limit from the start is fellowship, life, grace, and freedom in covenant relationship. When God asked Sue Miller to die to impostor syndrome (see the first chapter), it wasn't to harm her. It was for the sake of Sue's abundant life in God. This means that God's people may actually expect great benefits to emerge from faithful Sabbath-keeping. It also means that we need to distinguish clearly between the basis and the benefits of Sabbath observance.

After naming renouncing faith as the only proper basis for Sabbath observance, Barth goes on to name "two great benefits" that flow from Sabbaths based on renouncing faith:[58] (1) freedom from work; and (2) freedom for divine service (we might think here of participation in the life of a church).[59] Here again, we saw this in Sue Miller. Sabbath-keeping freed Sue from work and freed her for participation in worship in new ways. Barth subsequently articulates why neither of these benefits provides a proper basis for Sabbath observance.[60]

The problem with making either rest from work or divine service the basis for the Sabbath commandment is that both risk removing God from the Sabbath. Both can be reduced to a question of mere human action. Freedom from work (i.e., rest) and freedom for divine service gain their force and strength only insofar as they are based in God's work, not ours.

We don't observe the Sabbath for the sake and purpose of rejuvenation, refreshment, and rest from work, though we may expect to receive these benefits. We don't observe the Sabbath for the sake of rendering service to God in the congregation, though we will surely do so joyfully in our freedom before God. Why not? Because both can be reduced to matters of human effort. And, as Barth says, "a Sunday which has only a humanitarian basis and is celebrated merely as a day of rest can have no power, because, having itself only a humanitarian basis, it cannot be more than a humanitarian denial."[61]

Barth uses the term "humanitarian" here to designate "the necessities of physical, psychological, or social hygiene," and he recognizes that "rest from work does correspond to a genuine and well-founded human need."[62] In contemporary medical terms, we may look back to the sleep science from Chapter 2 and recognize both the absolute necessity of adequate sleep and the great benefits that come along with sufficient rest. But Barth insists that while these benefits may be expected, they don't provide our primary reason for Sabbath observance.

The problem is that to make rest from work the basis for Sabbath observance is to make the self the basis. Sabbath suddenly points to something other than God.[63] To refuse, then, is merely to refuse a human invitation. It thus strips the Sabbath of its power. If from the dawn of creation Sabbath rest has come about by God's will and invitation, then a human-initiated and human-focused Sabbath simply misses the power that brought about Sabbath in the first place.

Regarding divine service, Barth makes a similar argument. "Divine service in itself and as such is a work like any other."[64] Without a basis in God's life and action, even our divine service becomes a merely human endeavor. We have a critical distinction to make at this point. Is Barth utterly demeaning all human activity? Can humans, then, do anything? This brings us back to Barth's understanding of human life and freedom. The point is not the worthlessness of human effort and action. The point is that from the dawn of time, humankind was created not for itself, but for fellowship and covenant relationship with God. In relationship with God is the only place we can find our true identity. Proper Sabbath observance simply reflects this reality.

Our Sabbath observance loses its power and merely becomes another manifestation of endless human effort if it finds its basis in anything other than the radical grace and life of God. This is Barth's argument, and it repeats Sue's story from Chapter 1. In her grandmother's strict Sabbath legalism, Sue observed only the futility of endless human effort. It may or may not have been that for Sue's grandma, but for Sue we can see a close reflection of what Barth writes. If Sabbath amounts to mere rules and regulations, then refusal of the Sabbath presents no divine offense; it merely casts off a human construction. This brings us back to renouncing faith as the only proper basis for Sabbath-keeping.

Renouncing faith affirms that our being, identity, life, joy, and festivity emerge not in human autonomy or individualism, but in covenant relationship with the gracious creator God. Renouncing faith acknowledges "that God [our] Creator is in the right in all that [God] does . . . and it means we may entrust ourselves wholly to God and render obedience to God alone."[65] This sets definite limits around our being and activity, including our work.[66]

The Sabbath command "forbids [us] to be satisfied with [self-affirmation]. It forbids [us] faith in [our] own plans and wishes, in a justification and deliverance which [we] can make for [ourselves], in [our] own ability and achievement. *What it really forbids [us] is not work, but trust in [our] work.*"[67] As it forbids us to trust in our work, it sheds light on all our days, both working and resting.

On the holy day, the day made holy by God, we rejoice that God loves us simply and purely because God made us and we are God's. We rejoice that our identity is found not primarily or principally in our work, but in our relationship with God. Here, too, our understanding of the Sabbath contrasts one popular view. Sabbath is not self-care. In fact, on the Sabbath, we are free from the weight of having to care for ourselves and abandon ourselves to God's care.

Here we are not satisfied with mere self-affirmation; we receive God's affirmation. We turn away from faith in our own plans and trust God's instead. We deny any justification or deliverance we might make for ourselves and instead cast ourselves on the mercy of God's justification and deliverance. We put no faith in our own ability and achievement, but trust wholeheartedly in God's ability and achievement. We trust not our work, but God's.

This is renouncing faith. It is faith that renounces every other possible ground of faith for the sake of faith in the all-powerful and all-gracious God.

This doesn't abolish our work—it enlivens it. We work, as Barth notes, also at the command of God. Yet the Sabbath command unequivocally proclaims that our work cannot hold us captive, and our work may actually be undertaken in the light of God's grace. On the Sabbath, a certain relationship between humankind and work dies, and a very particular identity comes to life:

> [The Sabbath commandment] thus demands of us that we believe in God as our Ruler and Judge, and that we let our self-understanding in every conceivable form be radically transcended, limited and relativised by this faith, or rather by the God in whom [we believe].
>
> It demands that we know ourselves only in our faith in God, that we will and work and express ourselves only in this imposed and not selected renunciation, and that on the basis of this renunciation we actually dare in it all to be . . . new creature[s], . . . new [people]. This is the astonishing requirement of the Sabbath commandment.[68]

Here Barth cuts to the core of the question of human identity. Who are we? Sabbath "demands that we know ourselves only in our faith in God." Who are we? Before and above every other possible identity, we are God's. Before we are students, we are God's. Before we are pastors or parents, we are God's. Before we are consumers or achievers, athletes or musicians, we are God's. It is God who gives this limit, and God does so in order to make us new. This means the renunciation or death of every lesser identity.[69] Neither the autonomous self nor any work, achievement, or human striving suffices as a ground for true human identity. Our lives utterly consist in their relationship with God. For Barth, this is a statement of basic fact made manifest in creation.

We have no life apart from God. Only God gives us life. "On our own" is a fundamental impossibility, and every effort at autonomy is an exercise in loss and captivity. We are free only as we surrender ourselves utterly to God's care, and the breadth of the Sabbath tells us that God's care comes by absolutely no effort of our own.[70] Sabbath observance on the basis of renouncing faith thus moves through death to newness of life, that we may be new creatures, new people.

We observe the Sabbath for the sake of exercising the faith that responds joyfully and humbly to the God who created the universe, who rested on the seventh day, and who was incarnate in Jesus Christ.[71] In other words, we observe the Sabbath for the sake of exercising the faith which insists that our freedom, joy, rest, and our very life take place not in some sphere separate from God's grace, but only as we are confirmed and confronted by God's grace. We know ourselves truly and rightly only in the light of God's grace. As we have already seen, Sabbath points us to the "monstrous range" of God's grace from the beginning of time to its end. True life and true freedom exist only in relationship to this God, who has chosen unrelentingly to be our God, to be with us, to be for us, to be all-powerfully gracious toward us.

This is truly good news, and it should sound wonderful to our ears. The Sabbath journey is a good journey; it is for our life and well-being, and for the flourishing of our life with God. Yet as Barbara Brown Taylor and Karl Barth have shown us, and as the young people from the previous chapter sense, the Sabbath journey of life leads us through death. The vast story of the Sabbath in Scripture includes this, and we return now to the Israelites in the wilderness. Their story gives us concreteness and a narrative to clarify the connections among God's action, Sabbath, identity formation, and life and death.

Life in the Wilderness: Dying to Captivity, Rising to Faith

If in Genesis we found a pristine image of the Sabbath, free from the distortions and perversions of sin, in Exodus we find Sabbath thrust into the mess, stress, and struggle of life in a broken world. In Exodus, we find Sabbath in the midst of the nitty-gritty of life.

We need this image and this story because this is where we live—after the first Sabbath on the seventh day of creation and prior to the final Sabbath at the end of time.

The journey of the Israelites from captivity in Exodus 1 to wilderness, manna, and Sabbath in Exodus 16 echoes the accounts of Sabbath and death found in Barbara Brown Taylor and Karl Barth. It is a story of enslaved identities that need to die so that true identities can come to life. As the drama opens, the Exodus narrative goes to great lengths to establish the lost or misplaced identity of the Israelite people. While the Israelites initially entered Egypt quite literally as the children of Israel—i.e., Jacob and his immediate offspring—and as welcome guests, a new ruler in Egypt doesn't know or remember Joseph (Exod. 1:8).

The Israelites have multiplied greatly, and out of fear of their numbers, the new Egyptian leadership has chosen to enslave the Hebrew people. As we noted in Chapter 1, the Israelite identity has changed dramatically; they have gone from welcome guests to slaves, and along with the change in relationship to Egyptian political powers, the text also suggests a shift in the identity of the Israelites as it concerns the God of Abraham, Isaac, and Jacob. Exodus 2:23 brings the account of the suffering of the enslaved Israelites to a head: "The Israelites groaned under their slavery, and cried out."

But to whom or what did the Israelites cry? This cry doesn't fit with other cries in Scripture. It stings with hopelessness. In Scripture, a cry for help "is usually directed to the Lord (Judg. 3:9; Ps. 22:6). But since this cry is not directed to anyone, Israel seems not to know Yahweh. The people simply cry out."[72] No mention of Yahweh . . . or Abraham, Isaac, Jacob, or Joseph. The Israelites, it appears, have forgotten who they are.

Pharaoh, then, isn't the only one who has forgotten Joseph and the story of the Israelites' entry into Egypt. Generations of captivity have left the Israelites bereft of any identity rooted in God. Though they cry out, they fail—perhaps from forgetfulness, perhaps from hopelessness—to cry out to God. Nonetheless, God hears their cries and calls Moses and Aaron to enter Egypt and lead the Israelites to freedom. In response, Moses and Aaron arrive in Egypt with repeated reminders of the broader story of the Israelites' lost or misplaced identity.

Why have they come? They have come to lead the people to the wilderness to worship and make sacrifice to the God of Abraham, Isaac, and Jacob. In stark contrast to the forgotten history of Joseph—the forgotten longer history of this enslaved people—the first six chapters of Exodus mention Abraham, Isaac, and Jacob seven times.[73]

When Moses and Aaron finally reach the leaders of the Hebrew people with news of God's plans for deliverance, the Israelites "bow down and worship" (Exod. 4:31). It appears that they are ready and willing to embark on the journey toward freedom, yet as the story continues and as Pharaoh resists, it becomes clear that the birth of a renewed identity will not come easy. Faced with the challenges of liberation, the Israelites petition Moses for the comfort of the familiar: "It would have been better if we had died in Egypt" (Exod. 16:3).

Indeed, the literal death of their bodies in captivity looks preferable to the death they are called to on the journey toward freedom and renewed identity. They rightfully fear death on the journey out of Egypt. They mirror—it appears—the sum of humanity in their preference for the captivity of the familiar to the disorientation of God's grace and deliverance. The encounter with God's deliverance, provision, and grace requires a very real death among the Hebrew people.

They have left Egypt geographically, but their sense of identity remains deeply embedded in Egyptian rhythms and values. The Sabbath rhythm that God gives in tandem with the manna challenges this old identity to the core and ushers in the hope of an identity rooted firmly in the grace and provision of God. The Sabbath rhythm in the wilderness challenges the identity that has been forced upon the Israelites for generations.

While a quick read of Exodus 16 may make us roll our eyes at the inability of the Israelites to follow simple manna-gathering instructions, a closer look at their lives and ours reveals unsettling similarities. The Israelites have been in the desert for approximately one month when—in fear of death—they cry out for food. At this point, it seems safe to assume that their rhythms of life have been utterly discombobulated. They have gone from strict predictability at the hands of Egyptian taskmasters to apparently aimless following of clouds and pillars of fire. In the midst of this apparent aimlessness and chaos, God provides in a manner that just might have elicited the joy of the familiar.

Through the manna, God provides both food and the familiar opportunity to meet a quota: one omer per person per day. Imagine the relief! The Israelites have known quotas in Egypt for generations. Finally, the Israelites have productive work to do in the desert.[74] But here there will be a critical difference. While the taskmasters in Egypt demanded continual productivity, God limits the work the Israelites are supposed to do in the wilderness.

As the text plainly states, God intends the provision of manna and Sabbath as a test. And the Israelites struggle with it. Some save manna overnight; others go out to gather manna on the Sabbath. But when we remember the Israelites' misplaced and malformed identity, we may look upon them (and ourselves) with more compassion. They come to the wilderness as slaves who have only ever known endless work for generation upon generation. Surely the taskmasters in Egypt would have been thrilled by any Israelites willing to pull more than their fair share of the weight. Surely increased productivity cashed out in favors with the Egyptian overlords.

Perhaps the Israelites employ this very logic in their approach to the manna. Perhaps they think, "If God commands us to gather one omer of manna per person per day, surely God will be even more pleased if we save a bit for tomorrow! If God commands us to gather manna for six days, gathering for all seven days must be even better." On this read, the Israelites intend no disobedience; they perceive their own efforts not as a failure of God's test, but as extra credit.

Here we must stop and recognize how often we do exactly the same thing, particularly those of us in ministry. We think that if God is pleased with six days of work, God will be even more pleased with seven. After all, God told us to do this work in the first place. In the manna we might recognize that the same action that is commanded on six days is prohibited on the seventh. It is prohibited so that we may remember the true source of our daily bread.

For the Israelites, it takes the stench of rotting manna and the literal absence of manna on the seventh day across the span of an entire generation—forty years—to reshape and reform them to rhythms of grace that are attuned to the continual action and provision of God. As it turns out, old identities die hard. Somehow, we prefer the props of endless work, stench and all, to the death of the old identity and the anxiety and grief such death brings about.

What If It's True?

At this point it seems clear that a therapeutic or human-centered view of the Sabbath will not suffice. God doesn't give the Sabbath simply as a means of making us feel good. Yes, Sabbath brings rest, grace, and life. It also brings ceasing. That ceasing, in and of itself, may cause as much anxiety as it does comfort. We saw this in the last chapter, and need to acknowledge it here. The gift of the Sabbath is the gift of an identity rooted in God's grace and provision, yet for that identity to take root, all lesser identities must be up-rooted and replaced.

We allow ourselves to be tempted by false identities rooted in human effort, labor, busyness, and productivity. In theological terms, we reduce the covenant to the law, to a mere list of dos and don'ts. God's grace is simply too vast for any such reduction. The aim of God's grace today is the same as it was for the Israelites in the Exodus: worship, festival, and celebration. Such a life—such an identity—inevitably eludes us when we reduce our lives to endless activity and fail to receive the radical, disorienting, and identity-altering grace of God. When we cease our labors and rest in God, we say "yes" to the death of our lesser selves.

Through the Sabbath command, God dares us to stop our work, toils, and cares and be still and consider . . . what if it's true? What if God really made us? What if God not only created us, but also—and prior to our existence—chose to be our God? What if we really are God's? What if God really and actually loves us? Barth scholar Eberhard Busch proclaims the glad implications:

> From the beginning, [God] is the God of the covenant who has chosen
> [God's] creature to be [God's] companion. From the beginning, [God]
> refuses to be neutral and have an existence that can be manipulated
> by our arbitrariness. For the love of God for [God's] creature precedes
> [the creature's] existence. How wonderful! The creature cannot enter
> into existence without being loved.[75]

What if death, even the death of God's own Son, even our own death, cannot separate us from God's love? What if our Sabbath-keeping directs us concretely and repeatedly to the resurrection work that is God's alone—the work that brings life from death, that breathes life into lifeless dust, that sets us free from greater-than-human powers so that we may actually stand up straight and praise God?[76]

On the Sabbath we consider all of this in light of Jesus Christ, in light of the resurrection, in anticipation of the consummation, and we confidently proclaim, "Yes! It is true: we are not our own!" We die to autonomy and the captivity it imposes, and we live, rest, and work freely in faith in the all-powerful, surpassingly gracious God who loved us before we existed.

This means coming face-to-face with the ways we attempt—intentionally or unintentionally, knowingly or unknowingly, slightly or severely—to know ourselves by way of that which is not God. In other words, it means coming face-to-face with that which is not grace. This understandably causes anxiety, but then, as we receive and embrace God's gracious invitation to rest, we die to all lesser gods, and we find ourselves in the wondrous presence of a God who loved us before we existed, who sanctifies us apart from anything we can do, who calls us every week to stop, remember, and wait—to remember the salvation history from creation, Exodus, and the prophets to the Incarnation, all of which came about by God's own action; and to wait . . . wait for the end, the return of Christ and the final consummation. And to joyfully celebrate that God has chosen to be this kind of God with and for us.

Sabbath is thus a marker and a reminder of our truest identity. We are covenant partners with the Creator of the universe, and this at the choosing and grace of the Creator, not the created. It is a boundary to our work and thus frees us from and for work. It is grace. It cannot be earned; it is given freely. In all these things, it is also an invitation to surrender and yield. As we remember the limits of our work and the bounties of God's grace, we surrender and yield our will to God's, thus proclaiming that true life and freedom are found in God alone. Recognizing the limits and therefore the freedom that God gives through the Sabbath, we are wise to think of Sabbath quite literally as something that holds us together, both personally and communally.

Before proceeding to the next chapter, we pause and consider the current chapter in light of the vision for practical theology in the first chapter. We want to live faithfully in the world in response to God. As we prepare to close this chapter, we recap the contours that have already emerged:

- If we follow Genesis 1:1–2:3, Sabbath begins with God and God's own rest.
- All creation—and humankind in particular—remains unfinished and incomplete (Gen. 2:1–3) apart from Sabbath rest.
- Sabbath points us to the covenant relationship between God and humankind by pointing us to a broad swath of covenant history from creation to the Exodus, the giving of the Ten Commandments, and then to Christ's life, death, and resurrection.
- Sabbath points forward to the end of time, the eternal Sabbath.
- In pointing backward to salvation history and forward to the *eschaton*, Sabbath highlights God's all-powerful grace at work in the world.
- In God's invitation to humankind to participate in the Sabbath, God invites humankind both to remember God's all-powerful grace and to partake of that grace by partaking in the freedom, rest, and joy of God's own rest.[77]
- Insofar as the Sabbath insists that we root our identity in God's grace, it simultaneously insists that all lesser identities die.

In short, the practical theological vision which is emerging insists that faithful living utterly depends on the Sabbath. The story of God's grace and salvation remains incomplete without it.

It is possible that Sue Miller in her youth and the young people from the previous chapter could hear the potential for legalism in this vision. "So, we *have* to practice Sabbath?" Such a question sees Sabbath like a weight around someone's neck. Oxygen provides a better metaphor. Without oxygen, human life fails. What if Sabbath rest is like emerging from a claustrophobic closet where, no matter how hard you try, you can't get your breath, and into an open, sunlit field where fresh air fills your lungs and literally brings you to life? The greater effort is not in receiving this gift, but in refusing it.

If you've been reading this chapter closely, you may have noticed a significant missing piece. In our attempt to take God seriously in our Sabbath exploration, we've spent time in Genesis and Exodus, and even a little in Deuteronomy, but we have yet to look closely at the New Testament. What about the Gospels? What about Jesus and Sabbath? Did Jesus actually keep the Sabbath? Or did he overturn it? What might we discover if we approach the Gospel texts involving Jesus and the Sabbath in the same way that Barth approached the creation text? What might we learn about God, humanity, and the relationship between the two? These questions will guide us as we turn the page to the next chapter.

5 Jesus and Sabbath

In the first chapters of the First Gospel in the New Testament, Matthew paints a picture of Jesus which brings to mind the life of Moses, that first-bearer of the Sabbath commandment to God's people. Like Moses, Jesus spends childhood years in Egypt. His family escapes to Egypt after Herod issues a murderous decree which echoes that of Pharaoh at Moses's birth. Jesus, like Moses, endures the testing of the wilderness, and as the fifth chapter of Matthew begins, Jesus goes "up the mountain" like Moses at Sinai, and Jesus's experience upon the mountain—like Moses's—has everything to do with God's law.

Moses descends Mount Sinai with the law; Jesus ascends a mountain to interpret this law. This interpretation, more commonly known as the Sermon on the Mount, turns out to be the lengthiest discourse of Jesus in any of the Gospels, and his interpretation challenges traditional understandings of the law to the core. One way he does this is through what biblical scholars refer to as the Matthean antitheses. [1]

These antitheses follow a pattern that begins, "You have heard that it was said . . . ," and later continues, "but I say to you. . . . " Of the six Sermon on the Mount antitheses, two quote the Ten Commandments directly:

You have heard that it was said to those of ancient times, "You shall not murder"; and "whoever murders shall be liable to judgment." But

> I say to you that if you are angry with a brother or sister, you will be liable to judgment; and if you insult a brother or sister, you will be liable to the council; and if you say, "You fool," you will be liable to the hell of fire. (Matt. 5:21–22)

> You have heard that it was said, "You shall not commit adultery." But I say to you that everyone who looks at a woman with lust has already committed adultery with her in his heart. (Matt. 5:27–28)

These are the first two antitheses. Both directly quote Old Testament law, and they come directly on the heels of Jesus's statement that he has come not to destroy the law but to fulfill it (Matt. 5:17). In each of the antitheses Jesus seems to raise the bar for what is expected of those who seek to abide by the law.[2] Jesus moves the focus from the externally observable to the more challenging matters of the heart. This pattern remains for each of the antitheses, yet neither the antitheses nor the remainder of the Sermon on the Mount addresses the Sabbath.[3]

Jesus offers no Sabbath antithesis. He never says, "You have heard it was said, 'Six days you shall work and one day you shall rest,' but I say to you four days you shall work and three days you shall rest." He also never says, "Seven days you shall work and none shall you rest."[4] But this doesn't mean that Jesus leaves the Sabbath untouched. Rather, as we look across the Gospels, we see Jesus repeatedly disrupting people's conceptions of what the Sabbath means and what it entails. In this sense, Jesus's Sabbath ministry seems continuous with the antitheses. Jesus certainly seems to move the bar when it comes to the Sabbath.

Still, the history of interpretation regarding Jesus and the Sabbath stands in stark contrast to the interpretation of the other antitheses. There remains no consensus about how Jesus moves the bar. No one interprets Jesus's teaching on murder or adultery to inaugurate an era when murder and adultery suddenly become permissible. But when it comes to Sabbath, some have seen Jesus as a turning point in history, after which Sabbath-keeping no longer remains an obligation and no longer stands as a marker of God's people.[5]

This chapter aims to address this conundrum. What do we do with Jesus and the Sabbath? To be clear, Jesus hasn't been absent from the discussion up to this point. Along with Barth and the Christian tradition, we have affirmed Jesus's involvement in creation, which culminates in God's Sabbath rest; from the perspective of the first creation story in Genesis, we have viewed the coming fall of humanity and the prospect of sin Christologically—arguing that the ultimate perfection of the world through Christ provides the only basis for God's rest on the seventh day; and we have considered Christ's resurrection as a foretaste and a sign of the final Sabbath consummation at the end of time. Even so, the many Gospel texts that involve both Jesus and Sabbath remain unexamined. Thus, our focus here turns specifically to the Gospels' account of the life and ministry of Jesus and its intersection with the Sabbath.

Repeating the Questions

As we begin this exploration, we continue the trajectory we began in the previous chapter with its exploration of the creation saga. Our aim—echoing Barth and our broader project framework—is practical theological interpretation.[6] This means that we ask the same questions that we put to the Genesis text. What do these texts reveal about God, humanity, and the relationship between the two? How do divine and human action relate in these texts? While the examination of Genesis 1:1–2:3 focused very closely on the account of the seventh day in Genesis 2:1–3, our focus here spans a much broader corpus—all four Gospels. As we look across the Gospels, we find fifty references to the Sabbath day.[7] By way of comparison, the Gospels mention the Sabbath more frequently than they mention murder, adultery, idolatry, stealing, coveting, and bearing false witness combined.

What do the Gospels teach us about the Sabbath from Jesus's life and ministry? What theology or theologies of Sabbath do the Gospels provide? How might these texts relate to the previous interpretation of the seventh day of creation or the story of the Israelites in the wilderness?[8] Will they affirm the radical and all-powerful grace of God? What patterns emerge?

Jesus, Sabbath, and Healing

Barely two full chapters into the Gospel of Mark, we find Jesus in the synagogue on a Sabbath. "And a man was there who had a withered hand" (Mark
3:1). The Pharisees watch to see if Jesus will cure on the Sabbath. Jesus does,
and it irks the Pharisees. These two themes—healing and confrontation between Jesus and the Pharisees—recur throughout the Gospels' Sabbath texts.
We will return to the theme of confrontation in a moment. For now, we
focus on Sabbath healing.

Twelve separate passages tell stories of Jesus healing on the Sabbath day.
In addition to curing the man with the withered hand, Jesus heals a man
with an unclean spirit (Mark 1:21-28; Luke 4:31-37), cures the fever of Simon's mother-in-law (Mark 1:29-31; Luke 4:38-39), heals "a few sick people"
in his hometown (Mark 6:1-6), heals a woman who has been crippled by a
spirit (Luke 13:10-17), cures a man with dropsy (Luke 14:1-6), heals a man
who has been ill for thirty-eight years (John 5:1-18), and heals a man blind
from birth (John 9:1-12). All on the Sabbath.

One simply cannot read the Sabbath texts in the Gospels and fail to notice the overwhelming prominence of Jesus healing as a recurring theme.
Jesus, Sabbath, and healing simply go together. Since healing will reappear
in many of the remaining themes, and since it will factor prominently into
our discussion of grace, we leave our exploration of healing relatively brief
here. For now, suffice it to say that the Gospel picture of the Sabbath is a
picture of miraculous, gracious, and often unexpected healing at the hands
of Christ.[9]

Confrontation

If we follow Mark's account of Jesus healing the man with the withered
hand, we see it is not as simple as happily-ever-after. As noted, the Pharisees watch to see if Jesus will cure on the Sabbath. He does, of course, but
before healing, Christ asks a question that cuts to the core of the Pharisees'

identity as experts in the law: "Is it lawful to do good or harm, to save life or kill on the Sabbath?" Yet Jesus's question leads only to silence. The situation escalates quickly—emotions soar. The silence grieves and angers Jesus, who proceeds to heal the man, yet this only inflames the Pharisees, who immediately plot to destroy Jesus. This Sabbath healing leads to a significant confrontation—a confrontation that repeats itself across many stories of Jesus and the Sabbath.

Though they're not alone in taking offense at Jesus's Sabbath ministry, the Pharisees do often take the lead. At issue is the law. We saw this in Jesus's question to the Pharisees. Both the Pharisees and Jesus—as seen in the Sermon on the Mount—take the law very seriously. Confrontation emerges around the question of interpretation, and in the case of the Pharisees, the questioning of their interpretation equals the questioning of their power and authority. The question of power and authority thus stands at the heart of the confrontation that takes place within Jesus's Sabbath ministry.

Jesus frames the matter of Sabbath authority starkly. In the verse immediately preceding the story of the healing of the man with the withered hand, Jesus asserts, "The Son of Man is lord even of the Sabbath" (Mark 2:28).[10] Jesus shows no partiality in his willingness to confront the powers by displaying his Sabbath lordship. He confronts both the religious elite and the marginalized.[11] Each of the Gospels vividly portrays both the intensity and the stakes involved in this confrontation. When the Synoptics (Matthew, Mark, and Luke) conclude their respective versions of the story of Jesus healing the man with the withered hand, they all note the fervor of the Pharisees' response. "The Pharisees went out and immediately conspired with the Herodians against him, how to destroy him."[12] In Matthew, Mark, and Luke, this Sabbath confrontation signals the beginning of the broader confrontation that ultimately leads to Jesus's crucifixion. Something is clearly at stake here.

The Sabbath confrontation that John's Gospel portrays is no less intense. In the wake of Jesus healing one "who had been ill for thirty-eight years" (John 5:5), the religious leaders sought "all the more to kill [Jesus], because he was not only breaking the Sabbath, but was also calling God his own

Father, thereby making himself equal to God" (John 5:18). John would thus have us recognize within Jesus's Sabbath ministry both his divinity and the superiority of his power and authority over every other power and authority, whether religious, systemic, natural, or cosmic. The superiority of Jesus's power and authority puts every other power and authority in perspective, and as the fervent response of Jesus's opponents indicates, his Sabbath ministry bears life-and-death significance. Jesus's own life is on the line.

The challenge that Jesus issues to the religious leaders can be seen in still another light. Yes, Jesus confronts the religious and imperial systems and structures that uphold and empower the Pharisees. Yet a close reading of these texts—particularly in light of the Old Testament Sabbath texts—reveals another relevant question regarding power. Recall Barth's emphasis on God's all-powerful grace and action made manifest in and through the Sabbath. The Sabbath on the seventh day of creation comes about by God's grace and action alone; God delivers the Israelites from Egypt and provides manna and a Sabbath rhythm with a mighty hand and outstretched arm; the Exodus version of the Sabbath commandment points to God's rest on the seventh day of creation as the basis for the Sabbath rest of God's people; and the Sabbath commandment in Deuteronomy looks to God's deliverance of his people from slavery in Egypt as the basis of the Sabbath rest of God's people. In every case, the power, action, and grace of God stand as the unquestionable basis for the Sabbath rest of God's people.

In this light, the confrontation between Jesus and the Pharisees that takes place on the Sabbath may be interpreted through a question that is basic to practical theology: How do divine and human action relate here? The Pharisees have taken a gift that rests completely upon God's all-powerful grace and reduced it to rules and regulations—to a matter of human effort and action. In other words, Jesus insists that the error of the Pharisees is not that they take the Sabbath too seriously, but that they have missed the point and reduced it to a matter of mere human power and choice.[13] Jesus confronts this reduction head-on. As he miraculously heals on the Sabbath, he simultaneously proclaims both the superiority of his own power and lordship—making himself equal to God—and the insufficiency of merely human power and agency for attaining God's all-powerful Sabbath grace. Jesus confronts the Pharisees with this disorienting grace.

Jesus's Sabbath grace also confronts those with little apparent power—even those held captive by super-human forces. The Gospel of Mark portrays this vividly. Jesus's first healing in Mark takes place a number of stories before the healing of the man with the withered hand, but also on the Sabbath and in the synagogue. This time, it involves one who is clearly subject to powers beyond himself: "Just then there was in their synagogue a man with an unclean spirit, and he cried out . . ." (Mark 1:23-24). Yet when the speech comes forth, it becomes clear that the man with the unclean spirit isn't in control. The voice cries, "What have you to do with us, Jesus of Nazareth? Have you come to destroy us? I know who you are, the Holy One of God" (Mark 1:24). The unclean spirit controls the man's speech, and Mark contrasts for us the uncleanness of the spirit with the holiness of Jesus.

Mark then establishes the clear hierarchy of power. Though this man may be subject to an unclean spirit with greater-than-human powers, the power of the unclean spirit is no match for the Holy One, Jesus, who rebukes it and commands it to leave the man. Luke tells the same story (Luke 4:31-37), and adds the story of a woman "with a spirit that had crippled her for eighteen years" whom Jesus heals on the Sabbath (Luke 13:10-17). Other Sabbath healings repeat the theme that Jesus heals, delivers, and frees people from conditions against which mere human actions and capacities are powerless: one blind from birth receives sight (John 9); one paralyzed for thirty-eight years walks (John 5); one with a withered hand has it restored (Matt. 12; Mark 3; Luke 6); one with dropsy is cured (Luke 14). In each case, Jesus confronts the powers that compromise these people and in so doing confronts the lowly, marginalized, and powerless with their full humanity.

The teaching that Jesus offers during the Sabbath in Luke 14 summarizes well the confrontation that takes place at the intersection of Jesus and the Sabbath. As Jesus partakes of a Sabbath meal at the home of a leader of the Pharisees, Jesus professes that "all who exalt themselves will be humbled, and those who humble themselves will be exalted" (Luke 14:11). Jesus's Sabbath ministry does just this. It humbles the exalted and exalts the humble; it insists that the Sabbath involves powers and capacities which far exceed the power and capacity of humanity; and it confronts the exalted, the humble, and every power and authority with the superiority of Jesus's power and the reality of Jesus's lordship.[14]

Sabbath in Community

Jesus's confrontation of both the lowly and the exalted points to the communal nature of Jesus's Sabbaths. In fact, the Gospels give only one account of Jesus spending the Sabbath alone. It is the Sabbath that follows his crucifixion, when his body lay lifeless and alone in the tomb. We will tend to that cosmos-altering Sabbath below. For now, we recognize that the Sabbaths of Jesus's life and ministry were spent in community with others. Jesus interacts with disciples, those on the margins, those in need of healing, Pharisees, scribes, and crowds. Jesus gathers with others in the synagogue on the Sabbath, and he partakes of shared Sabbath meals.

In addition, when Jesus teaches on the Sabbath, he focuses overwhelmingly on the ethical—on how people should relate to each other and creation. For example, Luke marks the very beginning of Jesus's ministry with Jesus teaching on the Sabbath. This teaching proclaims the contours of the community under Jesus's lordship. Jesus goes to the community gathered in the synagogue, receives the scroll, and reads from Isaiah:

> The Spirit of the Lord is upon me,
> because the Lord has anointed me to bring good news to the poor.
> The Lord has sent me to proclaim release to the captives and recovery of
>   sight to the blind,
> to let the oppressed go free, to proclaim the year of the Lord's favor. (Luke
>   4:18–19)

If we follow these verses from Isaiah line by line, they provide something of an outline for what Jesus does on the Sabbath:

- *Gives good news to the poor*: Jesus's Sabbath healings come to those who would have been economically disadvantaged because of their conditions. The blind and the lame would have been exceedingly limited in their ability to provide for themselves or others. Jesus's Sabbath ministry overturns these conditions and empowers the poor for economically viable work.[15]
- *Gives release to the captives*: The man with an "unclean spirit" in Mark 1:21-28 and Luke 4:31-37 illustrates this. Though the story begins with the unclean spirit clearly in control of the man, it ends with Jesus releasing the man from that captivity. We may also see in Jesus's Sabbath ministry a drive to release God's people—and the Pharisees in particular—from laws and regulations that have come to hold them captive.[16]
- *Grants recovery of sight to the blind*: In John 9, Jesus gives sight on the Sabbath to a man blind from birth.
- *Lets the oppressed go free*: Jesus's healing of the woman in Luke 13 uniquely lifts up freedom. When the religious leaders question Jesus after he heals the woman, he responds by pointing to the religious leaders' certain practice of untying livestock to drink water on the Sabbath, and then insisting that this woman, too, should be set free on the Sabbath from that which binds her.

In every case, Jesus's Sabbath ministry emerges in the context of a gathered community with implications for the character of the community.

As already noted, Jesus challenges the religious elite and lifts up those on the margins, and along the way he insists on a particular shape of common life where all are welcome. At a Sabbath meal at the home of a Pharisee, Jesus commands hospitality particularly for those society tends to ignore:

> When you give a luncheon or a dinner, do not invite your friends or your brothers or your relatives or rich neighbors, in case they may invite you in return, and you would be repaid. But when you give a banquet, invite the poor, the crippled, the lame, and the blind. And

you will be blessed, because they cannot repay you, for you will be repaid at the resurrection of the righteous. (Luke 14:12–14)

In a way that echoes the all-inclusive Sabbath commandment of the Old Testament, Jesus's Sabbath ministry may be seen as a ground for extending grace and mercy to all in the community, not an excuse for withholding it.[17]

Thus, by virtue of Jesus's interactions with others and the ethical focus of his teaching on the Sabbath, Jesus refuses the reduction of the Sabbath to a matter of mere private devotion and insists instead on a Sabbath inclusive of a broad community. In glancing back to the Old Testament Sabbath texts, we see their overwhelming affirmation of the Sabbath's communal and ethical dimensions. On the seventh day, we have seen God at rest in fellowship with humanity and all creation; in the wilderness, God gives the Sabbath in its holiness to the entire Israelite community; and the Sabbath commandment in both Exodus and Deuteronomy expands the communal dimension beyond the Israelites and their sons and daughters to male and female servants, resident aliens, and livestock. Sabbatical and Jubilee years extend Sabbath to even the land. In every case, Sabbath takes place in the context of the community of faith for the good of creation and for the purpose of the formation of the community.

On the Sabbath, Jesus Teaches

We have already seen this in the synagogue and at the table of the Pharisee: Jesus teaches on the Sabbath. If we return again to the account of Jesus rebuking the unclean spirit in Mark 1, we see Jesus's action in the passage that precedes the rebuking. Jesus has just called his first disciples. They travel to Capernaum, "and when the Sabbath came, he entered the synagogue and taught. They were astounded at his teaching, for he taught as one having authority." After this, the one with the unclean spirit appears and cries out, leading to Jesus's rebuke of the spirit and the restoration of the man. The crowds then reiterate the force of Jesus's teaching. They ask, "What is this?

A new teaching—with authority! He commands even the unclean spirits, and they obey him."

When the Gospels tell Sabbath stories, the plot frequently involves Jesus teaching. In some sense, the aims and purposes of this teaching have already been named. This formation moves the community toward healing; it humbles the exalted and exalts the humble. Nine different Gospel passages reference Jesus teaching on the Sabbath. Five simply note that Jesus was teaching but don't tell us what Jesus taught. For example, Luke 13:10 notes rather blandly, "Now [Jesus] was teaching in one of the synagogues on the Sabbath."[18] In other cases, we do get the content of Jesus's Sabbath instruction. As noted above, in Luke 4 Jesus reads from Isaiah. In Luke 14, Jesus follows his Sabbath healing of the man with dropsy with teaching on humility and the parable of the great dinner (Luke 14:7–24), and Jesus's Sabbath healings in John 5 and 9 lead into discourses on Jesus's authority (John 5:19–47), spiritual blindness (John 9:35–41), and Jesus as the Good Shepherd (John 10:1–21).

Jesus's teaching on the Sabbath connects closely with the healing, confrontation, and community that have already been named. In some sense, healing, confrontation, and community emerge as the methods and curriculum of Jesus's Sabbath teaching. All of these point to a broader aim of Jesus's teaching on the Sabbath: life itself. Jesus insists that nourishment, restoration, and preservation of life fulfill rather than violate the Sabbath.[19] In Mark 2, Jesus and the disciples pluck grain and eat it to nourish their bodies. In Mark 3, Jesus asks, "Is it lawful to do good or harm on the Sabbath, to save life or kill" (Mark 3:4); and in a more implicit way, life is on the line with the livestock to which Jesus refers in Luke 13:15: "Do you not untie your donkey and lead it to water?" In other words, do you do what's necessary for life for your animals on the Sabbath? What do you do if your sheep falls into a pit (Matt. 12:11) or if a child or an ox falls into a well (Luke 14:5)? You pull them out!

In each case, the Gospels connect Sabbath with life itself. Jesus points his listeners to the ways the Sabbath already intersects matters of life and death, and he challenges every tendency to stifle life. In keeping with the themes noted in previous chapters, the distinctiveness of the life that Jesus brings about on the Sabbath necessitates the death of lesser forms of life. That which stifles life—be it illness, blindness, pits, water wells, spirits, or Sabbath legalism—must die. Ultimately, the aim of Jesus's Sabbath teaching echoes the content of his teaching during a Sabbath in John 10—that God's people "may have life, and have it abundantly" (John 10:10).[20]

Formation through Death

The connections among life, death, Sabbath, and all-powerful grace never appear more overtly than in Jesus's passion. Earlier, we noted the life-and-death implications that arose in the context of Jesus's confrontation with the religious leaders. In response to Jesus's life and ministry, the religious authorities conspire to kill Jesus (John 5:18); they set out to destroy him. Indeed, Jesus's Sabbath ministry puts his own life on the line, and this fact emerges with full force in the only Sabbath narrative that appears in all four Gospels: the story of Jesus's death and resurrection. This narrative recalls Barth's insistence on the ways the Sabbath points us to the vast history of the covenant relationship between God and humanity. Each Gospel account of Jesus's death and resurrection includes multiple references to the Sabbath. Matthew 28:1, Mark 16:1, Luke 23:54, and John 19:31, 41–42 all indicate that Jesus's body lay lifeless in the tomb on the Sabbath.

Yet the English language obscures another Sabbath reference that occurs in each of the Gospels.[21] To understand this, we need to look briefly at New Testament Greek. The same Greek word—*sabbatōn*—refers both to the Sabbath day and to the span of seven days—a week. Thus, though you can't see it in English, Matthew 28:1 includes *sabbatōn* twice: "After the Sabbath [*sabbatōn*], as the first day of the week [*sabbatōn*] was dawning, Mary Magdalene and the other Mary went to see the tomb."

The first instance of *sabbatōn* points to the day Jesus was dead; the second points to the new time of Jesus's resurrection. The text looked and sounded more literally like this: "After the Sabbath, as the first day of the

Sabbath was dawning, Mary Magdalene and the other Mary went to see the tomb." Granted, the first recipients would have distinguished the difference in usage, yet the significance remains. *Sabbatōn* points to both Christ's death and resurrection, and parallel verses occur in Mark 16:2, Luke 24:1, and John 20:1, 19. Thus the first recipients of each of these Gospels couldn't have heard the term *sabbatōn* without recalling both the death and resurrection of Jesus.

In retrospect, the death and resurrection narratives only make explicit what has been implicit across the Gospel texts and what has already been noted in the manna narrative from Exodus 16: life and death have been on the line all along. Jesus affirms the life-nourishing practice of the disciples in the grain fields and then extends newness of life to the man with the withered hand. The Pharisees respond with plans for Jesus's destruction because they perceive a threat to the vitality of their authority and power. Jesus's Sabbath ministry insists that the Sabbath cannot be reduced to a matter of human effort and law-keeping. Thus, Jesus's Sabbath mercies call for the death of the reduction of the Sabbath to a list of rules and regulations.

Jesus's Sabbath mercies also signal the death of the super-human powers that bind humanity. All of this echoes the essence of the Matthean antitheses. It's as if Jesus is saying, "You've heard it said that the Sabbath was all about what you can and can't do, but I say, it's about God's life, grace, and healing. It's about the death not only of your lesser identities, but also of the powers that are too great for humanity and that hold humanity captive."

Indeed, we may go so far as to say that the Sabbath signals the death of death itself! Here, Jesus's "It is finished" on the cross and the ceasing of his life echo the ceasing of God on the seventh day that finishes and completes creation.[22] Here the work of salvation and redemption belongs to God alone. Christ lays down his life, endures Sabbath death, and rises again in all-powerful grace on the first day of the *sabbatōn*.

Here we can affirm again that the Sabbath journey doesn't skirt death. It journeys through the bowels of death, but not so that death may have the last word. Instead, it makes this jouney so that God's people may know, experience, and be formed by God's all-powerful grace and resurrection life.

Yet again, the invitation to the death of all lesser gods is the invitation of disorienting grace.

Jesus, Sabbath, and Radical Grace

At the beginning of this chapter, we suggested that the Gospel accounts of Jesus and the Sabbath highlight the radical and all-powerful grace of God. That grace has been present in each of the aforementioned themes. Grace filled the healings, gave shape to the confrontation, enlivened the community, and stood as a marker of the content, methods, and aims of Jesus's Sabbath teaching. Even so, more must be said about the particularity of the grace that emerges at the intersection of Jesus and the Sabbath. In order to more fully glimpse this grace, we ask again how these texts portray the relationship between divine and human action. To do this, we affirm—along with the Christian tradition—the divinity of Christ. When Jesus acts, God acts.

This approach to the Gospel texts involving Jesus and Sabbath reveals the grace of the Sabbath all the more prominently because it illuminates again the priority and precedence of God's Sabbath action. In the twelve texts that tell stories of Jesus healing on the Sabbath, the sick or infirm do not initiate a single one. Jesus clearly initiates at least ten,[23] and in two of those ten stories, Jesus heals in the face of resistance from the spirit or power that possesses the infirm (Mark 1:21–28; Luke 4:31–37). When Mark and Luke recount the story of Jesus healing Simon's mother-in-law, they both follow this story with parallel texts that emphasize the unique way that Jesus initiates Sabbath healing. In Mark 1:32 and in Luke 4:40, we read that "as the sun was setting" or "at sunset," many people brought the sick and the lame to Jesus for healing. If we recall that the Jewish Sabbath ends at sunset, we recognize the shift in initiation that takes place when it ends. On the Sabbath, it is Jesus who initiates healing of a radically gracious nature.

In addition to coming at Jesus's initiative, these Sabbath healings take place among the inactive. Again, this stands in great distinction when compared to other healing texts in the Gospels. Healing on the Sabbath comes to those at rest. The Gospel writers seem to exhibit consistent intentionality in depicting the recipients of Jesus's Sabbath healing as passive. "A man was there with a withered hand" (Matt. 12:10); "Just then there was in their synagogue a man with an unclean spirit" (Mark 1:23); "Now Simon's mother-in-law was in bed with a fever" (Mark 1:30); "a man was there who had a withered hand" (Mark 3:1); "In the synagogue there was a man who had the spirit of an unclean demon" (Luke 4:33); "there was a man there whose right hand was withered" (Luke 6:6); "And just then there appeared a woman with a spirit that had crippled her for eighteen years" (Luke 13:11); "Just then, in front of him, there was a man who had dropsy" (Luke 14:2); "One man was there who had been ill for thirty-eight years" (John 5:5); "As he walked along, [Jesus] saw a man blind from birth" (John 9:1).

Not all Gospel healing stories go this way. In contrast to the hemorrhaging woman who spends all she has on doctors and pursues Jesus in the midst of a crowd (Luke 8:40–48), or blind Bartimaeus, who shouts for Jesus's attention (Mark 10:46–52), or the many healings that friends and family ask of Jesus (e.g., Mark 2:1–12 and Luke 9:37–43), the recipients of Sabbath healing simply "appear." No one intercedes on their behalf; they don't make requests of Jesus; and, astonishingly, none of the Sabbath healing narratives mention faith. In each case, Jesus's action precedes any action on the part of the one who receives healing.[24] We simply cannot conceive of these Sabbath healings as in any way being earned, achieved, or initiated by human effort. They are acts of sheer grace that echo the sheer grace of the seventh day of creation, the grace of manna and Sabbath in the wilderness, and the grace of Sabbath rest one day in every seven.

What do we make of the fact that none of the Sabbath healing narratives mention faith? While scholars generally frown on arguments rooted in absence, we must acknowledge that the Gospels mention faith with great frequency in other healing narratives. In Matthew 8:13, Jesus tells the centurion, "Go; let it be done for you according to your faith." To the woman suffering from hemorrhages, Jesus says, "Take heart, daughter; your faith has made you well" (Matt. 9:22). The healing of the paralytic in Mark 2 takes place after Jesus sees the faith of those who carry the man. To the blind beggar in Luke 18:42, Jesus affirms, "your faith has saved you," and John's Gospel notes that the royal official who approached Jesus on behalf of his dying son walked away exercising faith—"the man believed" (John 4:50).

The healing and restoration that Jesus extends on the Sabbath thus appear unique among healing narratives—not necessarily because of what Jesus is doing, but because of what the recipients are, or are not, doing. It seems that these texts provide a word of hope for those bound by powers greater than themselves—those who may not even know to hope or wish for healing or freedom, for whom bondage, captivity, or some dehumanizing force has simply become integral to their identity. Blind from birth; infirm for thirty-eight years; doubled over for eighteen years; weighted under the assumption that busyness is a good unto itself: these people surely have come to simply accept these conditions as part and parcel of their identity. But Jesus sees otherwise. Mark 6 and John 5 make the case to an even greater degree.

It turns out that one Gospel healing narrative involving Jesus and Sabbath does mention faith, but it mentions faith's absence, not its presence. In the sixth chapter of Mark, after Jesus teaches in his hometown on the Sabbath, he is "amazed at their unbelief [lit. lack of faith]." Nonetheless, Jesus "laid his hands on a few sick people and cured them" (Mark 6:5). In John 5, Jesus asks the man who had been ill for thirty-eight years whether or not he wants to be made well. The man responds to Jesus's question not with faith, but with an explanation of why healing remained impossible: "Sir, I have no one to put me into the pool when the water is stirred up; and while I am making my way, someone else steps down ahead of me" (John 5:7). Later in the narrative, after Jesus heals the man, it becomes clear that he didn't even know who Jesus was at the time of the healing (John 5:13).

So it appears that even overt lack of faith and confusion about Jesus's identity cannot stop the all-powerful and all-gracious healing which Jesus extends on the Sabbath. We simply have no way to conceive of these healings as being earned or achieved. They are radical acts of all-powerful grace.

Recognizing Response

Before moving on, we should recognize the continuity between the Old Testament Sabbath witness and that of the Gospels. In every case, the grace and action of God precede the achievement or initiation of humankind. From creation to redemption, the Sabbath saga proclaims God's all-powerful grace. However, we shouldn't interpret God's initiation and priority as the end of meaningful human action and response. They are, rather, their beginning. The Gospel Sabbath texts include two human responses to Sabbath grace that deserve attention here: faith and praise.

We've already noted the absence of the mention of faith in the healing narratives. This fact remains. Still, as noted earlier, John's Gospel provides two cases of extended discourse following Jesus's Sabbath healing. Both raise the matter of faith, though it is again difficult to see this in English translations. In the aftermath of Jesus's healing of the man who had been ill for thirty-eight years, Jesus responds to those who seek to take his life by affirming both his authority as granted by God and the life-and-death stakes of Jesus's lordship (John 5:19–29). This paves the way for questions of faith.

Jesus names the problem of his accusers sharply. They don't have God's word (*logos*) abiding in them because they don't believe—don't exercise faith in—Jesus (John 5:38).[25] The discourse concludes with Jesus mentioning faith four times in the final two verses (John 5:46–47). Though his accusers would profess strict adherence to the law as given by Moses, Jesus challenges this notion. "If you believed Moses, you would believe me, for he wrote about me. But if you do not believe what he wrote, how will you believe what I say?"[26] Every instance of "believe" or "believed" in English is a reference to faith.[27] Jesus stands in continuity with Moses, and the dominant question is one of faith. The response Jesus seeks to his Sabbath healing and teaching is not mere adherence to the law, but faith.

The passage in John 9 shifts the focus of faith from Jesus's opponents to the one Jesus heals. After the man born blind receives his sight, he finds himself embroiled in debate with Jesus's opponents, who, as the text notes, lack faith.[28] Here the man born blind bears simple witness to Jesus's healing:

"One thing I do know, that though I was blind, now I see" (John 9:25). After the debate, Jesus finds the man and raises again the question of faith: "Do you believe in the Son of Man?" (John 9:35). After Jesus reveals himself as the Son of Man, the now-seeing man responds: "'Lord, I believe.' And he worshiped him" (John 9:38).

This response of faith and worship echoes the response of the woman in Luke 13 who had been bound by a spirit for eighteen years. After Jesus sets her free, "immediately she stood up straight and began praising God" (Luke 13:13). Thus, the all-powerful Sabbath grace of God doesn't inhibit or squelch human action; it unquestionably invites it and serves as its basis. As God's people find themselves confirmed and confronted by this all-powerful grace, faith and praise stand as two ever-appropriate responses.

Both of these responses have clear precedents in the Old Testament. We have already seen God's provision of manna in Exodus 16 as a story of faith formation. Instead of a monotonous provision of manna every single day, God gives manna only six days, but promises provision for every day. The Israelites are challenged to exercise faith in God's provision anew each day. Will they trust that the double portion on day six won't rot? Will they exercise faith by resting on the seventh day? Do they trust God to provide anew on the eighth day?

Regarding worship, the Old Testament Sabbath became the day of the gathering of God's people. Even earlier, though, worship stands as the clear aim of the entire Exodus narrative. Moses repeatedly requests the release of the Israelites from captivity in Egypt so they may worship God.[29]

Why Sabbath? God's people Sabbath so that they may be known and know themselves as people of faith, as people who trust radically in God's all-powerful grace and provision. God's people Sabbath so that their identity may be rooted first and foremost in God's affirmation that they are God's beloved children. In recognition of this grace and this affirmation, God's people cannot help but praise God, from whom all blessings flow.

What about Rest?

Amid the all-powerful grace that has filled the pages of this chapter, we may notice a curious absence. What happened to Sabbath rest? What happened to Sabbath ceasing? Does Jesus affirm the Old Testament's invitation to Sabbath rest, or can we read the Gospels and conclude, "Oh, the Sabbath is about doing good and saving life—acts of mercy, healing, and teaching. Let's get busy! That's what Sabbath is all about!"

This line of thinking operates functionally in the lives of many in ministry—particularly ministry on behalf of youth. It operates equally in the lives of the young people we met in Chapter 3. They strive so endlessly after all the things their churches, schools, and the broader culture tell them they should that they, too, assume rest somehow falls outside the life to which they are called. If there is Sabbath, it's Sabbath work, not Sabbath rest.[30]

If we look again at the Gospels, this approach must contend with at least three realities. First, it fails to acknowledge the aforementioned pattern of Jesus's Sabbath healing coming to the inactive or those at rest. Second, the ceaseless work notion refuses Jesus's invitation to rest in Matthew 11. The very first instance of the term "Sabbath" in the Gospels occurs in Matthew 12:1, with the account of Jesus and his disciples walking through the grain fields. However, the verses that immediately precede Matthew 12 recount Jesus's invitation to rest. In a very real sense, these verses provide the prologue to all Gospel Sabbath texts.[31]

> [25]At that time Jesus said, "I thank you, Father, Lord of heaven and earth, because you have hidden these things from the wise and the intelligent and have revealed them to infants; [26]yes, Father, for such was your gracious will. [27]All things have been handed over to me by my Father; and no one knows the Son except the Father, and no one knows the Father except the Son and anyone to whom the Son chooses to reveal him.
>
> [28]"Come to me, all you that are weary and are carrying heavy burdens, and I will give you rest. [29]Take my yoke upon you, and learn

from me; for I am gentle and humble in heart, and you will find rest for your souls. [30]For my yoke is easy, and my burden is light." (Matt. 11:25-30)

These verses foreshadow many of the above themes. God's gracious will humbles the exalted—the "wise and intelligent"—and exalts the humble, the "infants."[32] These verses also attest to Jesus's authority, which comes directly from God. Yet Jesus's exercise of his authority starkly contrasts with the authority that the Pharisees will display in the Sabbath narratives. Contrary to the Pharisees, who impose "heavy burdens, hard to bear, and lay them on the shoulders of others,"[33] Jesus invites those with heavy burdens to come and receive rest.

Though religious and imperial powers impose heavy burdens, Jesus's reign invites rest. Jesus names this twice. In verse 28 he promises "I will give you rest," and in verse 29 he insists that all who receive his invitation "will find rest" for their souls.[34] Here the sense of the Greek term for "rest" repeats the very essence of the Hebrew Sabbath: to stop or to cease.[35] This prologue to the Gospel Sabbath texts thus paints a picture not in opposition to Sabbath ceasing and resting, but necessarily inclusive of the rest that Jesus himself offers.

The third problem with interpreting the Gospel Sabbath texts as giving license for never-ending labor is that it fails to contend with the simple reality that for Jesus and his followers, the Sabbath day clearly remained a day distinct from others. Luke notes the customary nature of Jesus's Sabbath observance: "When [Jesus] came to Nazareth, where he had been brought up, he went to the synagogue on the Sabbath day, as was his custom" (Luke 4:16).[36] The apostles continue the practice of teaching in the synagogue on the Sabbath in Acts,[37] and the unique nature of Jesus's Sabbath healings, as noted above, also signals a Sabbath day that is distinct from other days. Finally, Luke makes a point of recounting the Sabbath rest among Jesus's closest followers on the Sabbath coinciding with Jesus's death: "On the Sabbath [following Jesus's crucifixion] they rested according to the commandment" (Luke 23:56).

The point here is not Sabbath legalism; the point is that for Jesus and his closest followers, the Sabbath day remained distinct. A Sabbath that devolves into a work day like any other loses its distinction, definition, and identity. The sum of the Sabbath story suggests that God's people risk similar loss in the midst of endless labor.

Most importantly, we must ask this theological question: What kind of God does limitless work suggest? Limitless work implies that human life and thriving depend not on God's grace, but on human effort and achievement.[38] Yet if it's true that the world came into being apart from human striving, if it's true that Christ came to earth and conquered death apart from human striving, and if it's true that Christ will return to redeem the whole creation apart from human striving, then our ceaseless striving here and now simply cannot contain or convey God's all-powerful, creating, redeeming, and death-conquering grace.

Practically, the ceaseless work approach fails to recognize the possibility that we join in the work of God every bit as much through Sabbath rest as we do through the work of the other six days. It also fails to realize that our Sabbath rest both partakes of and bears witness to God's grace in a way that our labors never can. Something unique emerges through the Sabbath. It embodies grace in a way that stands distinct from the witness of our labor and striving.

Conclusion: All-Powerful Grace and the Faith It Invites

Imagine that you walk to work every day. And imagine that on your way, every day you pass an art gallery with magnificent paintings in the window. You know it's there. You could give directions to it or briefly describe it, but you've never stopped to look. Then one day, you do. You stop. You enter the gallery and let the beauty of the paintings wash over you. You notice things you've never noticed before—things that simply can't be noticed unless you stop and pay attention.

Our study suggests that the Sabbath is something like this. Through the Sabbath, God invites us to stop and consider God's mighty works, and in stopping we can perceive things we could never perceive if we just kept going. We perceive grace. We glimpse the very life of God. We saw it in the Old Testament, and we've seen it now in the New. From beginning to end, the Gospel Sabbath texts affirm the all-powerful grace of God.

On the Sabbath, Jesus takes the initiative to bring healing and life; Jesus confronts Sabbaths that have been reduced to mere rules, and he displays the superiority of God's power to every other power; in Christ, God calls for the passing away of every Sabbath that misses the point in order that new life and grace may thrive. We see this most dramatically in the death and resurrection of Jesus Christ, the dawn of the first day of the week (*sabbatōn*), and the inauguration of the death of death.

In and through the Sabbath, God promises not only to confront our lesser identities and call for their death, but also to journey with us through death to the promise of new life. As we cease our labors and practice the renouncing faith to which Barth pointed us, we may actually behold all of this, and we may be formed as people of faith. We may find ourselves in the very presence of God.

Recall Barth's interpretation of the seventh day of creation. He wrote that on the seventh day God "confirmed and confronted" creation. He also argued for the thoroughly gracious character of that confirmation and confrontation. On the seventh day, the first humans have no work of their own on which to reflect. God gives them Sabbath rest as a gift of sheer grace. God gives manna and Sabbath to the Israelites in the wilderness as gifts of grace, and God gives the Sabbath commandments in Exodus 20 and Deuteronomy 5 on the bases of God's gracious action at creation and through the Exodus.

We have seen this same grace in the Gospels' account of the Sabbath, and perhaps in the response of the man born blind in John 9; we have even seen the renouncing faith that Barth insists is the only proper basis for our Sabbath observance. After experiencing Jesus's all-powerful grace, the man declares his faith and falls down and worships.

In the end, our refusing to receive Sabbath rest is refusing an extraordinary invitation. In keeping with the view of the end of time as a great heavenly banquet, we may see our Sabbath refusal as a response that brings to mind Jesus's parable of the wedding banquet in Matthew 22. The king gives this banquet for his son, but those who are invited "made light of it and went away, one to his farm, another to his business, while the rest seized his slaves, maltreated them, and killed them" (vv. 5-6).[39] Among those who refuse the dinner invitation are those with business engagements and work to do—those who lord power over the powerless rather than empowering the lowly.

Again, we see the extraordinary nature of God's grace. It is extraordinary both in what it offers and in what it requires. It offers life, celebration, joy, festivity, and fellowship, but it does so by way of limits. To receive this invitation is to accept limits on our work and striving. Our endless busyness must die; our limitless pursuit of accomplishment and achievement must die; and our continual consuming must die. Yet this doesn't mean the death of all work and achievement. Instead, it means the radical reorientation of all human labor—indeed, all human living and human identity—around God's grace, which then becomes the basis and ground for who we are. We and our youth may then hear, along with Sue Miller, God's stunning and identity-rooting affirmation: "You are my beloved children."

Our endless effort on its own and of itself can never affirm this. God's invitation continues, but we must rest if we want to hear it. We must pull up a chair at the banquet. We must open ourselves to the joy, celebration, and fellowship—not because we've earned it or because we've completed enough work, but because the One who made us has graciously called us his own.

This is the stunning and all-encompassing invitation that God issues through the Sabbath. Come. Rest. Know that you are beloved and that you are God's.

What Do We Do Now?

A few weeks ago, I sat with two beloved friends. Of course, we didn't start out as beloved friends. In the beginning—over a decade ago now—one began as a professor of mine. Over the years, this professor-turned-friend has observed my Sabbath journey with a proximity that is second only to my family's. She read this book in a dozen different iterations long before it was a book. As my mentor and teacher, she understands my sense of the Sabbath as well as anyone. She has even confessed to being deeply convicted by it.

My other friend started out years ago as my student. She enrolled in a course that I taught during my doctoral studies. The subject of the course? Sabbath. As part of that course, she practiced Sabbath for the semester; she read Barth on Sabbath; she read about youth and technology; she journaled beautifully about her Sabbath experience; and she endured week after week of me rambling on about the Sabbath.

All of this is to say that there aren't very many people in the world who know my take on the Sabbath better than these two dear friends. When we met a few weeks ago, we didn't plan to talk Sabbath, but the conversation happened to turn in that direction. Years of friendship, shared adventures, and collaborative learning paved the way for these two to pull no punches. It didn't take long for both to shamelessly chuckle their way into confessions of Sabbath failure. Yes, they understand Sabbath. They even long for it, but actual practice eludes them more often than not.

The Sabbath journey is messier and more difficult than we thought.

If we're going to be true to the framework for practical theology we outlined in the first chapter, we have another decisive move to make—an all-important question to ask: What do we do now? What might faithful Sabbath practice actually look like? The story of my two dear friends reminds me of a sobering but hope-inspiring line from the end of the story of the Israelites in the wilderness: "The Israelites ate manna forty years" (Exod. 16:35). The rhythm of gathering and resting, gathering and resting, gathering and resting shaped them—worked on them—for forty years. Forty. Years. An entire generation.

I love this and I hate this. I hate it because I want to master the Sabbath right now or, better, yesterday. I want to add Sabbath to my list of life achievements. I love it because it reminds me that Sabbath isn't an achievement; it's a long, slow journey—a messy yielding to the slow, steady work of grace. The Sabbath offers no quick fix to our misplaced and fractured identities. It offers a steady diet of enough—daily bread to remind us of the source of our truest identity.

So, what *do* we do?

Over the years, I've had countless casual and formal conversations with hundreds of people about the Sabbath. When people first find out about my interest in the Sabbath, certain types of questions emerge with stunning frequency. Regarding the who, what, when, where, and why of Sabbath, people ask about the what and the when to the near exclusion of the who, where, and why. People want to know what counts as legitimate Sabbath practice? And when?

"Does it have to be on Sunday?"
"Can I mow the lawn on the Sabbath?"
"Is it OK to do laundry?"
"I suppose I shouldn't do homework?"
"Does Sabbath have to be every week?"

"What about doctors, nurses, and the wait staff at Denny's? They have
to work on Sunday, right?"

These questions suggest that I'm not alone in my temptation to reduce Sabbath to an achievement that can merely be checked off a to-do list. We want
to know what counts; we prefer to do Sabbath on our own time; and we tend
not to expect an encounter with the living God when we do Sabbath. No one
asks what God does during the Sabbath.

If we break Sabbath practices into questions of who, what, when, where,
and why, I hope it's clear that the previous chapters aim at the why. It's a
much-neglected question. Why do we Sabbath? We practice Sabbath because
of God's overwhelming and wonderful grace. We Sabbath because Sabbath is
an identity-rooting gift. We practice Sabbath in response to God's life-giving,
all-powerful grace. We Sabbath to encounter this God. That's why. But the
other questions remain. Who? What? When? Where? I promise we'll get
to the what, when, and who. Let's start with the where.

Sabbath in Communion

Where does Sabbath practice take place? In addressing this question first,
we lay bare another assumption within the questions that so frequently
surround Sabbath practice. The reduction of Sabbath practice to a matter of
lawn-mowing and Sunday shifts at work subtly assumes that each individual
possesses sufficient freedom and willpower to practice on his or her own.
If this is the case, then the question of where Sabbath takes place becomes
much less important.

In addition to assuming substantial privilege, this view of human freedom and power also repeats the definitions that consumer culture affirms
but the Sabbath resists. Consumer culture says, "Just give me all the options,
and I'll choose what's best." Through the Sabbath, God proclaims that existence without limits yields captivity and bondage, not freedom. To be clear,
we're not saying that Sabbath practice involves no personal choice. What

we're saying—in concert with the witness of the previous chapters—is that freedom happens in a very particular place, a place that utterly and starkly contrasts the ideals of consumer capitalism and any other cultural narratives that turn people away from God's grace.

The previous chapters point us to the place where Sabbath happens. It happens not in a bubble of autonomous, heroic willpower, but in the community of faith. This is the answer to the "where" question. Sabbath takes place in the community of faith. It comes to the first humans in God's company and the company of the very good creation; it comes to the entire Israelite community in the wilderness; it comes to both the religious and the broken in the Gospels; and it is promised for the whole new creation at the end of time. All of this points to the limits of individual effort and to the community of faith as a locus of human freedom.

Remember Matthew from Chapter 3. During the seven days he shared with us, he sent and received hundreds of texts a day; he slept less than six hours a night; he worked over twenty hours at a part-time job; he attended school each weekday; and at the end of the week he stayed up all night at his youth-group lock-in. Is this a picture of freedom or of captivity? At the end of an exhausting week, it seems that Matthew isn't entirely free to rest. Instead of getting a good night's sleep, he pulls an all-nighter at his church's invitation.

To be clear, we're not abandoning the reality of human choice. Matthew could have stayed home. He could turn off his phone. Or could he? Human choice rarely fits within the narrow constructs of simplistic yes-or-no binaries. We do have real choices to make, and we have a substantial amount of power to make them. At the same time, we may wish to make certain choices for which no amount of individual willpower will suffice. Something as serious as mental illness comes to mind, but so does Matthew's phone. He may not have the willpower to turn it off. Cultural and social influences may exert more power than Matthew can resist on his own.

Saying this doesn't belittle Matthew's power of choice. It puts it in proper perspective. We assume and ask too much of Matthew both developmentally and socially if we expect him to scan his options and then simply muster the willpower to choose what's best. The troubling fact is that Matthew hasn't been given the options. Both the culture and his church—at least in the case of the week he shared with us—don't appear to have given Matthew any clues that another life might be possible. Though our culture idolizes rugged individualism, human development and practical theology agree that individual achievement is an oxymoron. We cannot be who we are apart from the communities that nurture us.

Individual effort has its limits, and our tendency to refuse limits goes back as far as the Garden of Eden. Only one fruit is forbidden—only one limit. And yet the temptation to be god-like is too strong. We refuse the limit and thus refuse our freedom. To give in to such temptation is to fail to realize that human freedom takes place not beyond limits, but within them. The limits are, in fact, a gift from God.

The Sabbath commands in Exodus and Deuteronomy recognize the limits of individual effort. They insist on the thoroughly communal, egalitarian, ecological, and theological nature of Sabbath-keeping. This looks nothing like a lone individual privately mustering the courage to stop and rest. God gives Sabbath to all: you, your children, those in your service, the foreigners, the livestock, and the whole creation. Furthermore, God gives the commands on the basis of God's intimate and all-powerful interaction with God's people at creation and through the Exodus, not on the presumption of God's distance. We Sabbath with others . . . and with God!

By way of the Sabbath command, God acknowledges and accounts for the nature of human freedom: both limited and taking place within limits. We need an interdependent community of support along with divine power. We need God's invitation, example, and intimate presence in order to receive the rest that God modeled and gave on the seventh day. That's why the question of human choice remains blurred. We have real choices and real power, but we also recognize countless and complex influences that indicate the necessarily interconnected and interdependent nature of our existence. It will be important to remember this as we imagine faithful receiving of God's Sabbath rest in our current context.

Where, then, do we practice Sabbath? We practice Sabbath in intimate communion with the community of faith, the whole creation, and the God who is the source of all life and rest. Sabbath should lead us into fellowship and closer communion with God, neighbor, creation, and self. Any Sabbath that divides us from God, neighbor, creation, or self falls short of the practical theological vision articulated here. The answer to the "where" question already sheds light on the "who" of Sabbath practice.

Sabbath for All

The Sabbath commandments remind us that from beginning to end, the "who" of Sabbath practice is God. God rests. God gives rest to us, and God empowers us to both receive this gift and make it available to others. If the Sabbath journey is to be a journey of life through death, then it must be a journey that begins with the life of God, wraps within itself the brokenness and potential of God's people, bears the weight of sin and death, and emerges with resurrection power in the end. This is precisely the journey we have seen, and we have heard God's promise to travel today with the community of faith through the death-and-life journey of Sabbath rest.

All are welcome on this journey. God gives Sabbath rest to all. That means young people—not that they merely tag along, but that they contribute vitally to the process of imagining what faithful Sabbath practice might look like in the first place. The fact is that we've struggled with Sabbath practice. We've refused this grace. Yet if Daniel Siegel is right about the creative, novelty-seeking, socially engaged nature of adolescents, then our young people should be at the heart of the community of faith as it discerns the contours of faithful Sabbath practice.

When it comes time to consider the what, when, where, and why, difficult questions will inevitably arise. The journey of practical theological reflection will necessarily continue. The context will continue to evolve, and patterns of work, sleep, busyness, technology, and sociality will evolve as well. The journey will require travelers adept at thinking outside the box. Those of us who love and work with young people didn't need Daniel Siegel to tell us that they know how to think outside the box. Siegel's exploration may give us new language to use, but we've known this. We will most certainly need these gifts—the gifts that adolescents bring—as we embark or continue on the journey of God's Sabbath grace.

God forbid that we conceptualize Sabbath practice without young people's help. The "who" begins with God; it continues with young people.

It also includes us—those called to minister on behalf of young people. We musn't forget ourselves. We have the privilege and the challenge of traveling on this journey as well. I confess that this piece trips me up. I tend to make sure that everyone else is set for the journey, yet I lose sight of myself as a fellow traveler. I forget that I, too, am a beloved child of God, invited to stop, rest, and delight in that love. Youth workers, parents, pastors, volunteers, the whole community of faith—I include all of these in this last group of travelers. Sabbath is for us. We know what it is to work tirelessly on behalf of our young people, but do we know what it is to rest joyfully as well?

If we hope to join God and our young people on the Sabbath journey, then we must actually be willing to journey ourselves. We might fool ourselves into thinking that we can just assist everyone else on the journey, but we'll never fool our youth. The "who" of the Sabbath journey, then, begins with the God of all grace, rest, life, and joy, and by God's grace, rest, life, and joy the journey includes young people, those called to serve young people, and, indeed, all creation.

In this way the "where" and the "who" of Sabbath practice converge. We practice Sabbath in and with God, and in and with the community of faith, with the invitation extending beyond the community of faith to all people and all creation. With the "who" and the "where" clarified, we may finally turn to the "what." What do we actually do to keep the Sabbath?

Put Down the Duck

Early in this project, we noted that the term "Sabbath," at its roots, means literally to cease or to stop. On day seven of creation, God stops the work of creating. In the wilderness, the Israelites stop—or are supposed to stop—gathering manna on the Sabbath. If our lives, and the lives of our young people, are going to find a rooting in something other than going and going and going, something has to stop. But what?

In addition to the Sabbath conversations I have had over the past decade, I have also had the great privilege and responsibility of attempting to teach others about the Sabbath. When I do, I try to cover the who, what, when, where, and why. When it comes to the question of what—what do we actually do to practice Sabbath?—I draw on a somewhat underutilized theological resource: *Sesame Street*.

In an attempt to uncover concrete forms of Sabbath practice, I show—regardless of the audience—a *Sesame Street* video clip in which Ernie wants to play a musical instrument. He comes to bandleader Hoots the Owl for instruction, but Ernie has a problem. Though he wants to play the saxophone, his devotion to his rubber ducky gets in the way. Every time he tries to play the sax, he gets a squeak instead of a song. He attempts to play the saxophone without putting down his beloved duck. Hoots takes a look and a listen, and then sets about a lesson put to song that repeats the refrain, "You gotta put down the ducky if you wanna play the saxophone!"

As Hoots's song progresses, Ernie resists—his duck means too much to him. But finally Hoots convinces Ernie, who puts the duck down and then proceeds to join Hoots and the band in the toe-tapping tune. When the song ends, Ernie reunites with his rubber ducky while basking in the music that was made possible by putting down the ducky.

Ernie learned a vailuable lesson: that certain good and beautiful things can emerge only when other things are set aside. Ernie might be glad to know that he's in good company. The Sabbath stories of the Israelites and the Pharisees follow a similar script. When the Israelites are in the wilderness after God begins the provision of manna, they find themselves in a curious position regarding the life-and-death implications of their scenario. Their lives depend on manna. Yet in spite of—or perhaps because of—this fact, God asks that they not gather manna once every seven days. In terms of life-and-death realities, God asks them on the Sabbath to not do something on which it appears their lives depend. God asks them to put down gathering like Ernie had to put down his duck.

The same could be said about the Pharisees. They came to believe that their lives depended on the law and on diligent adherence to its rules and regulations. Jesus's Sabbath ministry challenges them to lay down these rules and regulations—not because they don't have a place in the life of faith, but because faith in rules and regulations is faith misplaced. Jesus asks the Pharisees to put down their faith in the law.

Here we need to recall Barth's insistence that only faith in God's omnipotent grace provides an adequate basis for our Sabbath practice. The problem of both the Israelites and the Pharisees is misplaced faith. Instead of surrendering themselves to God's grace and care, they seek to take matters into their own hands. They, like Ernie, need to put something down so they can receive the grace that sought them. Perhaps the manna of the Israelites and the laws of the Pharisees also provide some direction for us and our young people as we consider what Sabbath practice looks like today.

If it's true that God asks the Israelites and the Pharisees to put down something on which it appears their lives depend, and if it's true that God does this so that they may know that their lives ultimately depend on God's grace, provision, and care, then perhaps we can gain clarity on our Sabbath practice by asking the same question: What is it that tempts us to believe our lives depend on it? Work? School? Technology? Busyness? Achievement? Our résumé? College applications? What if our Sabbath practice begins by naming these goods that have become gods? What if these lesser gods—which are potentially good things—are like the rubber duck in Ernie's hand? We have to put them down in order for the sweet music of Sabbath rest to emerge.[1]

In this way, the Sabbath stories of the Israelites and the Pharisees guide our Sabbath practice positively. They provide a critical response to the question "What do we do?" On the Sabbath, we put down something on which it appears our lives depend so that we may know that our lives ultimately depend on God's grace, action, and provision, not on endless human striving.

The Israelites and the Pharisees also help us by providing examples of Sabbath practices that miss the point. The Pharisees, as we have seen, hold

Sabbath laws in high esteem, and they insist that for the roughly twenty-four hours of the Sabbath day, all rules and regulations be followed precisely. As soon as the sun sets on Friday, the action begins. Don't walk too far; don't carry your mat; go to the synagogue; don't pluck heads of grain; don't heal; don't come for healing; don't bury the dead—and the list could go on and on. If you successfully follow all of the minutiae of the law from sundown Friday to sundown Saturday, then—voila!—you've kept the Sabbath holy. Whatever you do, just make sure you practice Sabbath right!

The Israelites in the wilderness—or at least some portion of them—have a different struggle. They've been given exceedingly simple Sabbath instruction, but they struggle to obey. They recognize that their lives depend on the manna. Perhaps they believe that if a little gathering makes God happy, additional gathering will please God all the more. Either way, they forgo the rest that God offers on the Sabbath day. Their actions seem to say, "Sabbath? Sure, sure, but we've got really important work to do, and it's not just any work. God told us to do it. Maybe we'll rest when we get enough work done."

The Pharisees obsess about practicing Sabbath right; the Israelites obsess about getting enough work done. Both examples are ironic; both examples are common; and both remind us of the critical place of God's action and grace on our journey into Sabbath rest. Both remind us that the question "What do we do?" must be matched and integrated with the question "What is God doing?"

The irony of the Pharisees is that they work like crazy to keep the laws that are supposed to guide their rest. The irony of the Israelites is that in waiting to rest until all the work is done, they never rest. They both miss the point. The Pharisees think the Sabbath is about keeping their ducks in a row for twenty-four hours. The Israelites forfeit the Sabbath in their attempts to get their ducks in a row in advance. Both make the error of reducing the Sabbath to a matter of human choice and human power. They obscure God's action with their own.

The contemporary church includes examples of both. The young people in Chapter 3 have seen both. Many come from families that maintain some form of Sabbath observance, but virtually none have any sense of God's action and grace in and through the Sabbath. The Sabbath has become a tradition, a family meal, or a nap. These aren't bad things, but if they fail to convey the life and action of God, they also fail to convey the heart of the Sabbath as we have discerned it here. The young people are also quite familiar with their lists of things to do. They come from industrious families and industrious churches. They know how to get stuff done, and in many cases Sabbath rest simply gets set aside because of the illusion that too many other things demand their attention.

This leads us into tricky territory. We ask "What do we do?" in a context too frequently obsessed with getting things done. The theological explorations of the previous two chapters have failed miserably if they haven't already established the priority and precedence of God's action. We can only ever act in response, and we seek a distinctively practical theological response—one that grows from the fullness of the previous exploration into the absolute priority of God's grace, which stands at the heart of Sabbath practice. We seek a response in light of the developmental realities of adolescents, the cultural realities that surround them, and the broad and deep witness to Sabbath that we found in Barth and the scriptural narratives of creation, Exodus, and the Gospels. As we put it all together, we can actually imagine the contours of faithful Sabbath practice—and Barth would insist that the "what" of our Sabbath practice be full of faith not in our action, but in God's action. And so we turn to concrete forms of Sabbath practice. What might we do to receive this grace?

Sabbath Practices Worth Filling with Faith

As we turn to the "what" of specific Sabbath practice, we do so with great humility, but also with great courage, recognizing that we are not without resources. God has spoken, God has given the invitation, and we may actually heed this call. With this in mind, we turn to four paradigmatic Sabbath practices. I offer them as complements to the act of putting down our ducks, and I hope that they stir our imaginations toward further possibilities.

Worship and Liturgy

In the last chapter we saw worship as a response that erupted almost spontaneously from the "bent" woman in Luke 13 and the man blind from birth in John 9 after they experienced Jesus's Sabbath healing. The act of worship followed Jesus's Sabbath healing ministry. This simple sequence raises questions of our understanding of worship. Do we worship on Sunday mornings or other times under the impression that we initiate contact with God, or do we come at God's invitation?

If we recognize worship—whenever it happens—as a gathering of the body of Christ in response to God's all-powerful grace, we already embody much of the heart of the Sabbath. We gather to proclaim God's greatness. The congregation sets aside its labors to proclaim the greater worth of God's love and grace. The very notion of gathering as a believing body for the sake of worship beautifully reflects the conviction that our resting bears witness to God every bit as much as our laboring. Beyond that, our corporate worship bears witness uniquely to God's grace. It proclaims something that our endless labors never could. In worshiping the One who invites us to Sabbath rest, we put down productivity and efficiency, we put down achievement and busyness, and we exercise faith in the One who made us and reclaims us even when we go our own way.

In song and in prayer, in confessing, forgiving, and giving, and in stopping to listen to God's Word, we participate in an alternate rhythm of life. We receive the rest that gives definition and identity to the sum of our lives like rests give identity to the notes of a song. The students in Chapter 3 regularly stop classes for chapel services. Do they recognize this as a Sabbath practice? Do they realize the ways that worship time stops the productivity of class time? Might they receive that time as a gift of Sabbath rest?

Here again, we mustn't forget the "who" of Sabbath practice. Our practices of worship and liturgy—in chapel, church, youth group, and beyond—also need the gifts that adolescents bring, not in a way that excludes other gifts but in a way that fosters interdependence, integration, and worship experiences of meaning and significance. The fact that a church or chapel service exists provides no guarantee of Sabbath rest, but it certainly signals the potential. The deeper question involves the faith that Sabbath invites. Do we gather for the sake of the worship service, or to encounter a living, gracious, and loving God? Our theological exploration of the Sabbath suggests that the fidelity of our practice cannot be separated from the Sabbath stories that we tell.

Story-Telling

Though Sabbath figures prominently throughout Scripture, it has too frequently become an untold part of the faith stories we live and tell.[2] With Barth's help we have uncovered the prominence of the Sabbath within the broad narrative of Scripture and particularly within the history of the covenant. The story of the relationship between God and humanity is a Sabbath story.

We have also seen that Sabbath stories cannot be told apart from God's action in and interaction with the world and humankind. They are, overwhelmingly, the stories of God's action. From creation to the end of time, the story begins and ends with God's action. The stories and the way we tell them provide us and our young people with an alternative to the popular narrative that esteems busyness and the consuming it imposes. In telling these stories, we put down the false narratives and misshapen identities, and we learn new stories that have been our stories since the beginning. Busyness may mark the broader culture. God and God's people are known by their rest.

These are stories of life and death and life through death. They are stories of God's own life and death, and the life that God continually gives to creation. Our receptivity to this gift depends in part on our willingness to tell and retell, to narrate and re-narrate these stories. By now it should be clear that these stories are beautiful, messy, identity-altering stories. They are stories of anxiety and failure as well as stories of miraculous provision and all-powerful grace. We must tell these stories in the light of God's action and grace.

When has Sabbath been life for us? When has it been death? Are we telling the stories of creation, Exodus, Incarnation, resurrection, and *eschaton* as Sabbath stories? Are young people telling stories of their own rediscovery of Sabbath as life-giving and gracious? Perhaps their testimony will be central to the retelling of the Sabbath stories.

Breaking Bread

On the day of Christ's resurrection, the first day of the week (the *sabbatōn*), Jesus reveals himself to his disciples in the breaking of bread. Some disciples walk and talk unknowingly with Jesus on the road to Emmaus, but their eyes are opened when Jesus breaks bread (Luke 24:13–32). Bread unmistakably recalls God's provision for God's people, both through manna in the wilderness and through the daily bread that we ask for in the Lord's Prayer. To gather to break bread, whether for communion or more common meals, is to partake of God's provision. It also recalls the goodness and bounty of creation if we're willing to consider those who tended creation to bring forth the food that brings us life. In both cases, we recall that our lives depend on more than the accomplishment or achievement of any individual. God gives both life and bread; we return thanks and rejoice again.

Here we recall the overwhelming influence of families and parents on the youth in Chapter 3. Might not family meals provide a space for Sabbath rest and Sabbath receiving? When we pause to give thanks before we break bread, a gracious rhythm marks our meals and our days. We put down the work of the day and the work of meal preparation; we stop; we look to the One who has provided; and we partake with new conviction that we are not our own. We belong to God.

Families can do this, they can talk about why they do, and our youth and children might then know that we are a Sabbath people—our identity bears the marks of God's rest and grace. And even more, this attention to families reminds us how important parental expectations are in shaping the busyness of their young people's lives. We recall the stories of students whose parents seemed to believe that any sign of rest was a sign of laziness, weakness, or a lack of motivation. If breaking bread is to become a Sabbath moment, then parents will have to lay down expectations which communicate that achievement is a greater god than the God revealed in Jesus Christ.

Loving Neighbors

If the Sabbath points us beyond ourselves—to God, the community of faith, and the whole creation—then it necessarily points us to our neighbors far and wide. In so doing, it challenges us to ask difficult questions. How do our choices, habits, and lifestyles make Sabbath rest possible or impossible for others?

When the Israelites resided in Egypt, Sabbath rest was fundamentally impossible. Economic and political systems, structures, and forces utterly prevented their Sabbath rest. Our contemporary context, with its political and economic systems, structures, and forces, similarly prohibits vast swaths of people from ever resting: single parents, migrant farm workers, laborers in service industries, victims of human trafficking, refugees, undocumented immigrants—and the list could go on. While this project hasn't done justice to the justice dimension of the Sabbath, we must acknowledge it here.[3]

Look again at the Sabbath commandments in Deuteronomy and Exodus. The Israelites are commanded to rest, but they are also commanded to make that rest available to sons, daughters, slaves, livestock, and resident aliens. They must remember the days when Sabbath rest wasn't an option for them, and they must refuse to re-create those days for others. As we consider the "what" of our Sabbath practice, we must surely consider the implications of all our choices and of the political and economic systems that surround us. What would it look like for us to work, live, and rest in such a way that Sabbath rest is available to all people and the whole creation? How might we influence the systems and structures around us so that injustices pass away and justice and equity thrive?

But When?

One question remains on our journey of imagining contemporary Sabbath practice. When? When do we practice Sabbath? Must it always be Sunday . . . or Saturday? Here again our biases emerge in the question. To ask "Does it have to be [fill in the blank]?" might reveal a sincere desire for obedience, but it also misses the point. The point is not when we receive Sabbath rest; the point is that we receive it and receive it regularly. Every meal we share provides us with an opportunity, but we also have reason to reclaim weekly corporate worship as a vital and life-giving Sabbath practice.

For many contemporary youth and adults, Sunday still stands as a beautiful option with many opportunities for exercising Sabbath practices in the community of faith. But we also know that Sunday doesn't work for everyone. Many must work by no choice of their own, and others are involved in sports or other activities. To be crystal clear on this point, these activities and all our activity must be held up to the gracious light of God's Sabbath rest. Some activities—or at least our participation in them—will need to die, not because God forbids them, but because the activities forbid our participation in the life and grace of God and the sacred (i.e., holy, set apart) fellowship of the Sabbath community of faith.

Nonetheless, some people simply won't be able to practice Sabbath on Sunday. But the aforementioned practices lend themselves to being exercised on any day. There will also be times when circumstances dictate that we practice Sabbath without the blessing of the community of faith embodied in our presence. Hopefully, this is the exception, not the rule, and those times should not be interpreted as times of practicing in isolation. Christ has promised to be with us, and even if our bodies are alone, we remember the community of faith as we practice, and we anticipate practicing in the community again. Questions about Sunday obligations and practicing alone raise serious challenges, but they point us back to the "who" of Sabbath practice. Our young people have a unique perspective on these challenges, and they can join us and help us as we face them. By God's grace, the challenges themselves might provide opportunities for new experiences of Sabbath grace and rest.

Do Our Lives *Really* Depend on Sabbath Practice?

Worshiping, breaking bread, telling stories, and loving our neighbors aren't merely things we do. They are actions that seek to join God's action. They are forms of Sabbath that seek to join the Sabbath rest of God. We can't control or manipulate God by these practices, but we can humbly and gratefully join them in confidence that in so doing we partake of the very life of God and the life of Christ's body, the church.

At their best, these practices should help us put down the ducks of achievement, consumption, busyness, technology, and whatever else tempts us to believe our lives ultimately depend on them. In some sense we might say that our life depends on these Sabbath practices, but this point requires some clarification.

Throughout the chapters of this book, I've tried to make a strong case for the Sabbath. I believe that was partially the point. At the same time, our lives, both in fact and in theological perspective, don't depend on the Sabbath—at least not on the Sabbath as a merely human effort or accomplishment. Barth already said that. Our Sabbath practice can be or become a merely human endeavor like any other—like forfeiting sleep, loving busyness, or consuming technology. Our hope isn't in right practice—that would be the error of the Pharisees. Also, putting hope in right practice merely repeats the error of the Israelites, who just hoped to get enough done. Both place hope not in God's grace and provision, but in human effort. To enter Sabbath practice is to enter this apparent tension. We must, in fact, consider our ways. We do strive for right practice. If Christ cared nothing for right practice, he would surely have left the Pharisees alone. Yet in and through Jesus's confrontation with the Pharisees, there is the invitation to a paradigm shift in Sabbath observance.

Jesus sees the Pharisees.

Do we grasp this? Jesus. Sees. The Pharisees. And Jesus gives the invitation to lay down heavy burdens every bit as much to the Pharisees as to anyone. That much-maligned and weary group who strives so ceaselessly to observe the Sabbath are themselves observed on the Sabbath by the Son of God, who takes away the sins of the world and who says even to them, "Come to me, and I will give you rest."

The great hope of the Sabbath is not that we keep it or observe it with great diligence. Of course, we may cease our labors, we may shut off our phones, and we may enter this rest. Our young people can turn off their tablets, put away their résumés, and set aside their gym bags. These all point to the hope we have, but they are not our hope. No, our hope is not that we keep or observe the Sabbath rightly, but rather that in and through the Sabbath we are kept and seen. In and through the Sabbath, Christ himself sees us in our fractured efforts and brokenness, and Christ himself keeps us.

Remember again the story of the woman in Luke 13. Luke tells us she has been crippled by a spirit for eighteen years, and the spirit keeps her from standing up straight. The Greek suggests that she was doubled over. Like all of those whom Jesus heals on the Sabbath, this woman appears in the narrative quite passively: "Just then there appeared a woman. . . ." We know very little about her. She is bound by a force greater than herself; she is in the synagogue; but we don't even know if she's aware of Jesus's presence. Luke never mentions that this woman has any faith. In fact, until Jesus acts four times toward her, no action verbs are attributed to this woman:

> And just then there appeared a woman with a spirit that had crippled her for eighteen years. She was bent over and was quite unable to stand up straight. When Jesus saw her, he called her over and said, "Woman, you are set free from your ailment." When he laid his hands on her, immediately she stood up straight and began praising God. (Luke 13:11–13)

Jesus sees her, calls her over, speaks to her, and lays his hands on her. Jesus affirms the full humanity of this woman. His confrontation and confirmation come so near to the woman; they are intimate and personal. Jesus sees her, calls her, speaks to her, and then lays his hands upon the very brokenness that holds her captive, and in the process Jesus sets her free from that which binds her, from the powers beyond human power. Only then does the woman act. Her response? She stands up straight and praises God.

Again, our Sabbath hope is not that we observe or keep it rightly, though we do humbly and courageously offer our Sabbath practice. Our hope, like the hope of the woman in Luke 13, is that right in the midst of our brokenness, in the midst of powers too great for us, Jesus sees us.[4] Jesus calls us; Jesus speaks to us; and he lays his hands directly on our brokenness. Suddenly, we are free—free in the context of the One who made us and who confronts and confirms us in all-powerful grace, free to lay down our burdens, free to face death, and free to stand up straight and praise God.

Our response to a grace as radical as this is simply to receive with open hands. Bizarrely enough, this leads us back to those ridiculous rubber ducks. It is hard to receive grace, life, and rest in open hands while clinging to those blasted rubber ducks. The Pharisees clung to the law, and the Israelites clung to the work they were so sure they had to accomplish. They needed to stop; they needed to cease; they needed to let go and open their hands; and this meant dying to what they could achieve on their own. We cling to our phones; we cling to our to-do lists; we cling even to the work God gives us to do. Young people cling to their own to-do lists, résumés, college applications, and their pursuit of being just busy enough. We do all of this trying to avoid the anxiety that encroaches upon us at the thought of losing control, but this is not about seizing control.

This is about releasing control, letting go, responding to God with open hands rather than closed fists.[5] This is about learning to die.

Learning to Sit with Death

As we consider contemporary Sabbath practice, our framework must anticipate that the Sabbath community and its members will necessarily encounter both life and death, both hammock and hell. One may think these terms unnecessarily morbid, but unless we face anxiety and death openly and honestly, our whole project falters on the practical theological grounds that we outlined at the beginning. If we trace the contours of the preceding chapters, anxiety and death run like a thread through the whole—all the way from Sue Miller in Chapter 1 to the crucifixion in Chapter 5.

Most importantly for our broader project, we saw anxiety, pressure, worry, and stress in the lives of the young people in Chapter 3. They said that for rest to be rest, it had to reduce anxiety and stress, and yet they confessed that rest created its own anxiety. We've been listening on their behalf, and in this final dimension of our practical theological framework, we can do no less than consider a faithful response in the face of the experiences and understandings of those young people.

Contemporary culture offers its own responses. It sells plenty of distractions to keep young people awake, distracted, busy, and restless. The church, too, has offered its response. Too often it has attempted to outdo the culture on the culture's terms instead of engaging the world on the terms of God's life and grace.

Remember Matthew again. He attended school each weekday, worked twenty-six hours at a part-time job, slept less than six hours a night, and then stayed up all night on Friday night at his youth group's lock-in.

Remember Jessica. In the eyes of her teachers, she does it all with apparent ease—academics, athletics, music, church, faith. Yet in her life of continuous motion, Jessica struggles to slow down during rest. For her, rest provides another space for working through life's problems and challenges.

And then there's Jennifer. She seems to know something like Sabbath rest, but she hasn't learned it from the church.

Matthew, Jessica, and Jennifer all know anxiety and stress. One might say they've known more than their fair share. My observation is that they're being formed and trained to do good things. They will enter college having known a strong educational community that has helped them wrestle with questions of life and faith. They have learned English, science, math, and music. It is less clear that they have learned to rest. The anxiety that rest creates for them suggests that they, too, view rest as something opposed to rather than integral to their life and calling. The anxiety also signals the place where the church must be willing to journey if it is going to receive, and help its young people receive, a grace-rooted identity.

The sum of the Sabbath story insists that the journey to Sabbath life inevitably and necessarily leads through Sabbath death. Imagine again the Israelites in the wilderness and the anxiety they must have experienced on their Sabbath journey. The unfamiliar and the unknown threatened them to the point that they were ready to return to captivity. They feared for their lives; they knew hunger; the one thing by which they could measure their worth—productivity—had been taken away; their former identity was proving bankrupt; and then came manna and Sabbath. This couldn't have felt like grace.

Because they had numbed and distracted themselves with the busyness of productivity for generations, the stillness of rest must have been deafening and disorienting. It appears that God was quite content to let them sit in that anxiety. They were not alone; they had the signs of God's presence all around and the taste of God's provision on their lips. Yet surely the anxiety remained; surely the fact that some just had to get out on the seventh day to re-create the rhythms of the identity that needed to die signaled this anxiety.

Consider also the Pharisees. Consider their absolutely holy intention. They meant to protect the covenant—the relationship between God and God's people. Yet they seem to have reduced it to a matter of human effort and striving. They, too, displayed overwhelming anxiety in the face of radical Sabbath grace. Their reaction to Jesus's Sabbath ministry suggests that it is easier to destroy the threat that disorients than to sit in the disorientation and anxiety that brings the possibility of a new identity.

If we hope to receive God's Sabbath rest, if we hope to journey with our young people to receive God's Sabbath rest, then we must be ready and willing to sit in the anxiety and fear that accompany death. Old identities, inferior as they may be, often die hard. How do we do this? How do we respond to the anxiety and fear that rear their ugly heads on what we hoped would be a tranquil journey to sacred slumber? I humbly offer four movements for the Sabbath journey through death not as a formula for the individual, but as a guide for the Sabbath community:

1. Remember that we are not alone on the journey through death. The Sabbath coinciding with the death and resurrection of Christ proclaims with power and clarity that God will journey with us all the way through death and back. In the darkness of the death of our lesser identities, God is with us.

2. Honestly name the anxiety and fear when they arise and be willing to sit in the discomfort. There is no app for this. Contemporary quick-fix culture tempts us to seek numbing or distraction, to get up and move, to do something. But God says stop. Cease. Sit in the discomfort and name it to the God who accompanies us. Name it to trusted companions in the community of faith. Invite God on the journey. Invite God into the anxiety and fear.[6]

3. Sit with open hands—literally, if possible. If the quick-fix dimension of culture tempts us to find an easy out, the consumer dimension might tempt us to cling to the anxiety and fear with closed fists, but the fear and anxiety aren't ours to keep. We name them, we invite God into them, and we sit and listen for God's response. We sit and listen with open hands and listening hearts, not knowing how God will respond.

4. In the stillness, remember God's provision for God's people. Remember creation; remember the Exodus; remember Jesus; remember resurrection; and remember the promise that the great Sabbath banquet at the end of time is coming. Remember that we are God's beloved children by God's choice, not by ours. Even our anxiety and fear cannot alter God's love for us.[7]

In naming our discomfort, inviting God into it, remembering God's promise to journey with us, and sitting patiently in it, we open ourselves to the formation of a new identity. A willingness to sit patiently in the pain and discomfort applies equally to our journey with youth. We long to take their pain away; we desperately want to do something for them. But the best we can do is open ourselves to their anxiety, both the anxiety of all they feel they must accomplish and the anxiety that rest itself creates.

Here we face a crucial integrating question: Will we be honest about our anxiety and fear? The current framework insists that Sabbath makes space for us to sit with each other and with God in our anxiety, stress, shame, and fear, yet doing so presupposes both the courage of honesty regarding our fears and the safety of a loving and trusting community. Ironically, this is astonishingly difficult work. It is much easier—at least in the short run—to feign tranquility and rest and in so doing avoid the death to which we are called.

In many ways, our young people have become experts at this. They've learned to feign composure. They've learned it from those of us who have modeled it so diligently. The life and grace of God again provide our starting place. God has already journeyed through death on the cross and has promised to journey with us through death as well. The faithfulness and love of the community of faith, the church, must grow in recognition and response to the faithfulness and love of God. Thus we sit and rest together as a community of faith. We practice renouncing faith, the faith which insists that our life, joy, rest, and flourishing take place only in the context of God's all-powerful grace, and we trust that God's all-powerful grace is vast enough to see us, hold us, and keep us even in the darkness of anxiety, fear, and death.

And Joy!

In his account of adolescence and the journey toward integration, Daniel Siegel makes a fascinating point about being present to emotion. In essence, he says that we cannot selectively numb emotion.[8] If we numb and distract ourselves from anxiety and fear, we also numb and distract ourselves from joy and hope and love. If Siegel is right, then we have reason to believe that in honestly naming our fear and anxiety, and in learning to be present to them, we simultaneously open ourselves to knowing and experiencing joy and hope and love in ways that up until now remained impossible.

What if the Sabbath journey into anxiety, fear, and even death leads not only to a new capacity for being present with God in our pain and the pain of others, but also to new capacities and awareness of joy and life and peace? What if the good things aren't possible without the darker ones? The passion and resurrection of Christ echo again through the Sabbath saga. We journey through death not for the sake of death, but on the way to a life that no one imagined possible before—a life that bears both joy and pain, both suffering and delight, a life that comes to us not by way of limitless striving, but rather begins with rest.

The Sabbath journey includes death, anxiety, and fear, but it also unquestionably leads to new life, joy, feasting, and resurrection. The aforementioned framework makes space for joy as well as pain:

1. Remember that we are not alone in our joy and celebration. God initiated and accompanied the first humans as they rested and celebrated the very good creation on the seventh day. And God joins our Sabbath celebration now!

2. Honestly name the joy, hope, and peace when they arise, and be willing to sit with them and rejoice. Invite God into the rejoicing.

3. Rejoice with open hands. If the quick-fix culture deceives us into shirking even joy, consumer culture might tempt us to cling to the joy and hope with closed fists. But joy and hope are not commodities to hoard. On this side of the last great Sabbath, temporal experiences of the Sabbath will come and go. When the celebration comes, welcome it, but don't hold it hostage. Whether we rejoice or fear, God is with us.

4. In the rejoicing, remember God's provision for God's people. Remember creation; remember the Exodus; remember Jesus; remember resurrection; and remember the promise that the great Sabbath banquet at the end of time is coming. Remember that we are God's beloved children by God's choice, not by ours. Even our rejoicing can't alter God's love for us.

If all of this is true, then the stakes come into clearer focus. This is a matter of life and death, but not in a way that gives us a simple choice between life and death. The broad movement of the Sabbath is toward resurrection life and the great Sabbath at the end of time. We may receive Sabbath here and now as a foretaste of these, but death, for now, remains. So, to say that Sabbath is a matter of life and death implies no either-or choice. Until the end it will necessarily involve both. We will continually be challenged to put down lesser gods and false identities.

This brings us to a final point regarding the young people from Chapter 3. Many sought rest and referred to rest as an escape. It's true that the Sabbath gives us a refuge from powers and forces that are too great for us. But the problem with rest as escape is that it views rest as marginal rather than central to our life of faith. Surely the way we enter Sabbath rest signals something about its place in our lives. When we consider Sabbath rest, do we imagine it as an escape from or an entry into life, as a resisted last resort or a gracious beginning, as a guilty concession or a regular celebration? Our response must emerge from our theology.

In other words, our Sabbath rest must emerge from the very life and being of God.

If we recognize Sabbath as integral to the very being of God and to the very identity of the covenant relationship that God extends to humanity, then we will realize that our refusal of the Sabbath is not merely a failure of human development or human potential. It is more—it's a deformation of what it means to be human in the first place, which is another way of saying that it's a deformation of what it means to be a child of God. If God created humanity in the image of God for the purpose of covenant relationship, and that covenant relationship has been marked by Sabbath rest from the dawn of time, and if that covenant relationship will come to completion in Sabbath rest, then our refusal of Sabbath rest does nothing less than deform our very identity as God's children.

Our refusal roots human identity in mere achievement, productivity, efficiency, and accomplishment even as it divorces the life of humankind from the life of God. Our refusal to rest is killing us. It is killing our young. We saw this in the sleep science in Chapter 2, not to mention the anxiety in Chapter 3. It's leading to breakdowns in mental health, obesity, depression, broken relationships, broken families, and substance abuse. All of this is bad enough, yet the fullness of the mis-formation comes to light when we realize that those in ministry, those called to teach, train, pastor, and shepherd young people, engage equally in endless work and then point to God and say, "I'm doing this for God." So we shouldn't be surprised that our young people are dying in our wake.

It is true, as Bonhoeffer once wrote, and as we have already insisted, that when Jesus calls us, he calls us to come and die. Yet if the death that we and our young people experience is in service to achievement, productivity, and ceaselessness, or in avoidance of the disorientation of rest, then it isn't Jesus's call that we heed. Jesus still calls his followers to come and rest and to lay down the unbearable burden of a life rooted solely in human effort and accomplishment. Let that false self die! And let us rise anew to life and rest grounded each day, and particularly on the Sabbath, in the grace and love and faithfulness of God.

If we and our young people are going to embrace Sabbath rest for the gift that it is, we'll first need to stop blaming God for our continuous work and reject endless labor as a form of obedience. We will allow Barbara Brown Taylor's question, in all its terror and wonder, to confront us head-on: Why are we here? Our existence doesn't begin with what we can accomplish, and it won't end by what we can achieve. We are here because God made us, because God loves us, and because God has called us his own. That simple and identity-transforming affirmation provides more than enough motivation and rationale for our working and striving, yes, but first for our resting and celebrating in the love, grace, and care of God. Anything less forfeits our full humanity and threatens the full humanity of the young people in our care.

The invitation stands. Come and die. Die to ceaselessness. Die to gracelessness. Die to every definition of humanity that falls short of the one given to us by God . . . and rise to rest in the grace, power, and resurrection life of God.

Imagine. We are God's beloved children—not because of what we've achieved or what we ever will achieve, not because we've earned it, not because we got enough work done, not because our ducks are in a row, but because God graciously called us, formed us, and named us children of God. Because of this, we may actually lay down our burdens, we may set aside our work and the lesser gods that tempt us to look to them as the source of our identity. We may lay down even our Sabbath rules and regulations, and we may behold the work of God from creation to Exodus to Incarnation to cross to resurrection. And we may dare to hope that the rest we now enter is but a foretaste of the eternal rest, when we will all stand before God's throne and never question again that we are God's beloved children. Our provisional rest here and now reminds us of the promised rest that is to come. How can we but stand up straight and praise God?

Appendix:
What Is Practical Theology?

Because practical theology guides the layout of the chapters in this book and because practical theology can helpfully guide all of life and ministry, I want to explore it in this appendix in greater detail. As a discipline, practical theology can be drawn apart into distinct actions. Practical theology does four things:

1. It grows out of everyday, lived reality.
2. It draws on multiple disciplines or fields of study.
3. It takes God seriously.
4. It aims to live faithfully in the world in response to God.

To unpack these four characteristics and explain how they connect to each other, I want to draw on the example of my end-of-semester panic attack.[1]

Practical theology grows out of everyday, lived reality.

Life has a way of confounding us.[2] It brings us up short. And while some disciplines depend on a laboratory and an environment isolated from the world (think chemistry, molecular biology, and the life of a neurosurgeon), practical theology depends on everyday, lived reality. Or, as we said earlier, it emerges from the nitty-gritty of life.

My end-of-semester meltdown brought me up short. I didn't go looking for a near mental breakdown; it came to me. Life in ministry does the same thing. We don't go looking for situations beyond our comprehension. They simply go with the territory, and when these things happen, we know we need help. For this reason . . .

Practical theology draws on multiple disciplines or fields of study.

Our need for help drives practical theologians to learn new things or to learn things in new ways. Again, if you've been in youth ministry for more than twenty minutes, you've already done this. You know the kid who struggles with anxiety and depression, and so you've been online researching. You've talked with professionals in your community or your congregation to gain a deeper understanding of the situation.

Or maybe you know a young person who struggles with an eating disorder. Because you want to minister faithfully and because you love the kid, you learn everything you can about bulimia. You want to respond in a way that's informed and sensitive to the realities of the situation. You lean into the knowledge and expertise of those who know more than you or who have already faced similar situations.

In my end-of-semester panic attack, I wanted desperately to make sense of the situation, and I sought every possible resource in my quest. I called my sister-in-law, who works as a physician's assistant, to try to attain a medical perspective on what I was experiencing. She asked questions about my patterns of eating, sleeping, and exercise, and she recommended that I try exercising and taking over-the-counter sleep aids. I also talked with my professors. And I sought counsel from colleagues in the PhD program who had already survived their first year. As my closest friend and the one with the nearest perspective on my situation, my wife, Janel, provided another critical conversation partner and source of support.

Each of these dialogue partners provided new lenses for understanding my situation. They provided the language and perspective of other disciplines. As a whole, then, practical theology avails itself of whatever resources that prove helpful as we try to make sense of everyday, lived reality. In theory, no supplementary field of study is ruled out.[3]

So, as a discipline, practical theology aims for as thorough an understanding as possible of the scenarios and situations that we face along the way of life and ministry. To gain this understanding, we intentionally seek the resources of other disciplines.[4] Within our study of youth and Sabbath, the fields of sociology, neurology, sleep science, time-use studies, and empirical research all contribute. These fields shed light on everything from adolescent sleep patterns to teen technology usage to the development of the teenage brain. What they don't offer is any engagement with the Christian theological tradition. They generally don't consider who God is; they aren't attempting to reflect theologically. For that we turn to the next movement in practical theology.[5]

Practical theology takes God seriously.

This sounds simpler than it is.

Here I need to repeat the confession that I made when I first told the story of my panic attack: In the time leading up to that struggle and in the midst of that struggle, I stopped taking God seriously.

It wasn't intentional. I probably would have denied it in the moment, yet my actions spoke volumes. When it came to the work of the PhD program, I slowly but surely began living in a way which suggested that my life depended more on what I did and on what I accomplished than on God's grace and provision. Or maybe I started trusting the PhD program in and of itself. I thought my life depended on the degree.

Either way, I gradually misplaced my trust. I put it either in myself or in a degree more than I put it in God. In the midst of that struggle, I failed to perceive God at work around me. It took the panic attack to lay bare my misplaced trust.

181

Regrettably, we do this in youth ministry. We live as if the salvation of the young people we love depends more on us than it does on God. It can be disorienting to realize that we can't save our youth, but this doesn't mean that our work is meaningless. What it does is put our work in perspective. It shows us that we need regular reminders of God's presence and action. We need practices that keep us aware of the Spirit's presence. We need a community of faith to hold us and guide us when we lose our way.

And so, we seek the help and guidance of faithful companions.

We read and study Scripture.

We read the work of others who have thought diligently about ministry and theology.

We pray.

In all of this, we as practical theologians take God seriously. We reflect theologically. We believe that we have an actual relationship with a living God.

We dare to ask reality-shaking questions. What if it's true? What if a good and gracious God really does exist? What if this God really did form the heavens and the earth? What if this God took on flesh in Jesus Christ and enlivens all creation as Holy Spirit? And what if this God really is love?

What if it's true? If it is true, it changes everything.

Practical theologians dare to believe it's true—and we wrestle diligently with the implications.

We're willing to admit when we lose sight of God. We're willing to confess when we live our lives as if God isn't real or present or active.

We strive for that abundant life which breaks forth when we live our lives in communion with God. We recognize that we have real choices to make in life. We believe that God sees and hears us and responds dynamically to us.[6] We humbly acknowledge that we are not God, even as we rejoice in God's coming to humankind.[7]

This is profoundly challenging work. It is a lifelong journey.

In my panic attack, I found myself reflecting on Exodus 16 and asking questions about what God was doing in and through the story of the Israelites in the wilderness. I asked how God might be speaking to me and into my situation through the text. Ultimately, I sensed that God was challenging me in ways that echoed God's challenge to the Israelites. Would I radically trust God's provision? Was I willing to be a trusting child of God before I was a scholar or a PhD student?

But what would this look like? In what concrete ways would I live out my trust in God? These questions guide us to the fourth move of practical theology.

Practical theology aims to live faithfully in the world in response to God.

As I navigated my end-of-semester struggle, I sought the help of other disciplines, and I took God seriously, but I wasn't only seeking new understanding. I wanted to know what to do. I wanted to know what concrete actions I could take to move out of my panic attack and into a place of greater health and wholeness.

The process of practical theological reflection led me to take real actions:

- I recognized my misplaced trust, and I asked God for help.
- I asked for help from colleagues and professors.
- I continued practicing the Sabbath, but as I did, I tried to be more open to God through it.
- Most importantly, I reframed my experience of the PhD program. In a very real sense, I had to die to the PhD program. I had to recognize the ways in which I was putting too much trust in the degree. Ironically, as I shifted my trust from the degree to God, I was freed in new ways to actually do the work of the doctoral program.

Here I need to offer a word of caution. Practical theology isn't a foolproof formula for finding your way out of any struggle in life or ministry. Until Christ returns, struggles will remain. My panic attack could have led to a sustained breakdown in my mental health, yet such an outcome would not have altered God's love. It would have changed my responses and the responses of those who love me, but God's care would have remained steadfast.

Again, this is something we know in youth ministry. The struggles of life don't magically disappear. Our challenge is to live, work, and rest faithfully in the midst of struggles, yet, here again, practical theology can guide us. Rather than providing once-and-for-all solutions, practical theology provides a framework for navigating life and ministry.

Notes

FOREWORD

1. Ferris Jabr, "Why Your Brain Needs More Downtime," *The Scientific American*, October 15, 2013, https://www.scientificamerican.com/article/mental-downtime/ (accessed February 1, 2019).

2. "State of American Vacation 2018," *Project Time Off* (Oxford: Oxford Economics, 2018), 3, https://projecttimeoff.com/wp-content/uploads/2018/05/StateofAmerican Vacation2018.pdf (accessed February 2, 2019).

3. Clark Strand, "Bring On the Dark," *The New York Times*, December 19, 2014, https://www.nytimes.com/2014/12/20/opinion/why-we-need-the-winter-solstice.html (accessed February 2, 2019).

4. Michelle Shir-Wise, "Disciplined Freedom: The Productive Self and Conspicuous Busyness in 'Free' Time," *Time and Society*, April 22, 2018, 1-27.

5. Walter Elwell, "Anathema," in *Evangelical Dictionary of Theology* (1997), https://www.biblestudytools.com/dictionaries/eastons-bible-dictionary/anathema.html (accessed February 2, 2019).

6. Abraham J. Heschel, *The Sabbath: Its Meaning for Modern Man* (Austin: Noonday Press, 1994), 8.

CHAPTER 1

1. Danny, time diary, January 2013. I offer Danny's story with his permission. By mutual agreement, his name has been changed.

2. Walter Brueggemann, *Reverberations of Faith: A Theological Handbook of Old Testament Themes* (Louisville: Westminster John Knox, 2002), 180.

3. Paraphrased from Sherry Turkle, *Alone Together: Why We Expect More from Technology and Less from Each Other* (New York: Basic Books, 2011), 265–66.

4. A 2010 study by the Pew Research Center reports that 75 percent of all teens ages twelve to seventeen own a cell phone, and 88 percent of teens with cell phones text. See Amanda Lenhart et al., *Teens and Mobile Phones* (Washington, DC: Pew Research Center, 2010), 2. Available at http://pewinternet.org/Reports/2010/Teens-and-Mobile-Phones.aspx.

5. Turkle, *Alone Together*, 265.

6. Turkle, *Alone Together*, 265.

7. This claim is intentionally broad. Young people cannot live fully human lives apart from the Sabbath, and the vitality of every circle of relationships that surround young people depends on the Sabbath. While this proposal tends very closely to the contemporary realities of young people, it also grows out of a vast theological and scriptural tradition. Sabbath appears in the saga of Scripture before creation is finished; it recurs throughout the Pentateuch, the historical books, the prophets, and the Gospels; and while John the Revelator never mentions Sabbath explicitly, interpreters of the Sabbath have consistently viewed it as a foretaste in time of the culmination of all time. For example, Rabbi Theodore Friedman writes, "While it finds a variety of expressions in talmudic literature, all of them, in the end, give voice to the idea that the Sabbath is the anticipation, the foretaste, the paradigm of life in the world-to-come." Theodore Friedman, "The Sabbath: Anticipation of Redemption," *Judaism* 16 (1967): 443. See also Abraham Joshua Heschel, *The Sabbath: Its Meaning for Modern Man* (New York: Farrar, Straus and Giroux, 1951), 73–76.

Within the Ten Commandments, the Sabbath command provides the integrating link between the two tables. While the first table tends to the divine-human relationship and the second concerns the ethics of interpersonal dealings, the Sabbath command references both the divine-human relationship—"the seventh day is a sabbath to the LORD your God"—and the broader implications for relationships with and among humans and all creation—"you shall not do any work—you, your son or your daughter, your male or female slave, your livestock, or the alien resident in your towns" (Exod. 20:10). In the Gospels, Jesus recapitulates the entire Decalogue in the greatest and second-greatest commands: "The first is, 'Hear, O Israel: the Lord our God, the Lord is one; you shall love the Lord your God with all your heart, and with all your soul, and with all your mind, and with all your strength.' The second is this, 'You shall love your neighbor as yourself.' There is no other commandment greater than these" (Mark 12:29–31). The current project builds on this rich tradition of the Decalogue and the commands of Jesus to love God, others, and self. It goes so far as to claim that these relationships cannot be what God intended and created them to be apart from the Sabbath.

8. Latch-hooking is an art and craft whereby loops of yarn or thread are pulled through a stiff woven base to make a rug or the like.

9. In an April 2013 article in *The Chronicle of Higher Education*, "Joseph Kasper"—the pseudonym of an assistant professor in the humanities at a public university in the South—describes impostor syndrome as a condition "rooted in a constant fear of being discovered to be a fraud and a charlatan." "At its worst, it feels calamitous and smothering, feelings intensified by the awareness that my trial is one of my own making." Joseph Kasper [pseudo.], "An Academic with Impostor Syndrome," *The Chronicle of Higher Education*, April 2, 2013, http://chronicle.com/article/An-Academic-With-Impostor/138231/.

10. Sue, interviews by Nathan T. Stucky, March and July 2013. All interviews were conducted in confidentiality, and the names of interviewees have been changed by mutual agreement except where noted.

11. Romans 1:5; 16:26. Regarding sin, I recognize the immense potential for misinterpretation at this point. While explicit discussion of sin has fallen out of vogue in much contemporary theological literature, I believe that the church gives a great gift to the world by speaking candidly, humbly, and in dialogue with the rich resources of the Christian tradition about sin. Many of the problems related to contemporary rhetoric around sin stem from the fact that sin has too often only been located "out there." My intention here is to allow the light of grace to illuminate sin in order that the life and grace of God—the Kingdom of God—may flourish. For a contemporary scholarly treatment of sin and the variety of biblical and cultural portrayals of sin, see Gary A. Anderson, *Sin: A History* (New Haven, CT: Yale University Press, 2009).

12. See Hebrews 9:4.

13. See Genesis 15:13–14; Acts 7:6; Galatians 3:16–17.

14. Defining practical theology explicitly also allows individual practical theologians and communities of practical theologians to approach the task of practical theology in ways that more faithfully reflect their theological identity. Practical theologians from a variety of theological backgrounds may appropriate this understanding of practical theology, yet by having a grasp of its various dimensions, such a variety of people can actually do practical theology in ways that honor and reflect their respective theological convictions. A group of Catholic practical theologians will bring different theological starting points than a group of Anabaptist practical theologians. For more on practical theology, see the appendix at the end of this book.

15. Richard R. Osmer, *Practical Theology: An Introduction* (Grand Rapids: Eerdmans, 2008), x.

16. Daniel L. Migliore writes of "the christocentric and Trinitarian history of the covenant of God with humanity that provides for Barth the essential context, norm, and direction of all Christian ethical reflection and action." See Daniel L. Migliore, "Commanding Grace: Karl Barth's Theological Ethics," in *Commanding Grace: Studies in Karl Barth's Ethics*, ed. Daniel L. Migliore (Grand Rapids: Eerdmans, 2010), 9.

17. "Mennonites have underscored . . . interpretation of Scripture in harmony with Jesus Christ, in the sense that his life, teachings, death, and resurrection are essential to understanding the Bible as a whole." *Confession of Faith in a Mennonite Perspective* (Scottdale, PA: Herald, 1995), 24.

CHAPTER 2

1. This follows our outline of the movement of practical theology in Chapter 1.

2. Daniel J. Siegel, *Brainstorm: The Power and Purpose of the Teenage Brain* (New York: Penguin, 2013). Siegel teaches psychiatry at the UCLA school of medicine, where he is on the faculty at the Center for Culture, Brain, and Development. He also co-directs the UCLA Mindful Awareness Center and serves as Executive Director of the Mindsight Institute. He earned his medical degree from Harvard.

3. The interdisciplinary and rigorous nature of Siegel's work makes him a compelling dialogue partner for the interdisciplinary practical theological exploration of this chapter. Siegel's attention to interconnected life and action closely parallels the discussion of agency from the first chapter.

4. In terms of neuroscience and adolescence, Siegel's argument pushes back against recent neuroscience which implied that adolescents are simply at the mercy of their underdeveloped prefrontal cortices. For example, the 2002 PBS *Frontline* documentary "Inside the Teenage Brain" leans in this direction. *Frontline*, season 20, episode 11, "Inside the Teenage Brain," written and directed by Sarah Spinks, aired Jan. 31, 2002, on PBS, http://www.pbs.org/wgbh/pages/frontline/shows/teenbrain/.

5. Siegel, *Brainstorm*, 2–4. The term "adolescence" is itself contested, as are the markers of adolescence. Most developmental science views reproductive maturation (the onset of puberty) as the marker of the beginning of adolescence. The mark(s) of the end of adolescence creates more debate. Some combination of marriage, parenting, and economic independence has been identified as marking the end of that period. Jeffrey Arnett and Robert Epstein typify the debate surrounding adolescence. See Jeffrey J. Arnett, *Emerging Adulthood: The Winding Road from the Late Teens Through the Twenties* (New York: Oxford University Press, 2006); and Robert Epstein, *The Case against Adolescence: Rediscovering the Adult in Every Teen* (Sanger, CA: Quill Driver Books, 2007).

Siegel marks adolescence as occurring roughly between the ages of twelve and twenty-four, and along with much other contemporary research, he notes how contemporary adolescence has expanded in ways that have never been seen before in history. Whereas adolescence started as late as the mid-teen years in past centuries, contemporary young people commonly begin puberty before reaching double digits. In addition, prior centuries moved young people much more quickly from the onset of reproductive maturation to the onset of domestic responsibility. Young people could be financially independent, married, and have a family of their own by their early twenties or even their late teens. The time span from the onset of puberty to domestic responsibility and independence has grown from a few short years to nearly two decades.

6. Siegel, *Brainstorm*, 7–9.

7. Siegel, *Brainstorm*, 24.

8. While some previous views held that brain development—and, along with it, human development—essentially ended with the conclusion of adolescence, neuroscience now recognizes the reality of lifelong neuroplasticity, the continual process of brain development across the lifespan. The brain—and, along with it, the entire person—never quits evolving. See Daniel J. Siegel, *The Developing Mind: How Relationships and the Brain Interact to Shape Who We Are*, 2nd ed. (New York: Guilford, 2012), 252–56.

9. To be clear, rest doesn't stand as the centerpiece of Siegel's argument. Inner- and interpersonal integration (more on this soon) stand at the center of Siegel's thesis. However, Siegel insists that the ongoing work of integration depends on rest.

10. Siegel, *Brainstorm*, 67.

11. Siegel, *Brainstorm*, 67–71.

12. Siegel, *Brainstorm*, 69. Siegel makes the fascinating observation that intuition and non-rational thought provide antidotes for hyper-rationality. The hyper-rational person needs to consider intuition and "gut feeling" before proceeding. In terms of brain science and integration, Siegel is advocating the integration of the brain's hemispheres. Hyper-rationality leans too heavily on the left side of the brain and needs to tap into the supra-rational tendencies of the right brain.

13. In addition to changes in dopamine release, changes in the brain during adolescence also occur by way of two neurological processes that make the brain more efficient and that help the different parts of the brain interrelate in more sophisticated ways: pruning and myelination. Pruning "reduces the number of the brain's basic cells, the neurons, and their connections, the synapses." Pruning appears to be genetically controlled, shaped by experience, and intensified by stress. The connections that remain reflect the experiences of the person. "The more you use a circuit, the stronger it gets," says Siegel. Myelination, on the other hand, increases brain efficiency. During myelination, the brain "lays down 'myelin,' a sheath covering the membranes among interlinked neurons . . . to allow faster and more synchronized information flow." Siegel, *Brainstorm*, 81–82.

14. Siegel, *Brainstorm*, 40.

15. Siegel, *Brainstorm*, 87.

16. Siegel clarifies that adolescent brain development isn't just about the prefrontal cortex. It's more about integration—the differentiation and connection among the various regions of the brain. Adolescents still need the lowest part of the brain, the brainstem, for sleep function and for reactive states such as anger or fear. Healthy development involves distinguishing the various regions and functions of the brain, and then connecting them in a way that maximizes insight, empathy, and integration while avoiding the extremes of chaos and rigidity. Such development nurtures not only the life of the single person, but also the context and web of relationships that partially constitute the person. As

Siegel points out, "The frontal areas of the cortex also link our neural firing to the activity of other nervous systems, to other brains within other people." Siegel, *Brainstorm*, 88. Siegel argues compellingly that development in or toward autonomy—that is, the isolated individual—stands as a neurobiological anomaly. Isolation and autonomy may exist, but they don't promote human thriving or adolescent development.

Siegel continues, "During adolescence, the pruning and myelination and the remodeling that they create happen primarily in the cortical regions. While one of those areas is the prefrontal cortex, it is important to keep in mind that this most forward part of the frontal cortex is not super-special by itself; it is more accurate to say that the prefrontal region and related areas are important because they coordinate and balance other regions of the brain. In this way, we can say that the prefrontal cortex is integrative as it links differentiated areas to one another. This integration enables the 'whole to be greater than the sum of its parts.' With this integration we achieve more complex and useful functions. As we've seen, examples of these include self-awareness, empathy, emotional balance, and flexibility.

"As the prefrontal region serves as a master integrative hub . . . its rewiring during the adolescent period permits a more extensive form of integration to be achieved in the transition from childhood to adulthood. . . . [T]his hub is both for the networks within the brain and body as a whole, and for the networks of interconnecting brains we call relationships. Here we see how the integration of our inner networks and our interpersonal networks shapes our experience of mind. The mind is embodied within us and it is embedded between us. Our mind is within and between us." Siegel, *Brainstorm*, 100.

17. As Siegel points out, "What we focus our attention on and what we spend time doing directly stimulate [brain development]." Siegel, *Brainstorm*, 90–91.

18. Siegel, *Brainstorm*, 39–40. See also Siegel, *The Developing Mind*, 258–61. Note: For Siegel, integration describes a biological process (as in the prefrontal cortex). It also describes a skill.

19. Siegel, *Brainstorm*, 40.

20. Siegel's move in lifting up insight as a critical component to human development as evidenced by neuroscience reflects a much broader intellectual trend that has been taking place in recent decades. Whereas objectivity and some notion of pure reason guided intellectual thought after the Enlightenment, more and more contemporary thinkers—even within the "hard" sciences—recognize the fundamental impossibility of pure objectivity and value-less exploration. Human experience necessarily yields a set of values and norms, whether or not those values and norms are acknowledged. For more on the necessity of life experience and values within human thought and action, see Hans-Georg Gadamer, *Truth and Method* (London: Continuum, 2011); see also Charles Taylor, *Sources of the Self: The Making of the Modern Identity* (Cambridge, MA: Harvard University Press, 1989).

21. It also hints at the rest that Siegel sees as critical to development.

22. Siegel, *Brainstorm*, 50. In *The Developing Mind*, Siegel clarifies the distinction between mind and brain. "Brain is the embodied neural mechanism shaping [the flow of

energy and information within a person]; . . . mind is the embodied and relational process that regulates the flow of energy and information." Both mind and brain contribute to the broader process of energy and information flow. "This aspect of mind regulates the flow of energy and information as it is shared within relationships and moves through the physical mechanisms of the brain." Siegel, *The Developing Mind*, 1–45.

Nicholas G. Carr makes a parallel argument. See Nicholas G. Carr, *The Shallows: What the Internet Is Doing to Our Brains* (New York: W. W. Norton, 2010).

23. For more on attunement, see Siegel, *The Developing Mind*, 93–95.

24. Siegel, *Brainstorm*, 59–60.

25. By now, it should be clear that Siegel has no means of conceptualizing what it means to be human apart from human sociality and experience. Unlike some reptiles and amphibians that lay eggs, fertilize them, and let them fend for themselves, humans care for their young—in fact, human life depends on an extraordinarily long period of dependency. Even in cases where the broader culture sees sixteen- to eighteen-year-olds as fully functioning adults, roughly 20 percent of human life takes place prior to adulthood. Given current realities, many young people don't attain the markers of adulthood until departing the first third of life. The point here is that human living necessarily takes place in the context of human relationship. Those relationships may be more or less healthy, but no human life survives in isolated autonomy. Siegel's training in the social sciences predisposes him to seeing the necessarily social nature of human life; his experience with neuroscience has shown him parallel processes in the human brain and mind. Mental and neurological development (i.e., the development of the mind and brain) cannot be separated from the relationships that partially constitute human living. In other words, the human brain and the human mind are unavoidably shaped by the relationships that exist between a person, others, and the broader context.

While Siegel doesn't write theologically, he helps us raise important theological questions. How do we respond to and repair dis-integration in the theological realm where people feel abandoned or betrayed by God? The import of this question rises all the more as we remember the tendency of humans to project experiences and images of primary caregivers onto God. How do we help young people distinguish experiences of caregivers from experiences of God? The assets and challenges of adolescence make this period a critical time for this work.

26. Time-In "also helps to increase . . . levels of the enzyme telomerase, which repairs and maintains the ends of your chromosomes that help keep . . . individual cells alive and healthy." Siegel, *Brainstorm*, 282–84.

27. Siegel, *Brainstorm*, 288. Siegel goes on to note the neurology of focus time. "When we focus intensely, we do three things in the brain. One is that the part of the brain just above the brainstem . . . secretes an important chemical, acetylcholine, throughout the brain. A second thing is that paying close attention intensely activates specific circuits. When neurons fire together, they wire together. And this brings us to the third: When we pay close attention to one thing, the acetylcholine bathing those activating circuits

works with the localized release of . . . brain-derived neurotrophic factor, or BDNF, to optimize how genes become expressed to produce the proteins necessary to strengthen the connections among those firing neurons." Siegel summarizes, "In short, when you pay close attention, you optimize neuroplastic changes that are the basis for learning." Siegel, *Brainstorm*, 288–89.

28. Siegel, *Brainstorm*, 294.

29. As reported by John Medina in John Medina, *Brain Rules: 12 Principles for Surviving and Thriving at Work, Home, and School* (Seattle: Pear Press, 2008), 151–52.

30. Medina, *Brain Rules*, 152.

31. Richard T. Moore, Rachel Kaprielian, and John Auerbach, "Asleep at the Wheel: Report of the Special Commission on Drowsy Driving," February 2009, https://sleep.med.harvard.edu/file_download/103.

32. In a 2005 article in *Pediatrics*, Dr. Richard P. Millman summarizes the physiological developments of adolescent sleep. "These changes include a decrease in slow-wave sleep time (decreased by nearly 40% from prepubertal to late pubertal adolescents with a 10-hour sleep opportunity), an increase in the total amount of stage 2 sleep, and a decrease in the latency to the first episode of rapid eye movement (REM) sleep." See Richard P. Millman, "Excessive Sleepiness in Adolescents and Young Adults: Causes, Consequences, and Treatment Strategies," *Pediatrics* 115 (2005): 1774.

33. Mary A. Carskadon, preface to *Adolescent Sleep Patterns: Biological, Social, and Psychological Influences*, ed. Mary A. Carskadon (New York: Cambridge University Press, 2002), xiii; Mary A. Carskadon, "Factors Influencing Sleep Patterns of Adolescents," in *Adolescent Sleep Patterns*, 12.

34. Carskadon, "Factors Influencing Sleep Patterns," 5.

35. National Sleep Foundation, "Teens and Sleep," accessed February 28, 2014, http://www.sleepfoundation.org/article/sleep-topics/teens-and-sleep. According to Carskadon's Stanford research, teens need an average of 9.25 hours per night.

It should be noted that many in sleep science hold to the upper end of this range and recommend at least nine hours of sleep for adolescents. Martin Fisher is among them (see the next note below). Interestingly, because the onset of adolescence signals no change in the quantity of sleep needed, the question in developmental science regarding the markers of adolescence carries less significance in the field of sleep science.

36. Medical doctor Martin Fisher peruses the data and estimates that "the average [amount of nightly sleep] throughout adolescents is 7–7.5 hours, and only 20% sleep 9 hours or more per night" (Martin Fisher, "Fatigue in Adolescence," *Journal of Pediatric Adolescent Gynecology* 26 [2013]: 252–56). A 2013 "Stress in America" survey by the American Psychological Association found that thirteen- to seventeen-year-olds average 7.4 hours of sleep per night on school nights. American Psychological Association, "Stress in America: Are Teens Adopting Adults' Stress Habits?" American Psychological Association, February 11, 2014, http://www.apa.org/news/press/releases/stress/2013/stress-report.pdf.

A growing body of research suggests that this is a relatively recent historical phenomenon. Young people today average less sleep per night than young people thirty to one hundred years ago. In fact, I didn't find a single study that reports an increase in total sleep during adolescence over the course of recent decades. In a study of Swiss children, Iglowstein et al. report a "substantial decrease in sleep duration in younger children between the 1970's and 1990's," caused primarily by later bedtimes with wake times remaining constant through the decades. Ivo Iglowstein et al., "Sleep Duration from Infancy to Adolescence: Reference Values and Generational Trends," *Pediatrics* 111 (2003): 305. See also Lisa Matricciani, Timothy Olds, and John Petkov, "In Search of Lost Sleep: Secular Trends in the Sleep Time of School-Aged Children and Adolescents," *Sleep Medicine Reviews* 16 (2012): 203–11; and Carl Erik Landhuis et al., "Childhood Sleep Time and Long-Term Risk for Obesity: A 32-Year Prospective Birth Cohort Study," *Pediatrics* 122 (2008): 955–60.

Furthermore, 2014 data actually lowers the average amount of sleep per night to 7.9 hours for twelve- to fourteen-year-olds and to 7.1 hours for fifteen- to seventeen-year-olds. National Sleep Foundation, "2014 Sleep in America Poll: Sleep in the Modern Family: Summary of Findings," March 2014, http://sleepfoundation.org/sleep-polls-data /sleep-in-america-poll/2014-sleep-in-the-modern-family/.

37. According to the National Sleep Foundation, twelfth-graders average less than seven hours of sleep per night—more than an hour and a half less sleep per night than sixth graders. The Foundation notes that such sleep patterns among high school seniors add up to a weekly sleep deficit of nearly twelve hours. National Sleep Foundation, "National Sleep Foundation 2006 Sleep in America Poll: Highlights and Key Findings" (National Sleep Foundation, 2006), 1.

38. National Sleep Foundation, "National Sleep Foundation 2014 Sleep in America Poll Finds Children Sleep Better When Parents Establish Rules, Limit Technology, and Set a Good Example," National Sleep Foundation, March 3, 2014, http://stage.sleepfoun dation.org/media-center/press-release/national-sleep-foundation-2014-sleep-america -poll-finds-children-sleep.

39. Sleep scientists have been documenting the benefits of changes to high-school start times. See, for example, the work of Dr. Judith A. Owens and her colleagues at the Hasbro Children's Hospital in Providence, Rhode Island. At an independent high school in Rhode Island, Owens and her team convinced officials to delay the school start time a modest thirty minutes, from 8:00 to 8:30. Owens summarizes their findings: "After the start time delay, mean school night sleep duration increased by 45 minutes, and average bedtime advanced by 18 minutes . . . ; the percentage of students getting less than 7 hours of sleep decreased by 79.4%, and those reporting at least 8 hours of sleep increased from 16.4% to 54.7%. Students reported significantly more satisfaction with sleep and experienced improved motivation. Daytime sleepiness, fatigue, and depressed mood were all reduced. Most health-related variables, including Health Center visits for fatigue-related complaints, and class attendance also improved." Judith A. Owens, Katherine Belon, and

Patricia Moss, "Impact of Delaying School Start Time on Adolescent Sleep, Mood, and Behavior," *Archive of Pediatric Adolescent Medicine* 164 (2010): 608.

See also Kyla Wahlstrom, "Changing Times: Findings from the First Longitudinal Study of Later High School Start Times," *NASSP Bulletin* 86 (2002): 3–21.

40. Among other things, these changes also seem to emerge from a two-sided awareness gap. On the one hand, the general public makes the same assumption that Carskadon did prior to her research: adolescents need less sleep than children. On the other hand, many parents remain unaware of the actual sleep practices of their teens, with 90 percent of parents believing their children get adequate sleep "at least a few nights during the school week." National Sleep Foundation, "National Sleep Foundation 2006 Sleep in America Poll: Highlights and Key Findings," 1. See also Michelle A. Short et al., "Estimating Adolescent Sleep Patterns: Parent Reports versus Adolescent Self-Report Surveys, Sleep Diaries, and Actigraphy," *Nature and Science of Sleep* 5 (2013): 23–26.

Social psychologist Sanford M. Dornbusch suggests that the lack of awareness regarding biological needs for sleep drives the social reality among adults and teens which leads to reduced adolescent sleep. Sanford M. Dornbusch, "Sleep and Adolescence: A Social Psychologist's Perspective," in *Adolescent Sleep Patterns*, 2.

41. This change in biological rhythms has been observed across cultures, ethnicities, and geographies. See Carskadon, "Factors Influencing Sleep Patterns of Adolescents," in *Adolescent Sleep Patterns*, 11–17; and Millman, "Excessive Sleepiness in Adolescents and Young Adults," 1775.

42. Avi Sadeh, Reut Gruber, and Amiram Raviv, "The Effects of Sleep Restriction and Extension on School-Age Children: What a Difference an Hour Makes," *Child Development* 74 (2003): 444–55. Sadeh directs the Laboratory for Children's Sleep and Arousal Disorders at Tel Aviv University.

43. Sadeh, Gruber, and Raviv, "The Effects of Sleep Restriction and Extension," 444–55.

44. Lauren D. Asarnow, Eleanor McGlinchey, and Allison G. Harvey, "The Effects of Bedtime and Sleep Duration on Academic and Emotional Outcomes in a Nationally Representative Sample of Adolescents," *Journal of Adolescent Health* 54 (2014): 350–56; Julia F. Dewald et al., "The Influence of Sleep Quality, Sleep Duration, and Sleepiness on School Performance in Children and Adolescents: A Meta-Analytic Review," *Sleep Medicine Reviews* 14 (2010): 179–89.

45. As Matthew P. Walker and Robert Stickgold of Harvard Medical School note, neuroscience "provide[s] evidence of sleep-dependent memory consolidation and sleep-dependent brain plasticity." Matthew P. Walker and Robert Stickgold, "Sleep-Dependent Learning and Memory Consolidation," *Neuron* 44 (2004): 121.

46. Walker and Stickgold write, "Taken as a whole, these studies suggest a rich and multi-faceted role for sleep in the processing of human declarative memories. While contradictory evidence is found for a role in the processing of simple, emotion-free declarative memories, such as the learning of unrelated word pairs, a substantial body of evidence indicates that both SWS and REM sleep contribute to the consolidation of

complex, emotionally salient declarative memories embedded in networks of previously existing associative memories." Walker and Stickgold, "Sleep-Dependent Learning," 124. The importance of sleep for remembering motor learning, visual perceptual learning, and auditory learning has also been shown.

47. See Matricciani, Olds, and Petkov, "In Search of Lost Sleep," 203–11; and Landhuis et al., "Childhood Sleep Time and Long-Term Risk for Obesity," 955–60. See also Christine Acebo and Mary A. Carskadon, "Influence of Irregular Sleep Patterns on Waking Behavior," in *Adolescent Sleep Patterns*, 220–35; Avi Sadeh and Reut Gruber, "Stress and Sleep in Adolescence: A Clinical-Developmental Perspective," in *Adolescent Sleep Patterns*, 236–53; James T. McCracken, "The Search for Vulnerability Signatures for Depression in High-Risk Adolescents: Mechanisms and Significance," in *Adolescent Sleep Patterns*, 254–68; and Kyla L. Wahlstrom, "Accommodating the Sleep Patterns of Adolescents within Current Educational Structures: An Uncharted Path," in *Adolescent Sleep Patterns*, 184–85. Similar statistical relationships have been reported by Amy R. Wolfson and Mary A. Carskadon, "Sleep Schedules and Daytime Functioning," *Child Development* 69 (1998): 875–87. See also Dubi Lufi, Orna Tzischinsky, and Steve Hadar, "Delaying School Starting Time by One Hour: Some Effects on Attention Levels in Adolescents," *Journal of Clinical Sleep Medicine* 7 (2011): 137–43.

48. See Carol M. Worthman and Melissa K. Melby, "Toward a Comparative Developmental Ecology of Human Sleep," in *Adolescent Sleep Patterns*, 69–117.

49. Po Bronson and Ashley Merryman, *Nurture Shock: New Thinking about Children* (New York: Hachette Book Group, 2009), 44.

50. David Elkind, *The Hurried Child: Growing Up Too Fast Too Soon*, rev. ed. (Reading, MA: Perseus Books, 1988).

51. Alvin A. Rosenfeld and Nicole Wise, *The Over-Scheduled Child: Avoiding the Hyper-Parenting Trap* (New York: St. Martin's Griffin, 2001); William C. Crain, *Reclaiming Childhood: Letting Children Be Children in Our Achievement-Oriented Society* (New York: Times Books, 2003). For a balanced overview of the literature on youth and busyness and over-scheduling, see Stephen Hinshaw's chapter "Life in the Pressure Cooker" in his book *The Triple Bind: Saving Our Teenage Girls from Today's Pressures* (New York: Ballantine Books, 2009). It's worth noting that Hinshaw's concern for young people parallels that of Daniel Siegel. Hinshaw worries that a variety of cultural pressures, including the pressure to appear both busy and under control, prevents young people, and females in particular, from cultivating an inner life. He expresses concern that adolescent females give attention to the expectations of others to the exclusion of nurturing their own sense of self and intrinsic desires and interests.

52. Hofferth notes that while research does affirm the fact that contemporary young people have more scheduled, extracurricular activities than in decades past, very little empirical data exists that specifically evaluates the relationship between increased activity and well-being. Hofferth notes, for example, that between 1981 and 1997, "participation in sports rose 35 percent and participation in the arts (art, music, dance, drama)

rose 145 percent for children between the ages of nine and twelve." Sandra Hofferth, David A. Kinney, and Janet S. Dunn, "The 'Hurried' Child: Myth vs. Reality" (working paper, Maryland Population Research Center, University of Maryland, 2008), 5. See also S. L. Hofferth and J. F. Sandberg, "Changes in American Children's Time, 1981-1997," in *Children at the Millennium: Where Did We Come From, Where Are We Going?*, ed. S. Hofferth and T. Owens (New York: Elsevier Science, 2001), 193–229.

53. Hofferth, "The 'Hurried' Child," 4. Note that according to Elkind, over-scheduling has a particularly negative impact on preteens, the age group that Hofferth studied. We may also look to sleep research that focuses on the onset of puberty as a time when need for sleep potentially increases, thus potentially exacerbating the negative impact of excessive activity. Cf. Carskadon, "Factors Influencing Sleep Patterns of Adolescence," in *Adolescent Sleep Patterns*, 4-26.

54. Hofferth's team found that in a nationally representative sample, 25 percent qualified as hurried, 58 percent were either focused or balanced, and 17 percent were uninvolved. In the two Midwest towns that Hofferth's team analyzed, a somewhat larger percentage were hurried, the focused and balanced groups made up roughly the same proportion, and a somewhat smaller percentage were inactive. To the research team's surprise, their sample from these two towns revealed no relationship between socioeconomic status and activity level: family income didn't predict activity level. Variation in activity level occurred more within the communities than between them.

55. "Children's stress symptoms were measured by a subset of items from the 30-item Behavior Problems Index, a standard instrument used in the [nationally representative] Child Study to obtain primary caregiver reports of the incidence and severity of child behavior problems." Hofferth, "The 'Hurried' Child," 13.

56. "Parents worried when children did not have any activities." Hofferth, "The 'Hurried' Child," 31.

57. Hofferth's findings are consonant with time-use research which indicates that, on average, American teens have modest amounts of free time daily.

58. The intensity of the activity turns particularly toxic in situations where young people sense excessive pressure from parents. In Hofferth's sample, her team recognized the role that parental pressure played in the case of particularly young children involved in multiple activities.

59. Joseph L. Mahoney, Heather Lord, and Erica Carryl, "An Ecological Analysis of After-School Program Participation and the Development of Academic Performance and Motivational Attributes for Disadvantaged Children," *Child Development* 76 (2005): 811-25.

60. Joseph L. Mahoney, Angel L. Harris, and Jacquelynne S. Eccles, "Organized Activity Participation, Positive Youth Development, and the Over-Scheduling Hypothesis," *Social Policy Report, The Society for Research in Child Development* 20 (2006): 3-30.

61. Suniya S. Luthar, Karen A. Shoum, and Pamela J. Brown, "Extracurricular Involvement Among Affluent Youth: A Scapegoat for 'Ubiquitous Achievement Pressures'?," *Developmental Psychology* 42 (2006): 583–97.

62. Juliet Schor, *The Overworked American: The Unexpected Decline of Leisure* (New York: Basic Books, 1991).

63. Gershuny writes, "What emerges is the hypothesis that growth in busy feelings may in part reflect an increasingly positive view of 'busyness' that results from its association with the increasingly busy lifestyle of the most privileged groups in developed societies." Jonathan Gershuny, "Busyness as the Badge of Honor for the New Superordinate Working Class," *Social Research* 72 (2005): 289.

64. Gershuny draws on the work of Thorstein Veblen, Staffan Linder, and Gary Becker to suggest that an increase in productivity during the twentieth century led to a corresponding increase in consumption. The mechanism for this change has been theorized in different ways. One model sees manufacturing and advertising in tandem—as manufacturers produce ever more goods, the advertising machine convinces the public to consume more. Another model sees each class of society in constant pursuit of the goods and products of the class of society just above it, yet the "next class" of society is never reached because it, too, strives for the class above it.

65. Gershuny, "Busyness as the Badge," 292.

66. Gershuny, "Busyness as the Badge," 292.

67. As Gershuny notes, "There is a well-documented, cross-nationally consistent historical growth of busy feelings through the last part of the twentieth century. But there is an equally well-documented, long-term, and very substantial growth in leisure time in nearly every country for which we have appropriate evidence." Gershuny, "Busyness as the Badge," 287–88.

68. Derek Thompson, "Are We Truly Overworked? An Investigation—in 6 Charts," *The Atlantic*, May 22, 2013, http://www.theatlantic.com/magazine/archive/2013/06/are -we-truly-overworked/309321/.

69. Reed W. Larson, "How U.S. Children and Adolescents Spend Time: What It Does (and Doesn't) Tell Us about Their Development," *Current Directions in Psychological Science* 10 (2001): 161.

70. While some critics may question the historical validity of the minutiae of "Downton Abbey," the illustrative point stands. At the end of the nineteenth and the beginning of the twentieth century, upper-class persons were marked not by the excess of their busyness, but by the quantity and quality of their leisure.

71. The commercial is available at https://www.youtube.com/watch?v=04wNMO apzyw.

72. Consider global mobile-technology data. As of November 2018, the total number of global mobile connections approached 9 billion with the number of unique mobile subscribers surpassing 5 billion. GSMA Intelligence, Global Data, accessed November 6, 2018, https://www.gsmaintelligence.com/. As of 2010, there were three cell phones for

every computer with an Internet connection, and eighty mobile-phone subscriptions for every one hundred world inhabitants. See Jeffry A. Hall and Nancy K. Baym, "Calling and Texting (Too Much): Mobile Maintenance Expectations, (Over) Dependence, Entrapment, and Friendship Satisfaction," *New Media Society* 14 (2012): 316-17.

In the US, 2018 data from Pew Research states that "smartphone ownership has become a nearly ubiquitous element of teen life: 95% of teens now report they have a smartphone or access to one. These mobile connections are in turn fueling more-persistent online activities: 45% of teens now say they are online on a near-constant basis." This "near-constant" online activity represents more than a 20 percent increase compared to data from 2015. Monica Anderson and Jingjing Jiang, "Teens, Social Media & Technology 2018," Pew Research Center, May 31, 2018, http://www.pewinternet.org/2018/05/31/teens -social-media-technology-2018/; Amanda Lenhart, "Teens, Social Media & Technology Overview 2015," Pew Research Center, April 9, 2015, http://www.pewinternet.org/2015 /04/09/teens-social-media-technology-2015/.

The prevalence of SMS text-messaging has skyrocketed in the last decade. Consider, for example, that in 2006, Americans who used SMS averaged only sixty-seven text messages per month. By 2008, that number jumped 450 percent to over 350 messages per month. See the Nielsen Company, "In U.S., SMS Text Messaging Tops Mobile Phone Calling," September 22, 2008, http://www.nielsen.com/us/en/newswire/2008/in-us -text-messaging-tops-mobile-phone-calling.html.

The number of texts that teens send per day is disputed. The 2015 Pew Research says teens average thirty texts per day. In 2010, Nielsen said the average was 3,146 texts per month, or approximately 110 per day. See Roger Entner, "Under-Aged Texting Usage and Actual Cost," The Nielsen Company, January 27, 2010, http://www.nielsen.com/us/en/ newswire/2010/under-aged-texting-usage-and-actual-cost.html.

73. See https://en.oxforddictionaries.com/definition/technology.

74. Most often, technology does both. Researchers at the University of Kansas have chronicled the complexity of technology in the context of human relationships. They use dialectical theory to explain this complexity, and they refer to the influence of cell phones as ironic or "Janus faced." They note research which indicates that accessibility stands as both the most and least desired characteristic of cell phones. "Access is a double-edged sword: it is both the most commonly identified positive feature of mobile phones . . . and the most commonly identified negative feature of mobile phones." Hall and Baym, "Calling and Texting," 319.

75. MIT sociologist and longtime technology researcher Sherry Turkle has spent more than three decades researching technology by asking two primary questions: What do we do with technology? And what does technology do to us? Turkle insists that technology's impact can't be reduced to statistics or generalizations, that it demands exploration of concrete stories and real life. See Sherry Turkle, *Alone Together: Why We Expect More from Technology and Less from Each Other* (New York: Basic Books, 2011).

76. Jan Van den Bulck, "Adolescent Use of Mobile Phones for Calling and for Sending

Text Messages after Lights Out: Results from a Prospective Cohort Study with a One-Year Follow-Up," *Sleep* 30 (2007): 1220–23.

77. Sue K. Adams, "College Students and Sleep: The Effects of Living a 24/7 Lifestyle" (lecture, Wheaton College, March 2011). See also the National Sleep Foundation, "Annual Sleep in America Poll Exploring Connections with Communications Technology," March 7, 2011, http://sleepfoundation.org/media-center/press-release/annual-sleep-america-poll-exploring-connections-communications-technology-use-/page/0%2C2/.

78. Sandra Horowitz, "Sleep Texting: A New Variation on an Old Theme," *Sleep Medicine* 12, Supplement 1 (2011): S39.

79. National Sleep Foundation, "National Sleep Foundation 2014 Sleep in America Poll," National Sleep Foundation, March 3, 2014, http://stage.sleepfoundation.org/media-center/press-release/national-sleep-foundation-2014-sleep-america-poll-finds-children-sleep. The influence of such technology takes place in at least three ways. First, the light from electronic screens inhibits the body's secretion of melatonin, causing the body to delay sleep. The light essentially tells the brain, "It's daytime." Second, texting, talking, or playing a game on a mobile device stimulates the brain. Such stimulation tells the brain it's time to go, not time to rest, and thus delays the onset of sleep. Third, texts, calls, or alarms that occur after people fall asleep reduce total sleep time and interrupt the body's progression through natural sleep cycles.

CHAPTER 3

1. All interviews and focus groups were conducted in confidentiality, and the names of participants have been changed by mutual agreement except where noted. Transcripts of all interviews and focus groups are available upon request.

2. Jennifer, focus group by Nathan T. Stucky, transcript, May 2013.

3. Jennifer, time diary, May 2013.

4. The National Study of Youth and Religion defines the 8 percent of American youth who qualify as highly devoted along the following lines: "Attends religious services weekly or more; Faith is very or extremely important in everyday life; Feels very or extremely close to God; Currently involved in a religious youth group; Prays a few times a week or more; Reads scripture once or twice a week or more." Reported in Kenda Creasy Dean, *Almost Christian: What the Faith of Our Teenagers Is Telling the American Church* (New York: Oxford, 2010), 41. See also Christian Smith with Melinda Lundquist Denton, *Soul Searching: The Religious and Spiritual Lives of American Teenagers* (New York: Oxford, 2005).

5. Matthew, focus group by Nathan T. Stucky, transcript, May 2013.

6. Michael, focus group by Nathan T. Stucky, transcript, May 2013.

7. In the terms of social science, I engaged in qualitative research. I began with general questions and suspicions, but no specific hypotheses. The specific themes that

emerged and the ways that the young people brought them to expression were specific to the data. They emerged from the data. Lyn Richards writes about working "up from the data": "The most exciting and challenging processes in qualitative research require discovery and exploration of ideas from the data." This notion of discovering and exploring ideas within the data appropriately describes the research method I employed with these students. See Lyn Richards, *Handling Qualitative Data: A Practical Guide*, 2nd ed. (Los Angeles: Sage, 2009).

8. John P. Robinson's "The Time-Diary Method: Structures and Uses" served as a primary resource in the development of the time diary. Diaries were designed to be simple, portable (students would need to carry diaries with them), and feasible to use. In explaining the time diaries, I encouraged students to be specific enough in their recording in order to give a fair representation of their identity. I told them, "If your mother or friend picked up the time diary, they should be able to tell it's you." The actual number of entry lines in the blank diary struck a balance between giving students adequate space for recording the details of a day and keeping the diary to a reasonable size. See John P. Robinson, "The Time-Diary Method: Structures and Uses," in *Time Use Research in the Social Sciences*, ed. Wendy E. Pentland et al. (New York: Kluwer Academic, 1999), 47–90.

9. While just over 10 percent of the youth highlighted time on social media (four highlighted Facebook, one highlighted Twitter) as rest, almost 80 percent highlighted either movies or TV.

10. Amanda, focus group.

11. Jessica and Vince, focus group.

12. Michael and Taylor, focus group by Nathan T. Stucky, transcript, May 2013.

13. We can discern overlap here with Jonathan Gershuny's work on busyness. Michael and Taylor clearly have some discretionary time, but they fill it with the products of consumer culture.

14. Kaitlin, focus group by Nathan T. Stucky, transcript, May 2013.

15. Brian, focus group.

16. Taylor, focus group.

17. John, focus group.

18. This finding falls in line with other research on young people and music. See, for example, Heather C. North, David J. Hargreaves, and Susan A. O'Neill, "The Importance of Music to Adolescents," *British Journal of Educational Psychology* 70 (2000): 255–72.

19. This theme fits perfectly with Daniel Siegel's argument that creative exploration is a basic characteristic of adolescence.

20. Andrew, interview by Nathan T. Stucky, transcript, May 2013.

21. Andrew, interview.

22. Taylor, focus group.

23. Danielle, focus group by Nathan T. Stucky, transcript, May 2013.

24. Heather, focus group.

25. Vince, John, and Jessica, focus group.

26. Megan, focus group by Nathan T. Stucky, transcript, May 2013.

27. Heather, focus group. A word about sleep: While the time diaries provided concrete data regarding the hours these youth sleep and the patterns that govern their sleep, sleep came up only rarely in our focus group and interview conversations. These youth unanimously highlighted sleep as rest. Aside from this, one additional pattern emerged for a noticeable minority. In analyzing the time diaries, I was struck by the number of youth who were "sick" or who "felt sick" during the week. At least three marked in their diaries that they were sick in the morning, went back to sleep, and then ended the day in a way that seems to indicate something other than sickness. Nicole, for example, wakes up Friday morning at 7:00 and immediately goes back to bed for another four and a half hours. In the comment column she writes, "Sick ☹." After the extra sleep, she wakes up, gets ready for school, goes for a dress-fitting for the upcoming school banquet, heads to the school play, and then lands for the night at a sleepover. Similarly, David wakes up at 6:15 Wednesday morning, comments "felt sick" in his diary, and proceeds to go back to sleep for almost five hours. When he wakes up again, he immediately "got food, ate it," and "surf[ed] the web." He was at work by 5:30 to pull a five-hour shift as a busboy.

On Monday morning, Ashley wakes up at 6:00, then goes back to bed at 7:00 and comments "sick." She sleeps for three hours, then spends two hours online, then watches a movie. At 2:00 in the afternoon she goes to the dentist, then to her brother's concert, and finally feeds horses and goats before going to bed for the night at 10:30. Was she really sick or just exhausted? Or both? A pattern emerges: waking up, feeling sick, and returning to sleep, only to end the day in activities that don't seem to indicate any significant illness. At the risk of mere speculation, it seems that sickness—at least in these few cases—stands as an acceptable excuse for stealing a few extra hours of sleep or leisure. While a few of these youth do record naps with some regularity, simply being tired doesn't seem to function as an adequate cause for extra sleep in these cases.

In keeping with the broader themes of this chapter, anxiety and worry intersected with the conversations that did take place around sleep. Amanda commented, "I think [the reason] I sleep so little is because I am worried, and I can't get my mind to rest, and that's why I don't get as much sleep as I should." Amanda, focus group by Nathan T. Stucky, transcript, May 2013.

28. The busyness research from Chapter 2 helps us interpret the lives of these students. It helps us to recognize and name the valorization of busyness that so many of these young people clearly adhere to, and to acknowledge that this valorization stems not from the cosmos, but from social construction. Busyness as a badge of honor informs the lives of these young people, and it depends on a certain account of value and meaning. The fact that such a perception of busyness has been constructed means that it might also be deconstructed, but it will require an alternative narrative—a different account of value, meaning, and identity.

Siegel's account of adolescent development suggests that such a shift of values and structures of meaning becomes possible in adolescence in a way that may not be possible in any other phase of life. The adolescent ability to think creatively and abstractly and to engage with others sets them up for a new paradigm for understanding work, rest, and identity. The question is, what story might replace the current dominant story that valorizes busyness and demeans rest?

29. Heather, focus group.

30. Jennifer and Stephanie, focus group.

31. Brian, focus group by Nathan T. Stucky, transcript, May 2013.

32. Ashley, focus group by Nathan T. Stucky, transcript, May 2013.

33. Adam, Melissa, and Brian, focus group by Nathan T. Stucky, transcript, May 2013.

34. Nicole, focus group.

35. Jessica, interview by Nathan T. Stucky, transcript, May 2013.

36. Vince, John, and Stephanie, focus group by Nathan T. Stucky, transcript, May 2013.

37. Stephanie, interview by Nathan T. Stucky, transcript, May 2013.

38. James, focus group by Nathan T. Stucky, transcript, May 2013.

39. See, for example, Judith Rich Harris, *The Nurture Assumption: Why Children Turn Out the Way They Do* (New York: Free Press, 2009).

40. Jessica, focus group by Nathan T. Stucky, transcript, May 2013.

41. Jennifer, focus group by Nathan T. Stucky, transcript, May 2013.

42. The exploration of Sabbath and Scripture in upcoming chapters reveals that God frequently shows up through the Sabbath in unexpected ways.

43. James, interview by Nathan T. Stucky, transcript, May 2013. Again we see the valorization of busyness that Gershuny described (see Chapter 2).

44. In keeping with Siegel's framework for adolescent development, the term "identity" shouldn't be construed here as a static entity. The argument of this book as a whole resists any passive notion of identity. I spend a significant amount of time in the current chapter wrestling with the absence of stillness and ceasing in the lives of these young people. Again, this shouldn't be heard as an endorsement of mere being in opposition to acting, as if the two could be separated. In keeping with Barth and a number of his interpreters, I affirm the inseparability of being and action. In terms of the ceasing and stillness to which God invites us through the Sabbath, such ceasing and stillness must be known as acts in and of themselves, and as concrete responses of faithfulness to the ongoing faithfulness and provision of a gracious and loving God. The relationship between God and creation remains active and dynamic throughout.

45. Stephanie, focus group by Nathan T. Stucky, transcript, May 2013.

46. Nicole, focus group by Nathan T. Stucky, transcript, May 2013.

47. Melissa, focus group by Nathan T. Stucky, transcript, May 2013.

48. Betsy, focus group by Nathan T. Stucky, transcript, May 2013.

49. John, focus group by Nathan T. Stucky, transcript, May 2013.

50. Joseph and Justin, focus group by Nathan T. Stucky, transcript, May 2013.

51. Heather, focus group by Nathan T. Stucky, transcript, May 2013.

52. Brandon, focus group by Nathan T. Stucky, transcript, May 2013.

53. Though an explicit conversation about theological education falls beyond the purview of this chapter, the sum of the empirical research process that this chapter outlines includes significant implications for theological education. The exercise of keeping the time diary and gathering in focus groups to discuss the process provides students with an opportunity to reflect on their lives. Many of these young people are engaging the Sabbath from a theological perspective for the first time. They conflate Sabbath with relaxation, working at what one loves, and a host of other things that may or may not reflect a theologically robust sense of the Sabbath. At the same time, these conversations provide a concrete example of the willingness of young people to engage in theological reflection and conversation if they're given the chance, and if they're able to do so in a context that overtly and explicitly seeks their opinions, beliefs, experiences, and perspectives. They are unquestionably capable of such theological work. They engage it with interest and sometimes with passion. God forbid that we should avoid this conversation or any theological conversation with young people because of a misperception that they're unwilling or unable to participate. Both the experience of this research and the work of Daniel Siegel suggest otherwise.

54. Stephanie, interview.

55. James, interview.

56. Stephanie, interview.

CHAPTER 4

1. Barbara Brown Taylor, "Sabbath: A Practice in Death," http://www.theworkofthe people.com/sabbath-a-practice-in-death.

2. See, for example, Mark Yaconelli, *Growing Souls: Experiments in Contemplative Youth Ministry* (El Cajon, CA: Youth Specialties, 2007); Dan Kimball and Lilly Lewin, *Sacred Space: A Hands-on Guide to Creating Multisensory Worship Experiences for Youth Ministry* (Grand Rapids: Youth Specialties, 2008); and Carol Duerksen, *Keeping Sabbath* (Cleveland: Circle Books, 2010).

3. While Scripture figures prominently across the full spectrum of Christian traditions, my identity as a Mennonite practical theologian uniquely informs my approach here. Since the beginnings of the Radical Reformation in the sixteenth century, Anabaptists have sought a Christocentric interpretation of Christian Scripture. This means that all Scripture, both Old and New Testaments, are read "through the lens" of Jesus Christ, who is seen as the fullest and clearest manifestation of God. See General Conference Mennonite Church and Mennonite Church, *Confession of Faith in a Mennonite*

Perspective (Scottdale, PA: Herald, 1995), 21-24. This facet of Anabaptist-Mennonite tradition makes Karl Barth and his radical Christocentrism a logical dialogue partner for the current project. Barth's theological approach to Scripture and his insistence on the absolute priority of God's action provide a helpful corrective to some manifestations of discipleship among Mennonites whereby human agency is elevated sometimes to the point of excluding divine action.

4. Our turn to Scripture at this juncture is neither accidental nor incidental. Christianity across the centuries has consistently looked to Scripture as a place for encountering the living God. Given our framework for practical theology and our intention to discern the relationship between divine and human agency, it makes sense to begin our theological construction of Sabbath at a place where the agency of God has been consistently affirmed. The Christian tradition—and the Anabaptist tradition therein—also affirms our turning to Karl Barth as a guide for this endeavor. As much as any other modern theologian, Barth affirms the ongoing activity of God in the world, and he looks to Scripture as a primary locus for encountering the living Word of God.

5. Genesis 2:1-3.

6. Barth's translators use the English "saga" for Barth's "*Sage*," which comes "from the same root as *sagen* (to say or tell)." See the editor's note in *Church Dogmatics*, III/1, 42. For Barth's exposition on saga, see *Church Dogmatics*, III/1, 81-94. The full reference to the *Church Dogmatics* is as follows: Karl Barth, *Church Dogmatics*, ed. G. W. Bromiley and T. F. Torrance (Edinburgh: T. & T. Clark, 1936-75). Hereafter I refer to it as *CD*.

7. Barth writes in his section heading, "Since [the creation account] contains in itself the beginning of time, its historical reality eludes all historical observation and account, and can be expressed in the biblical creation narratives only in the form of pure saga." Barth, *CD*, III/1, 42.

8. Within the field of biblical studies, Barth is seen as a pioneer in a broad interpretive school known as theological interpretation of Scripture. Theological interpretation sees the Bible as Scripture—as the Word of God. As such, the interpreter seeks more than historical-factual data, though the interpreter will certainly be open to such data. The interpreter seeks the living God, and expects to encounter God's voice within Scripture. See Daniel J. Treier, *Introducing Theological Interpretation of Scripture: Recovering a Christian Practice* (Grand Rapids: Baker Academic, 2008); Joel B. Green, *Practicing Theological Interpretation: Engaging Biblical Texts for Faith and Formation* (Grand Rapids: Baker Academic, 2011); Richard E. Burnett, *Karl Barth's Theological Exegesis: The Hermeneutical Principles of the Römerbrief Period* (Grand Rapids: Eerdmans, 2004).

9. Barth, *CD*, III/1, 98-213.

10. Barth, *CD*, III/1, 42-329.

11. Note the repetition of the phrase "of every kind" in the NRSV. It occurs ten times in the first chapter of Genesis.

12. Barth, *CD*, III/1, 213.

13. Barth insists, "The fathers thus betrayed a great obtuseness, and narrowed the

horizon with serious consequences, when in their handling of creation they usually confined themselves to the *hexaemeron* [six-day story], although both externally and internally everything points to the fact that the story of creation is to be understood as a *heptaemeron* [seven-day story], and that the record of the seventh day is quite indispensable." Barth, *CD*, III/1, 220.

14. Barth, *CD*, III/1, 213.

15. Barth, *CD*, III/1, 214.

16. Barth, *CD*, III/1, 215.

17. Barth, *CD*, III/1, 215.

18. To be clear, though Barth argues that freedom happens only by way of limits, he isn't saying that limits automatically equal freedom. Limits, too, can be for our good or our ill. The point is to recognize that there is no life apart from limits. Even God abides by them.

19. Barth, *CD*, III/1, 215.

20. Barth, *CD*, III/1, 215.

21. Barth, *CD*, III/1, 215.

22. Sherry Turkle, *Alone Together: Why We Expect More from Technology and Less from Each Other* (New York: Basic Books, 2011), 189–90.

23. Barth, *CD*, III/1, 215.

24. For Barth, this decision has taken place already within God's eternal being. God's "creative will was divine from the very outset just because it was not infinite but had this specific content and no other. [God's] creative work must now be discontinued because [God] did not will it. [God] could rest from all [God's] works because from the very outset [God] had willed and planned these and no other works." Barth, *CD*, III/1, 215.

25. Barth, *CD*, III/1, 216.

26. "God could not and would not return to an existence without the world and [humankind], since the rest, freedom and joy of this seventh day are described as the completion of [God's] creation of the world and [humankind]." Barth, *CD*, III/1, 214.

27. Barth insists that God's being remains the same before, during, and after the first six days of creation. Yet at the close of the sixth day, God reaches a self-imposed limit and ceases God's creative work. As already noted, at this point God's self-limitation reveals God's freedom. God isn't bound to ceaseless activity. The limit also signals a complexity to the divine character that mere creative activity cannot contain. God not only exercises God's agency through the creative work of the first six days; God also exercises God's agency by ceasing and resting (*shabat*) on the seventh day. On the seventh day, God continues being who God has always been, but now in relationship to the created order. With the beginning of time, God chooses to take on or associate with time. God chooses to be God's self in time and in relationship to the created order. God doesn't turn away from creation, but categorically chooses to be God of creation—to be our God. "What God was in [God's self], and had done from eternity, [God] had now in some sense repeated in time, in the form of an historical event, in [God's] relationship to [God's] creation, the world

and [humankind]; . . . the completion of all creation consisted in the historical event of this repetition." Barth, *CD*, III/1, 216.

God's eternal being and action—God's rest—take on time through the Sabbath, and through this rest, creation reaches completion. Barth's interpretation here parallels that of Jewish scholar Abraham Joshua Heschel, who notes the traditional Jewish interpretation of the Sabbath as "holiness in time." To refer to the Sabbath as holiness in time is to refer to the Sabbath as a temporal locus of God's presence. See Abraham Joshua Heschel, *The Sabbath: Its Meaning for Modern Man* (New York: Farrar, Straus and Giroux, 2005), 8–10.

28. Barth, *CD*, III/1, 214–15, italics in original. Barth contends that creation provides the context *ad extra*—outside of God's own being—for God's revelation, action, power, and grace.

29. "That God rested on the seventh day, and blessed and sanctified it, is the first divine action which [humankind] is privileged to witness." Barth, *CD*, III/1, 219.

30. Barth, *CD*, III/1, 219.

31. Daniel L. Migliore, *Faith Seeking Understanding: An Introduction to Christian Theology*, 2nd ed. (Grand Rapids: Eerdmans, 2004), 409.

32. Jewish Sabbath interpretation has consistently included an eschatological dimension. See, for example, Heschel, *The Sabbath*, 73–76. Barth comments, "When the first Christians called their holy day 'the day of the Lord' they were certainly not unaware that in the Old Testament 'the day of Yahweh' denoted the day of all days, on which there would be concluded in joy and calamity the history not only of Israel but also of the other nations, in a comprehensive and decisive act of God's judgment, but in righteousness, in the restoration of the order willed by [God], in the fulfillment of [God's] promise, in the execution of [God's] will which had this as its goal from the very first, and therefore to [God's] glory and to the salvation of [God's] people and all creation." Barth, *CD*, III/4, 56.

Early Christians adopted a similar interpretation, but with direct reference to Christ's resurrection. "The eschatological connexion and significance of the New Testament holy day . . . are manifest in the fact that it has been put on the day of the resurrection of Jesus. . . . [T]he first Christians saw in the resurrection of Jesus the first and isolated but clear ray of his final return in judgment and consummation. . . . On this special day they waited specially upon him because, in their remembrance of the past on this particular day, they were summoned by him to wait for that other and great particular day of his future as the last day." Barth, *CD*, III/4, 57.

33. Barth, *CD*, III/1, 218.

34. Cf. Gen. 1:31.

35. Barth, *CD*, III/1, 217. Barth sees this invitation in Genesis 2:3—"God blessed the seventh day and hollowed it"—which then becomes God's own rationale for Sabbath observance in the Decalogue in Exodus 20. The Israelites are to keep the Sabbath holy (*qdsh*) because God did so at creation (Exod. 20:8, 11). Barth goes so far as to suggest that because

of the intimate association between God's activity on the seventh day and the institution of the Sabbath for God's people, we cannot hope to understand the seventh day apart from the institution of the Sabbath. Barth, *CD*, III/1, 214.

36. Barth, *CD*, III/1, 214.

37. Barth insistently connects the command of God to the grace of God. God's command is grace and is for the sake of human freedom and life. Earlier in the *Church Dogmatics*, Barth writes, "The command of God sets [humankind] free. The command of God permits. It is only in this way that it commands. It permits even though it always has *in concreto* the form of one of the other commands, even though it, too, says, 'Thou shalt' and 'Thou shalt not,' even though it stands before [humankind], warning, disturbing, restraining, binding and committing. The command of God and other commands do the same thing, but it is not really the same. No matter in what guise the command of God meets us, in accordance with its basis and context, it will always set us free along a definite line. It will not compel [us], but burst open the door of the compulsion under which [we have] been living. It will not meet [us] with mistrust but with trust. It will not appeal to [our] fear but to [our] courage. It will instill courage, and not fear into [us]. This is the case because the command, as we have seen, is itself the form of the grace of God, the intervention of the God who has taken the curse from us to draw us to [God's self]—the easy yoke and the light burden of Christ, which as such are not to be exchanged for any other yoke or burden, and the assumption of which is in every sense our quickening and refreshing. This is what God prepares for us when [God] gives us [God's] command. The [one] who stands under the jurisdiction of all those other commands of God and is not refreshed is not the obedient [one] but the [one] who disobeys God, who, instead of living according to his determination to be the image of God, and therefore in conformity with the grace of God, has succumbed and succumbs to the temptation to eat of the tree of the knowledge of good and evil, which is forbidden [humanity] for [humanity's] own good, and in this way to exalt [humanity] to a spurious divine likeness." Barth, *CD*, II/2, 586. See also Daniel L. Migliore, "Commanding Grace: Karl Barth's Theological Ethics," in *Commanding Grace: Studies in Karl Barth's Ethics*, ed. Daniel L. Migliore (Grand Rapids: Eerdmans, 2010), 1–25.

38. Barth, *CD*, III/1, 222, quoting Dutch theologian H. F. Kohlbrügge.

39. Barth, *CD*, III/1, 222.

40. Barth, *CD*, III/1, 225. Barth continues, "its [creation's] history is in order; it is possible, without destroying the creaturely world, as a sequence of divine self-attestations with their revelations, miracles, signs and new creations." Barth's move here has everything to do with his broader insistence on the reality of God as the self-revealed God. In a world created in this way, with the inclusion of the Sabbath, revelation occurs not in contradiction to the created order, but in a way that maintains the created order even as it brings creation to completion. Creation stands incomplete and unfinished apart from God's self-revelation and self-witness. For Barth, Sabbath points inextricably to this at the very dawn of time.

41. This theme will emerge repeatedly in the Gospel texts involving Jesus and the Sabbath. See Chapter 5.

42. Heschel, *The Sabbath*, 9.

43. Heschel, *The Sabbath*, 104n7.

44. See Chapter 1.

45. In this chapter, the exploration of human response by way of the Sabbath remains somewhat general. It paves the way for further theological exploration of the Sabbath in the next chapter. The most explicit work regarding faithful human Sabbath-keeping will come in the final chapter.

46. Although we move directly from Barth's exegesis of the seventh day to his ethics of the Sabbath, the reader should know that Barth doesn't make these moves in simple succession. Two full part-volumes fill the space between Barth's exegesis of day seven in III/1 and the Sabbath section of his special ethics in III/4. His broad movement across the sum of the *Church Dogmatics* parallels the moves he makes with the Sabbath: begin with God, then consider human response.

47. Throughout the *Church Dogmatics*, Barth has tirelessly expounded on who God is, beginning unequivocally with the threefold word of God in Volume I of the *Dogmatics*, then proceeding to his Doctrine of God in the second volume, and now in the third volume, the Doctrine of Creation. This leads directly into theological anthropology: who are humans in light of who God is? Finally, in III/4, the question of ethics: What is good human action—not considered abstractly—but considered in light of God the Creator? The starting place of our proper response to God lies not in work or achievement or even in our love of others. It lies in the exercise of self-renouncing faith by way of keeping the Sabbath holy. Here human response comes face-to-face with the radical grace of God.

Part of Barth's hesitation in offering specific guidance stems from a tendency and temptation toward elevating Sabbath rules and regulations above the covenant relationship that the guidelines are supposed to preserve. Barth writes, "No ethics of the holy day can come between God and the individual, nor can the particularity of the Sabbath commandment, as God himself proclaims it, be reduced to general rules, thus telling the individual indirectly what is [her] obedience to this commandment." Barth, *CD*, III/4, 65. Ethics must be an outgrowth of and in service to the covenant relationship. Similarly, the reduction of the Sabbath to "general rules" perverts the covenant relationship by allowing humanity to skirt God in favor of rules and regulations. The Pharisees' relationship to the Sabbath will provide a concrete example of this, which we'll consider in the next chapter.

48. Bromiley and Torrance help clarify what Barth means by "special ethics": "Ethics arises where the vertical claim of God encounters [humanity] in [their] horizontal relationships, i.e., in the concrete situations of life, nature and history, in the continuities of daily life and work. Special ethics is the exposition of this encounter." G. W. Bromiley and T. F. Torrance, "Editor's Preface," *CD*, III/4, ix. Barth writes at the beginning of III/4, "The task of special ethics in the context of the doctrine of creation is to show to what

extent the one command of the one God who is gracious to [humanity] in Jesus Christ is also the command of [humanity's] Creator and therefore already the sanctification of the creaturely action and abstention of [humans]." Barth, *CD*, III/4, 3.

As we saw in the previous section, the Sabbath intersects with holiness (*qdsh*) at many points. Most importantly, God makes the Sabbath holy—sanctifies it—on the seventh day (Gen. 2:3) and invites his people to keep it holy. Thus, Barth refers to this section simply as "The Holy Day." Barth, *CD*, III/4, 47–72.

49. Barth, *CD*, III/4, 53.

50. Barth, *CD*, III/4, 55.

51. We will focus specifically on this in the next chapter.

52. Matthew 26:28. The commentary in *The New Interpreter's Study Bible* for Matthew 26:28 notes, "The forgiveness of sins [which Jesus names in the words of institution] does not only denote personal sins. The term 'forgiveness' is used fourteen times in Leviticus 25 to denote the year of Jubilee, the year of societal restructuring, freeing slaves, canceling debt, returning property. Jesus's death anticipates a just society at his return and establishment of God's empire." See *The New Interpreter's Study Bible: New Revised Standard Version with the Apocrypha* (Nashville: Abingdon, 2003), 1794.

53. Matthew 28:1; Mark 16:1; Luke 24:1; John 20:1.

54. Acts 20:7; cf. 1 Corinthians 16:2.

55. Barth, *CD*, III/4, 57.

56. Continuing the theme of Sabbath as joy and celebration, Barth writes, "The meaning of Sunday freedom is joy, the celebrating of a feast. It is this as and because it is significantly concerned with freedom for God, with the remembrance of [God's] rest and enthronement after the completion of creation, and with the remembrance of the resurrection of Jesus Christ from the dead, and therefore significantly with the expectation of the eternal kingdom." Barth, *CD*, III/4, 68.

57. This understanding of faith resonates deeply with the early Anabaptist notion of *Gelassenheit*. Anabaptist historian C. Arnold Snyder describes *Gelassenheit* as "an emphasis on how one must 'yield' one's will and creaturely impulses in trust to God." See C. Arnold Snyder, *Following in the Footsteps of Christ: The Anabaptist Tradition* (Maryknoll, NY: Orbis Books, 2004), 65. Barth echoes this very idea in his exposition of the Sabbath commandment: "The aim of the Sabbath commandment is that [we] shall give and allow the omnipotent grace of God to have the first and the last word at every point; that [we] shall surrender to it completely, in the least as well as in the greatest things; that [we] shall place [ourselves], with our knowing, willing and doing, unconditionally at its disposal. It aims at this complete surrender and capitulation by singling out one day, the seventh, and thus the seventh part of the whole life-time of every [person], from the succession of [our] work days, by forbidding [us] to make this day another work day, and by bidding [us] place [ourselves] on this day directly as it were in relation to the omnipotent grace of God and under its control." Barth, *CD*, III/4, 54–55.

58. In using language like "special activity and inactivity," "concrete," "particular,"

and "specific," Barth wants to guard against every conception of the Sabbath—and, more broadly, of the life of Christian faith—that gets lost in abstraction and fails to bear concretely and specifically on the day-to-day and moment-to-moment life of the believer. Early in his section "The Holy Day," Barth writes, "Here too, and particularly, religious profundity may become the enemy and destroyer of the concreteness of practical Christian knowledge." Barth, *CD*, III/4, 47-48.

59. Barth, *CD*, III/4, 60.

60. "We may well say that without rest from work and participation in divine service there is no obedience to the Sabbath commandment. But we cannot say that obedience to the Sabbath commandment consists in resting from work and participation in divine service. When we obey the Sabbath commandment, in and with the fulfilment of the one great promise, we can and will realise and enjoy the benefits of resting from work and divine service. But we cannot wish to keep the Sabbath commandment merely for the purpose of enjoying these benefits." Barth, *CD*, III/4, 60. Barth also contends that the "special Sabbath act of renouncing faith" is possible even without rest from work and divine service.

61. Barth, *CD*, III/4, 62.

62. Barth, *CD*, III/4, 60.

63. To recap a prior point, the notion of a self-referential Sabbath carries two meanings, both of which fall flat on theological grounds. To what does the Sabbath point or direct us? This is the critical question. A self-referential Sabbath might point either to the day itself or to the human who observes the Sabbath. Either referent remains theologically deficient. In theological perspective, Sabbath must point us to the God of Sabbath rest and to the relationship enacted by God between God and humanity.

64. Barth, *CD*, III/4, 64.

65. Barth, *CD*, III/4, 47.

66. Barth is raising core questions about what it means to be people of faith—people who trust in God the Creator. For Barth, this inevitably leads to questions about what it means to be human creatures. As creatures, we did not bring ourselves or the world into existence. We were created in and through Jesus Christ. We are not our own. We belong to the Creator. To be human is to be in relationship with the Creator. The Sabbath—the holy day—inexorably reveals the gracious character of the relationship between human creatures and Creator.

67. Barth, *CD*, III/4, 54, italics added.

68. Barth, *CD*, III/4, 58.

69. Thus, Barth argues for the utter insufficiency of all "self-positing, self-affirming, self-expression, self-help, and self-justification." Barth, *CD*, III/4, 58. Contemporary resources on the Sabbath frequently frame Sabbath as a mode or method of self-care, and Barth radically challenges this notion. While not altogether dismissing the notion of self-care, Barth emphatically insists that the autonomous self remains utterly insufficient as the basis of Sabbath observance. Beyond that, the self is insufficient for life

itself. Life consists in its relationship to God and all creation. Sabbath on the basis of self-renouncing faith is the utter opposite of self-help or self-care. God does not leave us alone to care for ourselves in and through the Sabbath. Rather, in and through the Sabbath, we utterly surrender ourselves to the "omnipotent grace of God." We place ourselves unconditionally in God's care. We allow God's care for us and grace toward us to radically transcend all our self-care.

70. The reality revealed in Jesus Christ is that God is unequivocally with and for humanity. God has chosen from eternity to be our God; time provides the context in which we may actually respond to the love and grace of God. No activity or inactivity on our part can change the fact of God's grace, love, and fidelity toward humankind. In freedom before God, we are given the choice to bear witness to God's grace. Keeping the Sabbath, the holy day, provides the starting point for all responsibility of humankind before God.

God's command is all-encompassing. Barth begins his exposition on the holy day this way: "To be [human] means to be caught up in responsibility before God." Human responsibility before God stands, for Barth, as a fundamental fact of reality (what is more academically referred to as Barth's ontology). All human activity is "freedom for God and responsibility before [God]." Yet this responsibility isn't vague. In the commanded holy day, "it is most palpably and extensively revealed that God claims not only the whole time of [humankind] but also, because the whole, a special time, not only [our] whole activity but also, because the whole, a particular act. We thus enter the special sphere denoted by the fourth Mosaic commandment." Barth, *CD*, III/4, 49. Here Barth guards against the loss of particularity that yields no distinction in our time—no distinct spheres of activity where all is responsibility and therefore nothing is responsibility. Barth moves the other direction. If in the broadest and most comprehensive sense, all our being is responsibility before God, then it must be true that we are responsible before God in particular ways as well. The exposition of the particular ways in which humankind finds itself responsible before God marks the realm of special ethics for Barth. The Sabbath commandment—the command to keep the holy day—stands at the very beginning of Barth's special ethics.

71. Barth's guidelines for Sabbath-keeping flow from his insistent Christocentrism. Barth ultimately insists that each person will have to discern the contours of faithful Sabbath practice by listening to the ever-speaking Word of God. Yet even saying it this way falls short of Barth's theological impulse. We follow Barth more closely if we give God's action precedence: The ever-speaking Word of God will make the specific contours of Sabbath observance clear to all who listen. God's Word comes to each person and community in a way that preserves the integrity of the true Word who is Jesus Christ.

This means that the specifics of Sabbath obedience must come to each person and each community just as Christ incarnate came to earth—in a way that both ensures that God is God and remains God, and is utterly particular to the context of its manifestation. Jesus Christ came as fully God and fully human; Christ does not compromise God's being or integrity; Christ reveals God's true being. At the same time, Christ comes as a very specific person to a very specific context: first century, Nazarene, Jew, and so on. Barth trusts and insists that the ever-speaking, living Word of God will similarly come to each person who willingly receives God's Sabbath commandment.

"The Sabbath commandment . . . reaches and encounters each [person] in direct reference to [their] person, [their] situation, [their] ability, task and surroundings at this specific time and in these specific circumstances. . . . Thus in the question what is entailed by obedience the [person] who is called to obedience in this matter is not left to [their] own devices or opinion, but set on a definite path by God and required to take definite positive and negative steps. The only open question can and will be whether [one] hears the Word of God and hears it rightly, whether [one] obeys it and obeys it fully." Barth, *CD*, III/4, 65.

72. *The New Interpreter's Study Bible*, 89.

73. Exodus 2:24; 3:6; 3:15; 3:16; 4:5; 6:3; 6:8.

74. Here we see, in terms that parallel the insights of missional theology, the infinite translatability of the grace of God. God's grace comes to the Israelites in terms that are utterly familiar, yet in ways that subvert lesser gods—in this case, ceaseless labor, productivity, trust in human striving, meritocracy, and so on.

75. Eberhard Busch, *Barth* (Nashville: Abingdon, 2008), 49.

76. See Luke 13:10-17.

77. Exodus 20:8: "Remember the Sabbath day, and keep it holy." See also Deuteronomy 5:15, within the Sabbath commandment: "Remember that you were a slave in the land of Egypt. . . ."

CHAPTER 5

1. For more on the Matthean antitheses, see W. D. Davies and Dale C. Allison Jr., *Matthew 1-7* (New York: T. & T. Clark, 2004), 72. See also Luke Timothy Johnson, *The Writings of the New Testament: An Interpretation*, 3rd ed. (Minneapolis: Fortress, 2010), 178-79.

2. Given both traditional Anabaptist emphasis on the Sermon on the Mount and my identity as a Mennonite, the relationship between the Sabbath and the Sermon on the Mount bears even greater personal significance. For more on Mennonite and Anabaptist emphasis on the Sermon on the Mount, see Abe J. Dueck, "Sermon on the Mount," in *Mennonite Encyclopedia*, vol. 5 (Harrisonburg, VA: Herald, 1989), 811-12; and Harold S. Bender, "The Anabaptist Vision," *Mennonite Quarterly Review* 18 (1944): 67-88. It's no coincidence that Bender penned his now-famous (among Mennonites) work during a time of war. The draft, a nation at war, and the possibility of military conscription have a way of raising pointed questions about peace, violence, and the ethics of Jesus. Bender holds Jesus's Sermon on the Mount and grace together to insist on peace and nonviolence. "We shall not believe, [the Anabaptists] said, that the Sermon on the Mount or any other vision that He had is only a heavenly vision meant but to keep His followers in tension until the last great day, but we shall practice what

He taught, believing that where He walked we can by His grace follow in His steps."
Bender, "The Anabaptist Vision," 88.

3. Questions about the law figure with special prominence in the interpretation of
Gospel texts involving Jesus and the Sabbath. Lutz Doering, a scholar of the New Testament and ancient Judaism, highlights two recent streams of interpretation regarding the
relationship between Jesus and the law, and specifically the Sabbath.

Ernst Käsemann represents a confrontational or conflictual interpretation. According to this school, Jesus actually leaves the boundaries of Judaism—he overturns the law.
Such an interpretation could yield a contemporary interpretation that rendered Sabbath
practice utterly superfluous: Jesus overturned the law and the Sabbath along with it. E. P.
Sanders, David Flusser, and others represent a second approach that sees no serious conflict between Jesus and Sabbath law. According to this view, Jesus doesn't actually break
Sabbath law because he "heals with a word."

See Lutz Doering, "Much Ado about Nothing? Jesus' Sabbath Healings and Their Halakhic Implications Revisited," in *Judaistik und Neutestamentliche Wissenschaft: Standorte,
Grenzen, Beziehungen,* ed. Lutz Doering, Hans-Günther Waubke, and Florian Wilk (Göttingen: Vandenhoeck & Ruprecht, 2008), 217–41. See also Ernst Käsemann, *Essays on
New Testament Themes* (London: SCM, 1964); E. P. Sanders, *Jesus and Judaism* (Philadelphia: Fortress, 1985); and David Flusser, *Jesus* (Jerusalem: Magnes, 1998).

4. One wonders which would count as antithesis.

5. For example, dispensationalist thought perceives a new era that stretches from
Christ's resurrection to Christ's return, during which the obligation to practice the Sabbath is abolished. See, for example, Joel T. Williamson Jr., "The Sabbath and Dispensationalism," *Journal of Dispensational Theology* 11 (2007): 77–95.

Incidentally, my primary critique of dispensationalist Sabbath interpretation has less
to do with differing eras of time and more to do with a general Sabbath posture that sees
Sabbath as a burden (cf. Matt. 11:28) to be cast off rather than as a gift of life and grace. In
some sense we can affirm—echoing dispensationalist thought—that Christ does remove
Sabbath as a burden. As we will see, Christ affirms the inability of rules and regulations—i.e., the law—to contain the radical grace that is the Sabbath. The question then
becomes, Why refuse a gift of such extraordinary grace? The dispensationalist school
also struggles to account for the institution of the Sabbath prior to the giving of the law
(theoretically a different dispensation), namely at creation and in Exodus 16.

Beyond dispensationalist thought, another Christian argument against Sabbath obligation looks to Hebrews 4. This line of thought perceives Christ as our eternal Sabbath in
whom all time is Sabbath time. Though this view maintains some theological viability,
in it the Sabbath tends to lose its distinctiveness in a way that reflects neither the life and
ministry of Christ nor those of his closest followers.

6. As noted in the previous chapter, our approach to Scripture follows the school of
thought within biblical studies known as theological interpretation. In following this
school—which looks to Barth as a pioneer—we trace the broad contours of the canon

and embrace the texts as containing more than mere history or historical account. This means that we focus not only on the "historical Jesus," but on the second person of the Trinity, who is affirmed to be fully divine and fully human. In addition, our exploration is not merely for the sake of exploration, but for the sake and in the context of the church. We listen for God's voice within these texts with the youth from Chapter 3 in mind. See Daniel J. Treier, *Introducing Theological Interpretation of Scripture: Recovering a Christian Practice* (Grand Rapids: Baker Academic, 2008); Joel B. Green, *Practicing Theological Interpretation: Engaging Biblical Texts for Faith and Formation* (Grand Rapids: Baker Academic, 2011); and Richard E. Burnett, *Karl Barth's Theological Exegesis: The Hermeneutical Principles of the Römerbrief Period* (Grand Rapids: Eerdmans, 2004).

7. The word in Greek is *sabbatōn*. Considering each instance of Sabbath is but one approach among many possible methods for discerning a theological understanding of the Sabbath in the Gospels. Gospel texts that recall God's provision of manna in Exodus 16 (e.g., Jesus's temptation in the wilderness, the Lord's Prayer, John 6, etc.) provide another potentially fruitful pathway. All Greek text is taken from the Bible Works New Testament, *Novum Testamentum Graece*, Nestle-Aland 27th edition (Stuttgart: Deutsch Bibelgesellschaft, 1993).

The Greek—including the longer ending to Mark—includes fifty-six (56) instances of *sabbatōn*. The discrepancy between the Greek (56) and the English (50) comes about because New Testament Greek uses the same term for the Sabbath day and for the span of seven days—a week. We will consider the implications of this linguistic reality in the pages ahead. By way of distribution of references to the Sabbath day, Matthew includes ten; Mark includes eleven; Luke includes eighteen; and John includes eleven. Though it surpasses the purview of this chapter, it is worth noting that Luke—particularly with the inclusion of Acts (nine additional references to the Sabbath day)—references the Sabbath disproportionately compared to the other Gospel authors. The themes explored in this chapter emerge from an examination of all fifty references to the Sabbath day in the Gospels except one in Matthew 24:20, which occurs in the context of Jesus's eschatological discourse preceding his death and resurrection. Within the discourse, Jesus advises, "Pray that your flight may not be in winter or on a Sabbath."

8. Here we follow the example of Jaroslav Pelikan and his commentary on Acts in the Brazos Theological Commentary on the Bible. Pelikan engages a single theological issue (a *locus communis*) that recurs throughout the book of Acts in a single portion of commentary. For example, even though angels appear throughout the book of Acts, Pelikan considers angelology within Acts in a single section of commentary. We intend something similar regarding the question of Jesus and the Sabbath in the Gospels. In other words, we seek theological insights that emerge when the sum of the Gospels is considered as they portray the relationship between Jesus and Sabbath. See Jaroslav Pelikan, *Acts* (Grand Rapids: Brazos, 2005), 29-31.

To be clear, the aim is not to homogenize the witness of the Four Gospels when it comes to the Sabbath. Each Gospel contains a unique perspective, and each in all likelihood was originally intended for a unique audience. We receive them as part of one canon, but this doesn't mean that we seek to flatten the unique perspective and contribution of each. To borrow Daniel Siegel's framework, that would lean more toward chaos or rigidity than integration. In listening across the four voices, the harmony that emerges depends in part on the distinctiveness of each voice. John tells different Sabbath stories than the Synoptics. The Synoptics don't always tell the same Sabbath stories, and when they do, they tell them in their own ways and with particular emphases. The common themes that do emerge across the witness of the Four Gospels are made all the more rich by the distinctiveness of each of the Gospel voices.

9. In Exodus 15:26, in the verses that come just before the manna narrative, God reveals a new dimension of his character. God has just provided a way to make the bitter water at Marah sweet—a reversal of the plague story—and has promised to protect the Israelites from disease if they will listen carefully to God and obey. God grounds this promise in God's own being: "I am the LORD who heals you." On the heels of the revelation of God as healer, God provides manna and Sabbath. Perhaps even at this Old Testament juncture—and particularly in light of the wounds of Israel's Egyptian captivity—the Sabbath includes a healing dimension.

10. Cf. Matthew 12:8; Luke 6:5. Within our immersion in the Sabbath, Jesus's proclamation that he is "lord even of the Sabbath" provides a simple but all-important reminder. Jesus is Lord. Sabbath is not.

11. Cf. Luke 14:1-24.

12. Mark 3:6. Mark's mention of the Herodians—an unknown group presumably affiliated with devotion to Herod—simply reinforces the confrontation that takes place between Jesus and the systemic powers contemporary to his earthly ministry. The confrontation includes both religious and imperial powers. Cf. Matthew 12:14 and Luke 6:11, which note that the Pharisees "were filled with fury" following the healing of the man with the withered hand.

13. This was precisely Barth's point when considering divine service or "humanitarian" benefits as a basis for Sabbath observance. They can be reduced to matters of human power and agency. The point of renouncing faith is that it surrenders all human power and achievement into the hands of God's all-powerful grace.

14. A glance at the Old Testament shows continuity regarding this theme. In the creation narrative, the rest and the holiness of the seventh day utterly contrast with the chaos and disorder of the "formless void" in Genesis 1:2, thus overcoming chaos with rest and peace. In the manna narrative, the Sabbath rhythm confronts the "formless" drone of ceaseless work and the misshapen identity of the Israelites, and the radically egalitarian nature of the Sabbath commandment—for sons, daughters, livestock, servants, and foreigners—confronts the possibilities and realities of systemic powers of injustice and economic oppression.

15. This highlights a dimension of the Sabbath commandment that has received little attention. The command not only prescribes rest; it also prescribes work. "Six days

you shall work" (Exod. 20:9; Deut. 5:13). The empowerment that Jesus extends through these Sabbath healings unquestionably brought economic implications. In the account of Jesus healing the man with the withered hand (Matt. 12:9-14; Mark 3:1-6; Luke 6:6-11), Jesus instructs him to stretch out his hand. Interpreters note the raising of the hand as a symbol of power, and Jesus's healing of the hand both empowers and enables the man for productive and economically viable work. See Duncan M. Derrett, "Christ and the Power of Choice," *Biblica* 65 (1984): 168-88.

16. See the discussion on the heavy burden of the law below.

17. Jesus's critique of the Pharisees on the Sabbath in Matthew 12:7 is that they didn't understand the priority of mercy over sacrifice.

18. See also Mark 1:21-28 and 6:1-6; Luke 4:31-37 and 6:6-11.

19. Here we note parallels with the Matthean antitheses that opened this chapter. Jesus doesn't discard the Sabbath; he fulfills it in keeping with his proclamation in Matthew 5 that he has come not to destroy but to fulfill the law.

20. In John 9, Jesus speaks of abundant life in the discourse that follows his Sabbath healing of the man blind from birth.

21. See Matthew 28:1; Mark 16:2; Luke 24:1; and John 20:1, 19.

22. With gratitude to Richard Adam DeVries, who first suggested to me parallels between Jesus's cry on the cross and the seventh day of creation.

23. The only possible exception to this pattern comes in the story of Jesus healing Simon's mother-in-law (Mark 1:29-31; Luke 4:38-39), though the text leaves the question of initiation open.

24. Again, one possible exception to this pattern occurs in the brief narrative of Jesus healing Simon's mother-in-law. Both Mark and Luke include this account:

> As soon as they left the synagogue, they entered the house of Simon and Andrew, with James and John. Now Simon's mother-in-law was in bed with a fever, and they told him about her at once. He came and took her by the hand and lifted her up. Then the fever left her, and she began to serve them. (Mark 1:29-31)

> After leaving the synagogue he entered Simon's house. Now Simon's mother-in-law was suffering from a high fever, and they asked him about her. Then he stood over her and rebuked the fever, and it left her. Immediately she got up and began to serve them. (Luke 4:38-39)

The texts don't reveal the nature of the conversation that takes place between Jesus and the disciples concerning Simon's mother-in-law. In Mark, they tell Jesus about her; in Luke, they ask him. We cannot categorically exclude the possibility that the disciples ask Jesus to heal her. It is similarly impossible to insist that they do. As noted above, what does seem clear in both Mark and Luke is that things change at sundown or, according to Jewish law, after the Sabbath has concluded. In both Mark and Luke, the verses that immediately follow the story of Simon's mother-in-law mention the setting of the sun.

25. For an explication of the significance of John's use of the term *logos*, see Herman N. Ridderbos, *The Gospel According to John: A Theological Commentary* (Grand Rapids: Eerdmans, 1997), 17–59.

26. Though Matthew typically receives most attention for depicting Jesus in a manner continuous with the law and Moses, John echoes that emphasis here.

27. The Greek language holds the advantage of including both noun and verb forms of its term for faith. English, quite unfortunately, has no verb form for faith.

28. John 9:18: they "did not believe."

29. Exodus 4:23; 5:1; 8:1, 20; 9:1, 13; 10:3, 24, 26; 12:31.

30. As noted above, some Christians interpret the intersection of Jesus and Sabbath as the end of Sabbath rest.

31. I want to thank Jessica Winderweedle for her astute exegesis of this passage. See Jessica Winderweedle, "A Pervasive Sabbath Rest: A Close Reading of Matthew 11:25-12:14," unpublished paper, Princeton Theological Seminary, 2013. See also Ulrich Luz, *Matthew 8-20: A Commentary*, trans. Wilhelm C. Linss (Minneapolis: Augsburg Fortress, 2001).

32. The Greek term *nēpios* can be translated either literally as "infant" or "child" or metaphorically as "childish," "unskilled," or "untaught." Regardless, it connotes the marginal, the humble, and the powerless.

33. *The New Interpreter's Study Bible* notes that Jesus's language in Matthew 11:25-30 is also imperial. Thus, Jesus's reign and authority contrast with both the burden of the Pharisees and the burden of the empire. See *The New Interpreter's Study Bible: New Revised Standard Version with the Apocrypha* (Nashville: Abingdon, 2003), 1766-67.

34. The Greek term that gets translated here as "rest" means "1) to cause or permit one to cease from any movement or labor . . . 2) to give rest . . . 3) to keep quiet, of calm and patient expectation." See Joseph H. Thayer, *Thayer's Greek-English Lexicon of the New Testament* (Peabody, MA: Hendrickson, 1996), 40-41.

35. F. Wilbur Gingrich, *Shorter Lexicon of the Greek New Testament*, ed. Frederick W. Danker, 2nd ed., BibleWorks, vol. 8 (Chicago: University of Chicago Press, 1983).

36. Cf. Jesus's presence and ministry in the synagogue on the Sabbath in Matthew 12; Mark 1, 3, and 6; and Luke 6 and 13.

37. Acts references the Sabbath day nine times. Most of these texts reference synagogue gatherings where the apostles teach and interpret Scripture.

38. In the realm of youth ministry, this has been called a Messiah complex.

39. See also the parable of the great dinner in Luke 14, which Jesus actually tells on the Sabbath during a meal.

CHAPTER 6

1. This matter of "putting down the duck" in order to allow something else to emerge corresponds to the questions of agency and freedom that have frequently arisen in this

project. To shamelessly philosophize on Ernie and his duck, we might say that as long as Ernie refuses to put the duck down, Ernie simultaneously refuses his own freedom and agency. He refuses a limit in his relationship to the duck, and thus gives greater agency to the duck than to himself. The duck acts on Ernie like technology apart from intentionality acts on us. Ernie is free neither toward the duck nor toward the saxophone as long as the duck is in his hand. When he puts the duck down, he actually acts. He becomes free toward the duck, the saxophone, and the possibility of something emerging—music—which couldn't have emerged in any other way. At the same time, when Ernie puts down the duck, the duck in some way becomes free to just be a duck. In Siegel's terms, Ernie's relationship to the duck becomes more thoroughly integrated as soon as he puts it down. Before Ernie does it, his life displays the rigidity or chaos of dis-integration. After he does it, it displays the distinction, connection, freedom, and flexibility of integration.

2. In the terms of educational philosophy, we have relegated Sabbath to the null curriculum.

3. For a recent treatment of the Sabbath that considers economic justice, see Walter Brueggemann's *Sabbath as Resistance: Saying No to the Culture of Now* (Louisville: Westminster John Knox, 2014).

4. It is worth noting that the system of religious laws operative in this narrative may be included in the list of powers that were too great for this woman to overcome on her own. The religious leaders object to Jesus's healing and instruct the crowd to come on the other six days for healing. Whether demonic, systemic, or religious, Jesus overcomes the powers that bind us through his Sabbath healing and ministry.

5. I thank my mentor, Dale Schrag, for sharing with me the image of holding our convictions in open hands rather than closed fists.

6. Not all anxiety and fear are equal. My assumption here—based on the research and work of the previous chapters—is that the Sabbath journey occasionally leads us through anxiety and fear. These experiences shouldn't be conflated with clinically diagnosed anxiety and depression. Sabbath anxieties and other anxieties may connect or overlap, but my recommendations here shouldn't be received as a substitute for necessary clinical or other professional help. God's Spirit is unquestionably vast enough to work both through the guidance of this book and through the help of trained professionals. Either way, the aim is formation in community.

7. I am indebted to the late Marcus Smucker—professor, pastor, and spiritual director—for the overall arc of these four movements.

8. Daniel J. Siegel, *Brainstorm: The Power and Purpose of the Teenage Brain* (New York: Penguin, 2013), 205.

APPENDIX

1. My definition of practical theology is influenced substantially by Richard R. Osmer. See Richard R. Osmer, *Practical Theology: An Introduction* (Grand Rapids: Eerdmans, 2008).

2. To be clear, practical theology doesn't depend on a crisis to exist. Yes, the movements of practical theology can guide us when life confounds. They also help in the midst of the mundane. Indeed, some apparently mundane daily realities (e.g., taking out the trash) could benefit greatly from practical theological reflection.

3. Richard R. Osmer writes about the import of choosing dialogue partners wisely and provides guidance for discerning dialogue partners in relation to specific scenarios. See Osmer, *Practical Theology*, 100-103, 113-28, and 160-72. Fittingly, the choice of dialogue partners within the exercise of practical theological reflection also depends on context. In my case, the descriptive and interpretive partners who assisted me on my journey were those who were contextually close at hand.

4. As Osmer, Don Browning, Johannes van der Ven, and others have noted, practical theology tends intentionally and explicitly to context. At its best, practical theology allows context to guide the exploration and interpretation of context. For example, my case inherently brought with it a certain urgency. This meant that my interdisciplinary explorations were initially quite limited—I needed guidance quickly. Other contexts—like writing a book—allow for exploration and interpretation in a much more sustained manner. The point here is that practical theology isn't merely or formulaically sensitive to context. It is contextually sensitive to context. Concern for ongoing and future faithful action motivates this sensitivity. See Osmer, *Practical Theology*; Don S. Browning, *A Fundamental Practical Theology: Descriptive and Strategic Proposals* (Minneapolis: Fortress, 1991); and Johannes van der Ven, *Practical Theology: An Empirical Approach* (Leuven, Belgium: Peeters, 1998).

5. At this point, our exploration of practical theology as a discipline requires two critical clarifications. First, as noted, practical theology closely explores particular episodes, situations, and contexts, but this shouldn't be interpreted as though such contexts can be explored in isolation from other contexts and settings. As I journeyed through the end-of-semester scenario, I continued the rest of my life. I continued as a father to our children; I paid bills; and we went to church. Contexts are not discrete, and rigorous practical theological reflection recognizes the complexity of interweaving contexts and scenarios. Second, it must be reiterated that practical theology as I'm describing it necessarily involves the individual in community. Practical theology involves both scholarly and faith communities.

6. James Loder refers to the relationship between God's action and human action as the "generative problematic" for practical theology as a discipline. Andrew Root provides helpful commentary on Loder's thought: "It is problematic because divine and human actions are distinct and different—or, at the very least, we must admit that divine action

is hidden directly from the human knower. But it's also generative, because although these forms of action (praxis) are distinct, they nevertheless do relate." See Andrew Root with Blair Bertrand, "Postscript: Reflecting on Method: Youth Ministry as Practical Theology," in Andrew Root and Kenda Creasy Dean, *The Theological Turn in Youth Ministry* (Downers Grove, IL: InterVarsity, 2011), 219. See also James Loder, "Normativity and Context in Practical Theology," in *Practical Theology: International Perspectives*, ed. Friedrich Schweitzer and Johannes van der Ven (Berlin: Peter Lang, 1999).

The idea here echoes Barth's conception of divine providence in his *Church Dogmatics*. Barth insists repeatedly that God's providence is neither distant nor static. Rather, God remains dynamically involved in and throughout creation. "The Lord is never absent, passive, non-responsible or impotent, but always present, active, responsible and omnipotent. He is never dead, but always living; never sleeping, but always awake; never uninterested, but always concerned. . . . [God] co-exists with [the creature] actively, in an action which never ceases and does not leave any loopholes." See Karl Barth, *Church Dogmatics*, ed. G. W. Bromiley and T. F. Torrance (Edinburgh: T. & T. Clark, 1936-75), III/3, 13.

7. Here I echo Barth, recognizing his indebtedness to Kierkegaard. In Kierkegaard's terms, the presuppositions of practical theology are an offense to reason, yet they are the basis of hope for humankind. In Jesus Christ, God overcomes the "infinite qualitative difference" between God and humans. See Søren Kierkegaard, *The Sickness unto Death* (Princeton, NJ: Princeton University Press, 1980), 126-27.

Bibliography

Acebo, Christine, and Mary A. Carskadon. "Influence of Irregular Sleep Patterns on Waking Behavior." In *Adolescent Sleep Patterns: Biological, Social, and Psychological Influences*, edited by Mary A. Carskadon, 220–35. New York: Cambridge University Press, 2002.

Adams, Sue K. "College Students and Sleep: The Effects of Living a 24/7 Lifestyle." Presented at Wheaton College, March 2011.

American Psychological Association. "Stress in America: Are Teens Adopting Adults' Stress Habits?" American Psychological Association, February 2014. See http://www.apa.org/news/press/releases/stress/2013/stress-report.pdf.

Anderson, Gary A. *Sin: A History*. New Haven, CT: Yale University Press, 2009.

Anderson, Monica, and Jingjing Jiang. "Teens, Social Media and Technology 2018." Washington, DC: Pew Research Center, May 31, 2018. See http://www.pewinternet.org/2018/05/31/teens-social-media-technology-2018/.

Arnett, Jeffrey J. *Emerging Adulthood: The Winding Road from the Late Teens Through the Twenties*. New York: Oxford University Press, 2006.

Asarnow, Lauren D., Eleanor McGlinchey, and Allison G. Harvey. "The Effects of Bedtime and Sleep Duration on Academic and Emotional Outcomes in a Nationally Representative Sample of Adolescents." *Journal of Adolescent Health* 54 (2014): 350–56.

Barth, Karl. *Church Dogmatics*, ed. G. W. Bromiley and T. F. Torrance. Edinburgh: T. & T. Clark, 1936–75.

Bender, Harold S. "The Anabaptist Vision." *Mennonite Quarterly Review* 18 (1944): 67–88.

Bible Works New Testament. *Novum Testamentum Graece*. Nestle-Aland 27th edition. Stuttgart: Deutsch Bibelgesellschaft, 1993.

Bronson, Po, and Ashley Merryman. *Nurture Shock: New Thinking about Children.* New York: Hachette Book Group, 2009.

Brown Taylor, Barbara. "Sabbath: A Practice in Death." Accessed November 6, 2018. See http://www.theworkofthepeople.com/sabbath-a-practice-in-death.

Browning, Don S. *A Fundamental Practical Theology: Descriptive and Strategic Proposals.* Minneapolis: Fortress, 1991.

Brueggemann, Walter. *Reverberations of Faith: A Theological Handbook of Old Testament Themes.* Louisville: Westminster John Knox, 2002.

———. *Sabbath as Resistance: Saying No to the Culture of Now.* Louisville: Westminster John Knox, 2014.

Burnett, Richard E. *Karl Barth's Theological Exegesis: The Hermeneutical Principles of the Römerbrief Period.* Grand Rapids: Eerdmans, 2004.

Busch, Eberhard. *Barth.* Nashville: Abingdon, 2008.

Carr, Nicholas G. *The Shallows: What the Internet Is Doing to Our Brains.* New York: W. W. Norton, 2010.

Carskadon, Mary A. "Factors Influencing Sleep Patterns of Adolescents." In *Adolescent Sleep Patterns: Biological, Social, and Psychological Influences,* edited by Mary A. Carskadon, 4–26. New York: Cambridge University Press, 2002.

———. Preface to *Adolescent Sleep Patterns: Biological, Social, and Psychological Influences,* edited by Mary A. Carskadon, xiii–xvii. New York: Cambridge University Press, 2002.

Crain, William C. *Reclaiming Childhood: Letting Children Be Children in Our Achievement-Oriented Society.* New York: Times Books, 2003.

Davies, W. D., and Dale C. Allison Jr. *Matthew 1–7.* New York: T. & T. Clark, 2004.

Dean, Kenda Creasy. *Almost Christian: What the Faith of Our Teenagers Is Telling the American Church.* New York: Oxford University Press, 2010.

Derrett, Duncan M. "Christ and the Power of Choice." *Biblica* 65 (1984): 168–88.

Dewald, Julia F., Anne M. Meijer, Frans J. Oort, Gerard A. Kerkhof, and Susan M. Bögels. "The Influence of Sleep Quality, Sleep Duration, and Sleepiness on School Performance in Children and Adolescents: A Meta-Analytic Review." *Sleep Medicine Reviews* 14 (2010): 179–89.

Doering, Lutz. "Much Ado about Nothing? Jesus' Sabbath Healings and Their Halakhic Implications Revisited." In *Judaistik und Neutestamentliche Wissenschaft: Standorte, Grenzen, Beziehungen,* edited by Lutz Doering, Hans-Günther Waubke, and Florian Wilk, 217–41. Göttingen: Vandenhoeck & Ruprecht, 2008.

Dornbusch, Sanford M. "Sleep and Adolescence: A Social Psychologist's Perspective." In *Adolescent Sleep Patterns: Biological, Social, and Psychological Influences,* edited by Mary A. Carskadon, 1–3. New York: Cambridge University Press, 2002.

Dueck, Abe J. "Sermon on the Mount." In *Mennonite Encyclopedia,* vol. 5, 811–12. Harrisonburg, VA: Herald, 1989.

Duerksen, Carol. *Keeping Sabbath.* Cleveland: Circle Books, 2010.

Elkind, David. *The Hurried Child: Growing Up Too Fast Too Soon*. Rev. ed. Reading, MA: Perseus Books, 1988.

Entner, Roger. "Under-Aged Texting Usage and Actual Cost." The Nielsen Company, January 27, 2010. See http://www.nielsen.com/us/en/newswire/2010/under-aged -texting-usage-and-actual-cost.html.

Epstein, Robert. *The Case against Adolescence: Rediscovering the Adult in Every Teen*. Sanger, CA: Quill Driver Books, 2007.

Fisher, Martin. "Fatigue in Adolescence." *Journal of Pediatric Adolescent Gynecology* 26 (2013): 252–56.

Flusser, David. *Jesus*. Jerusalem: Magnes, 1998.

Friedman, Theodore. "The Sabbath: Anticipation of Redemption." *Judaism* 16 (1967): 443–52.

Gadamer, Hans Georg. *Truth and Method*. London: Continuum, 2011.

General Conference Mennonite Church and Mennonite Church. *Confession of Faith in a Mennonite Perspective*. Scottdale, PA: Herald, 1995.

Gershuny, Jonathan. "Busyness as the Badge of Honor for the New Superordinate Working Class." *Social Research* 72 (2005): 287–314.

Gingrich, F. Wilbur. *Shorter Lexicon of the Greek New Testament*. Edited by Frederick W. Danker. 2nd ed. BibleWorks, vol. 8. Chicago: University of Chicago Press, 1983.

Green, Joel B. *Practicing Theological Interpretation: Engaging Biblical Texts for Faith and Formation*. Grand Rapids: Baker Academic, 2011.

GSMA Intelligence (website). Global Data. Accessed November 6, 2018. https://www .gsmaintelligence.com/.

Hall, Jeffrey A., and Nancy K. Baym. "Calling and Texting (Too Much): Mobile Maintenance Expectations, (Over) Dependence, Entrapment, and Friendship Satisfaction." *New Media Society* 14 (2012): 316–31.

Harris, Judith Rich. *The Nurture Assumption: Why Children Turn Out the Way They Do*. New York: Free Press, 2009.

Heschel, Abraham Joshua. *The Sabbath: Its Meaning for Modern Man*. New York: Farrar, Straus and Giroux, 1951.

Hinshaw, Stephen. *The Triple Bind: Saving Our Teenage Girls from Today's Pressures*. New York: Ballantine Books, 2009.

Hofferth, S. L., and J. F. Sandberg. "Changes in American Children's Time, 1981–1997." In *Children at the Millennium: Where Did We Come From, Where Are We Going?*, edited by S. Hofferth and T. Owens, 193–229. New York: Elsevier Science, 2001.

Hofferth, Sandra, David A. Kinney, and Janet S. Dunn. "The 'Hurried' Child: Myth vs. Reality." Working paper, Maryland Population Research Center, University of Maryland, 2008.

Horowitz, Sandra. "Sleep Texting: A New Variation on an Old Theme." *Sleep Medicine* 12, Supplement 1 (2011): S39.

Iglowstein, Ivo, Oskar G. Jenni, Lusiano Molinari, and Remo H. Largo. "Sleep Duration from Infancy to Adolescence: Reference Values and Generational Trends." *Pediatrics* 111 (2003): 302-7.

Johnson, Luke Timothy. *The Writings of the New Testament: An Interpretation.* 3rd edition. Minneapolis: Fortress, 2010.

Käsemann, Ernst. *Essays on New Testament Themes.* London: SCM, 1964.

Kasper, Joseph [pseudo.]. "An Academic with Impostor Syndrome." *The Chronicle of Higher Education*, April 2, 2013. See http://chronicle.com/article/An-Academic-With -Impostor/138231/.

Kierkegaard, Søren. *The Sickness unto Death.* Princeton, NJ: Princeton University Press, 1980.

Kimball, Dan, and Lilly Lewin. *Sacred Space: A Hands-on Guide to Creating Multisensory Worship Experiences for Youth Ministry.* Grand Rapids: Youth Specialties, 2008.

Landhuis, Carl Erik, Richie Poulton, David Welch, and Robert John Hancox. "Childhood Sleep Time and Long-Term Risk for Obesity: A 32-Year Prospective Birth Cohort Study." *Pediatrics* 122 (2008): 955-60.

Larson, Reed W. "How U.S. Children and Adolescents Spend Time: What It Does (and Doesn't) Tell Us about Their Development." *Current Directions in Psychological Science* 10 (2001): 160-64.

Lenhart, Amanda. "Teens, Social Media & Technology Overview 2015." Washington, DC: Pew Research Center, April 9, 2015. See http://www.pewinternet.org/2015/04/09 /teens-social-media-technology-2015/.

Loder, James. "Normativity and Context in Practical Theology." In *Practical Theology: International Perspectives*, edited by Friedrich Schweitzer and Johannes van der Ven. Berlin: Peter Lang, 1999.

Lufi, Dubi, Orna Tzischinsky, and Steve Hadar. "Delaying School Starting Time by One Hour: Some Effects on Attention Levels in Adolescents." *Journal of Clinical Sleep Medicine* 7 (2011): 137-43.

Luthar, Suniya S., Karen A. Shoum, and Pamela J. Brown. "Extracurricular Involvement among Affluent Youth: A Scapegoat for 'Ubiquitous Achievement Pressures'?" *Developmental Psychology* 42 (2006): 583-97.

Luz, Ulrich. *Matthew 8-20: A Commentary.* Translated by Wilhelm C. Linss. Minneapolis: Augsburg Fortress, 2001.

Mahoney, Joseph L., Angel L. Harris, and Jacquelynne S. Eccles. "Organized Activity Participation, Positive Youth Development, and the Over-Scheduling Hypothesis." *Social Policy Report, The Society for Research in Child Development* 20 (2006): 3-30.

Mahoney, Joseph L., Heather Lord, and Erica Carryl. "An Ecological Analysis of After-School Program Participation and the Development of Academic Performance and Motivational Attributes for Disadvantaged Children." *Child Development* 76 (2005): 811-25.

Matricciani, Lisa, Timothy Olds, and John Petkov. "In Search of Lost Sleep: Secular

Trends in the Sleep Time of School-Aged Children and Adolescents." *Sleep Medicine Reviews* 16 (2012): 203–11.

McCracken, James T. "The Search for Vulnerability Signatures for Depression in High-Risk Adolescents: Mechanisms and Significance." In *Adolescent Sleep Patterns: Biological, Social, and Psychological Influences*, edited by Mary A. Carskadon, 254–68. New York: Cambridge University Press, 2002.

Medina, John. *Brain Rules: 12 Principles for Surviving and Thriving at Work, Home, and School.* Seattle: Pear Press, 2008.

Migliore, Daniel L. "Commanding Grace: Karl Barth's Theological Ethics." In *Commanding Grace: Studies in Karl Barth's Ethics*, edited by Daniel L. Migliore, 1–25. Grand Rapids: Eerdmans, 2010.

———. *Faith Seeking Understanding: An Introduction to Christian Theology.* Grand Rapids: Eerdmans, 2004.

Millman, Richard P. "Excessive Sleepiness in Adolescents and Young Adults: Causes, Consequences, and Treatment Strategies." *Pediatrics* 115 (2005): 1774–86.

Moore, Richard T., Rachel Kaprielian, and John Auerbach. "Asleep at the Wheel: Report of the Special Commission on Drowsy Driving." February 2009. See https://sleep.med.harvard.edu/file_download/103.

National Sleep Foundation. "2014 Sleep in America Poll: Sleep in the Modern Family Summary of Findings." March 2014. See http://sleepfoundation.org/sleep-polls-data/sleep-in-america-poll/2014-sleep-in-the-modern-family/.

———. "Annual Sleep in America Poll Exploring Connections with Communications Technology." March 7, 2011. See http://sleepfoundation.org/media-center/press-release/annual-sleep-america-poll-exploring-connections-communications-technology-use-/page/0%2C2/.

———. "National Sleep Foundation 2006 *Sleep in America* Poll: Highlights and Key Findings." National Sleep Foundation, 2006.

———. "National Sleep Foundation 2014 Sleep in America Poll Finds Children Sleep Better When Parents Establish Rules, Limit Technology and Set a Good Example." National Sleep Foundation, March 3, 2014. See http://stage.sleepfoundation.org/media-center/press-release/national-sleep-foundation-2014-sleep-america-poll-finds-children-sleep.

———. "Teens and Sleep." See http://www.sleepfoundation.org/article/sleep-topics/teens-and-sleep.

The New Interpreter's Study Bible: New Revised Standard Version with the Apocrypha. Nashville: Abingdon, 2003.

The Nielsen Company. "In U.S., SMS Text Messaging Tops Mobile Phone Calling." September 22, 2008. See http://www.nielsen.com/us/en/newswire/2008/in-us-text-messaging-tops-mobile-phone-calling.html.

North, Heather C., David J. Hargreaves, and Susan A. O'Neill. "The Importance of Music to Adolescents." *British Journal of Educational Psychology* 70 (2000): 255–72.

Osmer, Richard R. *Practical Theology: An Introduction*. Grand Rapids: Eerdmans, 2008.

Owens, Judith A., Katherine Belon, and Patricia Moss. "Impact of Delaying School Start Time on Adolescent Sleep, Mood, and Behavior." *Archive of Pediatric Adolescent Medicine* 164 (2010): 608-14.

Pelikan, Jaroslav. *Acts*. Grand Rapids: Brazos, 2005.

Richards, Lyn. *Handling Qualitative Data: A Practical Guide*. 2nd ed. Los Angeles: Sage, 2009.

Ridderbos, Herman N. *The Gospel According to John: A Theological Commentary*. Grand Rapids: Eerdmans, 1997.

Robinson, John P. "The Time-Diary Method: Structures and Uses." In *Time Use Research in the Social Sciences*, edited by Wendy E. Pentland, Andrew S. Harvey, M. Powell Lawton, and Mary Ann McColl, 47-90. New York: Kluwer Academic, 1999.

Root, Andrew, with Blair Bertrand. "Postscript: Reflecting on Method: Youth Ministry as Practical Theology." In Andrew Root and Kenda Creasy Dean, *The Theological Turn in Youth Ministry*, 218-36. Downers Grove, IL: InterVarsity, 2011.

Rosenfeld, Alvin A., and Nicole Wise. *The Over-Scheduled Child: Avoiding the Hyper-Parenting Trap*. New York: St. Martin's Griffin, 2001.

Sadeh, Avi, and Reut Gruber. "Stress and Sleep in Adolescence: A Clinical-Developmental Perspective." In *Adolescent Sleep Patterns: Biological, Social, and Psychological Influences*, edited by Mary A. Carskadon, 236-53. New York: Cambridge University Press, 2002.

Sadeh, Avi, Reut Gruber, and Amiram Raviv. "The Effects of Sleep Restriction and Extension on School-Age Children: What a Difference an Hour Makes." *Child Development* 74 (2003): 444-55.

Sanders, E. P. *Jesus and Judaism*. Philadelphia: Fortress, 1985.

Sanneh, Lamin. *Whose Religion Is Christianity? The Gospel Beyond the West*. Grand Rapids: Eerdmans, 2003.

Schor, Juliet. *The Overworked American: The Unexpected Decline of Leisure*. New York: Basic Books, 1991.

Short, Michelle A., Michael Gradisar, Leon C. Lack, Helen R. Wright, and Alex Chatburn. "Estimating Adolescent Sleep Patterns: Parent Reports versus Adolescent Self-Report Surveys, Sleep Diaries, and Actigraphy." *Nature and Science of Sleep* 5 (2013): 23-26.

Siegel, Daniel J. *Brainstorm: The Power and Purpose of the Teenage Brain*. New York: Penguin, 2013.

————. *The Developing Mind: How Relationships and the Brain Interact to Shape Who We Are*. 2nd ed. New York: Guilford, 2012.

Smith, Christian, with Melinda Lundquist Denton. *Soul Searching: The Religious and Spiritual Lives of American Teenagers*. New York: Oxford, 2005.

Snyder, C. Arnold. *Following in the Footsteps of Christ: The Anabaptist Tradition*. Maryknoll, NY: Orbis Books, 2004.

Spinks, Sarah. *Frontline*. Season 20, episode 11, "The Teenage Brain." Aired January 31, 2002, on PBS. See http://www.pbs.org/wgbh/pages/frontline/shows/teenbrain/.

Taylor, Charles. *Sources of the Self: The Making of the Modern Identity*. Cambridge: Harvard University Press, 1989.

Thayer, Joseph H. *Thayer's Greek-English Lexicon of the New Testament*. Peabody, MA: Hendrickson, 1996.

Thompson, Derek. "Are We Truly Overworked? An Investigation—in 6 Charts." *The Atlantic*, May 22, 2013. See http://www.theatlantic.com/magazine/archive/2013/06/are-we-truly-overworked/309321/.

Treier, Daniel J. *Introducing Theological Interpretation of Scripture: Recovering a Christian Practice*. Grand Rapids: Baker Academic, 2008.

Turkle, Sherry. *Alone Together: Why We Expect More from Technology and Less from Each Other*. New York: Basic Books, 2011.

Van den Bulck, Jan. "Adolescent Use of Mobile Phones for Calling and for Sending Text Messages after Lights Out: Results from a Prospective Cohort Study with a One-Year Follow-Up." *Sleep* 30 (2007): 1220-23.

van der Ven, Johannes. *Practical Theology: An Empirical Approach*. Leuven, Belgium: Peeters, 1998.

Wahlstrom, Kyla L. "Accommodating the Sleep Patterns of Adolescents within Current Educational Structures: An Uncharted Path." In *Adolescent Sleep Patterns: Biological, Social, and Psychological Influences*, edited by Mary A. Carskadon, 172-97. New York: Cambridge University Press, 2002.

———. "Changing Times: Findings from the First Longitudinal Study of Later High School Start Times." *NASSP Bulletin* 86 (2002): 3-21.

Walker, Matthew P., and Robert Stickgold. "Sleep-Dependent Learning and Memory Consolidation." *Neuron* 44 (2004): 121-33.

Williamson, Joel T., Jr. "The Sabbath and Dispensationalism." *Journal of Dispensational Theology* 11 (2007): 77-95.

Wilson, George, and Samuel Shpall. "Action." In *The Stanford Encyclopedia of Philosophy*, edited by Edward N. Zalta. Summer 2012 edition. See http://plato.stanford.edu/archives/sum2012/entries/action/.

Winderweedle, Jessica. "A Pervasive Sabbath Rest: A Close Reading of Matthew 11:25-12:14." Unpublished paper, Princeton Theological Seminary, 2013.

Wolfson, Amy R., and Mary A. Carskadon. "Sleep Schedules and Daytime Functioning." *Child Development* 69 (1998): 875-87.

Worthman, Carol M., and Melissa K. Melby. "Toward a Comparative Developmental Ecology of Human Sleep." In *Adolescent Sleep Patterns: Biological, Social, and Psychological Influences*, edited by Mary A. Carskadon, 69-117. New York: Cambridge University Press, 2002.

Yaconelli, Mark. *Growing Souls: Experiments in Contemplative Youth Ministry*. El Cajon, CA: Youth Specialties, 2007.

Index